HANDBOOK OF
IS MANAGEMENT

1994–95 YEARBOOK

ROBERT E. UMBAUGH
EDITOR

AUERBACH PUBLICATIONS
A Division of Warren, Gorham & Lamont
Boston and New York

Printed in the United States of America.
Published in the United States in 1994
by Auerbach Publications
Warren, Gorham & Lamont
31 St. James Avenue
Boston MA 02116 USA

15   14   13   12   11   10   9   8   7   6   5   4   3   2   1

Contributors

PHILIP L. ARTHUR, *A/D Consulting and Services Specialist, IBM's Dallas Systems Center, IBM Corp., Dallas TX*

RICHARD BASKERVILLE, *Assistant Professor, Binghamton University, Binghamton NY*

HOWARD C. BERKOWITZ, *Technology Manager, PSC Int'l, McLean VA*

MAC CLARK, *President, Management Strategies, Boston MA*

HOWARD A. CURLE, JR., *Information Systems Analyst, Virginia Power, Richmond VA*

HARRY B. DEMAIO, *National Marketing Director, Information Protection Consulting, Deloitte & Touche, Wilton CT*

JEFFERY M. FERGUSON, *Professor of Marketing, University of Colorado at Colorado Springs, Colorado Springs CO*

PHILIP FRIEDLANDER, *Assistant Director, Ernst & Young, Cleveland OH*

PETER C. GARDINER, *Associate Professor of Systems Management, Institute of Safety and Systems Management, University of Southern California, Los Angeles CA*

MACON GRIGSBY, *Principal, Output Strategies Consulting, San Francisco CA*

CYNTHIA D. HEAGY, *Associate Professor, University of Houston-Clear Lake, Houston TX*

GIL HELD, *Director, 4-Degree Consulting, Macon GA*

STEPHEN MCHENRY, *Vice-President, Consulting Services, Advanced Software Technologies, Morgan Hill CA*

MARTIN E. MODELL, *Technical Director, Unisys Corp., McLean VA*

NATHAN J. MULLER, *Consultant, The Oxford Group, Huntsville AL*

JACK B. MULLEN, *CPA, CISA, Wilmington Trust Co., Wilmington DE*

JOHN P. MURRAY, *Consultant, Famous Footwear, Madison WI*

RICHARD J. MURRAY, *Partner-in-Charge, Nolan, Norton & Co., Los Angeles CA*

ROM NARAYAN, *Principal Consultant, Narayan Systems Corp., Wellesley MA*

HOWARD NIDEN, *Partner, Price Waterhouse, Chicago IL*

PAUL NISENBAUM, *Independent Consultant, Los Angeles CA*

LOU RUSSELL, *President, Russell Martin & Associates, Indianapolis IN*

DANIEL F. SCHULTE, *Process Specialist, Information Systems, Southwestern Bell Telephone Company, St. Louis MO*

KENNETH A. SMITH, *Vice-President, SunGard Planning Solutions, Wayne PA*

STEWART L. STOKES, JR., *Senior Vice-President, QED Information Sciences, Inc., Wellesley MA*

CHRISTINE B. TAYNTOR, *Manager, Corporate Staff Applications, AlliedSignal Inc., Morristown NJ*

WILLIAM E. TOOTHMAN, *President, Software AnalySYS, Inc., St. Louis MO*

H. VAN TRAN, *Associate Professor of Information Systems, University of Houston-Clear Lake, Houston TX*

DOROTHY E. TREFTS, *Managing Consultant, Business Transformation Practice, The IBM Consulting Group, White Plains NY*

SHOUHONG WANG, *Associate Professor, University of New Brunswick, Saint John, NB Canada*

JAMES A. WARD, *Management Consultant, James A. Ward Associates, Mays Landing NJ*

ROGER B. WHITE, JR., *Senior Industry Analyst, Network Technical Services, Provo UT*

ROBERT A. ZAWACKI, *Professor of Management and International Business, KPMG Peat Marwick Distinguished Scholar in Residence, University of Colorado at Colorado Springs, Colorado Springs CO*

GEORGE W. ZOBRIST, *Faculty Member, Department of Computer Science, University of Missouri-Rolla, Rolla MO*

Contents

Contents

Introduction

IT IS VERY MUCH IN VOGUE right now to talk about the information superhighway. The inference is that a lot of something can be moved to many places at high speed and with a minimum of impedance. The analogy to superhighways used by motor vehicles is, on the surface, appealing. It would be wise, however, to take some lessons from our system of vehicular superhighways.

For example, we know that they were built at great cost, and that in many places they were deficient in their carrying capacity from the start. They are also subject to a great deal of rebuilding and maintenance. The other thing to remember about our superhighways is that because they bypass much of America's heartland, they sounded the death knell for thousands of small towns and villages. The superhighways changed the face of America, both for the good and, in some ways, to the detriment of a more refined pace of life.

The use of the analogy of the superhighway may make us guilty of simplifying a high-speed data and multimedia network that probably won't be that simple to create. The phenomenon that the term *information superhighway* is being used to describe is, nonetheless, well under way, and IS professionals are being swept along with it. Clearly, communication is the key and the computer is the driver.

WHO'S IN CHARGE HERE?

What isn't so clear is how the infrastructure for the information superhighway will be built and who will build it. A few companies have a solid vision of where they want to be—this alone is not an easy thing. Exactly where the IS department fits in isn't always clear; the cost of getting to where the company wants to be is probably the most obscure part of all. The all-encompassing vision of information anywhere, in any form, at any time, is a tall order, especially when you consider where most organizations are today.

THE CHALLENGE BEFORE US

I believe that the visionaries who see Valhalla just around the next bend on the information superhighway do not fully appreciate the deplorable condition of most of the computer-readable data that exists today. Yes, organizations have a lot of data, but it is not well integrated, so the job of making it universally available to all users in any form they want is a formidable one. The IS challenge is to meet the need of supporting today's strategic objectives while building systems for tomorrow. This requires drastic changes in the way we do business and how we organize to do it. The reengineering of work processes and the creation of customer value are needed.

INTEGRATING TECHNOLOGY

We are currently in the age of technology integration, having surmounted the age of technology implementation. The challenge that's bearing down on us is the successful integration of all the technology that organizations wish to apply, even as we recognize that there is usually more technology available than any one company can reasonably use.

The driving force of integration is data, and more precisely, the availability of information. Many IS departments specialize in producing data in great volume, but the leaders in the IS field recognize that their real task is adding relevance and purpose to the raw data to make it genuinely valuable to the organization.

WHAT TASK, YOU ASK?

The task that most IS managers face is demanding at the least and perhaps impossible in the extreme. An appealing path might be to choose submission—just let the users do whatever they want and clean up the mess later. That, of course, will not work. IS managers must take the initiative; they should and will continue to lead the way when adopting technology for the good of the enterprise.

The many subjects addressed in this book can help the IS professional, because the task for the IS person is to put everything together in the environment specific to the enterprise. The complexity and diversity of information technology is sometimes intimidating. IS must continue to maintain and change systems that were designed and built 10, 15, even 20 years ago and at the same time integrate them with state-of-the-art purchased software that is completely alien to the methodologies used on those old systems. Building complex communication systems and then maintaining them threatens to absorb hugh amounts of time and money, yet they are critical to the environment that organizations exist in today. Yes, the task is intimidating, but it can be done, and the material in this book can help.

USING THIS HANDBOOK

This book covers a wide range of topics of interest to the IS management team. It is intended to be used as a reference that the IS professional can turn to again and again for ideas and advice. Some IS organizations use the *Handbook of IS Management* and its yearly supplements as a training resource, by having various members of the IS staff lead discussions on topics of specific interest chosen from among these pages. In whatever way you may choose to use the book, it is my wish that it becomes a part of making your job more rewarding and easier than might otherwise be the case.

ROBERT E. UMBAUGH
Carlisle PA
September 1994

Section I
Strategy, Policy, and Planning

EVERY SURVEY DONE among IS managers during the last three years has listed the need to transform the business and to align IS with corporate business objectives among the top five issues of concern. That these actions are critical there can be no argument. What can be argued is how to go about them. This section of the yearbook deals with these two subjects in a manner that permits the IS manager to transfer ideas that can result in improved operations and, if implemented properly, a higher level of corporate participation.

Organizations need IS professionals who can generate results—and at a pace that can significantly leverage the organization's ability to create value. To meet this need, IS departments must transform their mode of operation. Chapter I-1, "IS Technology and Business Transformation," describes a new management process in which IS works with business management to establish organizationwide information technology initiatives.

Chapter I-2 addresses the role that a corporate information technology architecture can play in supporting high-level objectives. This chapter, "IS Support of Strategic Objectives," offers sound advice on formalizing the IT architecture that exists in every organization and bridging the IS architecture to the corporate one.

A documented corporate information technology architecture is a guide for current operations and a blueprint for future direction. With the backing of senior corporate management, the corporate technology architecture helps ensure that the IS organization meets the strategic business needs of the corporation. By providing a common source of information about the organization's existing and planned technology, the architecture ensures that standard information is available to all departments and employees and thus prevents the costs of time, money, and other resources associated with not having such information available.

I-1

IS Technology and Business Transformation

Richard J. Murray
Dorothy E. Trefts

FOR BUSINESS AND IS MANAGEMENT, the information technology imperative is to construct the organizationwide systems and capabilities needed by businesses to compete. For IS professionals, this means developing a totally new viewpoint regarding the role information technology (IT) plays in building the business of the future. The new viewpoint embraces the idea that without IS professionals' involvement in and significant understanding of the business—from strategy creation through systems implementation—the business itself will stand in jeopardy. IS and business management must act as true partners following this new management process, each supporting the other with goals well aligned toward a common end: creating the optimally performing company.

THE NEW MANAGEMENT PROCESS

To put into practice this notion of partnership and mutually supportive involvement, IS and business managers require a totally new way of working together. This is essential because the restructuring initiatives being undertaken by corporate America require change management on a scale never encountered before. Information technology is envisioned as the strategic enabling ingredient in this restructuring. Unless business and IS management agree to partner and work together, the corporation will never accomplish this goal.

Global Demands

Companies are being realigned to address global business opportunities. *Global* is not just another word to describe conducting business as usual, in autonomous, diversified, unintegrated entities around the world. Information technology is the key to transforming business capabilities from parochial to global. Unless IS and business management can put the pieces together, they will fall short of achieving the global corporation.

Most of corporate America is constrained by information technology islands of automation: solutions that effectively address single, localized, usually departmental issues but that are disconnected from and unresponsive to the needs of the integrated business. This problem is compounded by different processing platforms, programming languages, software packages, communications protocols, data base technologies, and skills—all of which prohibit easy connections between islands of automation. The result is a web of systems that make it impossible to leverage the organization's technology resources to generate true business advantage.

Managing the IT resource to move from these automation islands to organizationwide, global systems requires the development of a new management process—one that is based on a clearly articulated management template. Such a process enables the organization to establish and maintain a focus on those projects that are critical to developing and maintaining a competitive edge.

FUNDAMENTAL MANAGING PRINCIPLES

First, it is important to articulate the principles that govern the new management process. Paradigm shifts always present a challenge and require a more fundamental base of understanding from which to build. The new management process is not a cookbook approach to solving problems. It must be described and understood within the context of a dramatically different role for IT.

Six managing principles govern this new process of management:

- Linkage to strategy.
- A focus on business benefits.
- The concept of quickstrikes.
- Defined roles and responsibilities.
- Creeping commitment.
- Linkage to architecture.

Linkage to Strategy

Organizationwide IT initiatives must be:

- Driven by the business vision and strategy.
- Tied to specific quantifiable benefits.
- Based on the redesign of the business process.

This linkage to strategy clarifies what problems must be solved and, more important, how success is to be measured. Translation of vague corporate vision statements into specific performance goals permits the organization to grasp how information technology can play a leading role in vaulting the corporation ahead. Expectations are clearly understood at the beginning of the transformation process.

There are distinct implications for IS professionals. First, IS management must understand the full business vision (ideally by participating in its development) and be able to communicate it throughout the IS group. Second, business vision and strategy must be translated into conceptual statements of those tasks that the organization must perform exceptionally well to achieve its vision, as well as measurable business objectives (i.e., specific, quantified performance goals, most of which are nonfinancial) that in turn clearly set out the organization's goals. Finally, these new goals trigger a process of reevaluating the organization's strategic business processes. At present, many organizations may have no significant IT component, yet designing a new way of conducting business in the future is fundamental to doing business cheaper, better, and faster.

Focus on Business Benefits

Executive participation is essential to enable transformation; the ongoing measurement of performance and benefits against strategic objectives drives the transformation process.

Business transformation clearly requires investment. One of the missing ingredients in the management of traditional development efforts has been rigorous financial analysis at all stages of the development process, to revisit initial financial assumptions and to incorporate and test the new information. This process implies incremental funding, with go or no-go decision points. Also implied are sunk costs that may or may not be recovered.

The new management process is based on the assumption that program financials will be revisited and challenged at each phase of the process, so that the learning acquired at each phase becomes incorporated into the analysis. The corporation is able to continually answer the questions: Is this program accomplishing what it set out to achieve? Is it worth it?

Quickstrikes

Quickstrike initiatives—defined as small technical and nontechnical projects of short duration that produce immediate business benefits—can be implemented early on to speed the realization of overall program benefits. The underlying concept of the quickstrike is that benefits should not accrue solely at the end of a program; they should begin to be reaped in the early phases of a program and continue throughout its life. The intention is to move the program in the direction of becoming self-funding as soon as possible, thereby avoiding the traditional model of delayed realization of benefits. Interim benefits must be used to fund the program.

Defined Roles and Responsibilities

The new management process defines expectations about behavior that put performance goals on the table and ensure that all players are aware of their role. This principle is basic; however, it is an element of process design that is often forgotten. Ensuring that each group is aware of its role in the new management process facilitates the program and the organization's success. The explicit nature of this principle is what is important, so that individuals become aware of and accountable for their contribution to the whole.

Creeping Commitment

Work should be performed according to a standard work process, which produces interim deliverables that permit the continuous management of risk and capital investment. The organization's commitment to a specific transformation program should grow as the program moves through the various phases of the management process. As the strategic vision is defined and clarified and as ever more detailed pieces of the plan are fleshed out, the organization's commitment level—and financial appetite for the program—grow.

The new management process builds creeping organizational commitment through its rigorous gatekeeping requirements, which ensure that the process is managed and monitored. As a transformational program moves forward through the management process, the corporation takes the opportunity to identify and test its assumptions about the program's inherent risk and rewards. Only at the point of maximum information, when the risks have been well calculated, is major capital committed.

Linkage to Architecture

A technological and business architecture is needed to coordinate and integrate individual projects over extended periods of time. New business processes and information systems must be consistent with this architecture.

The new management process embraces the concept of architectural standards for organizationwide information technology to guide the development of new systems capabilities. These standards—as they relate to technologies, data, communications, applications, and systems—are analogous to the plumbing, heating, ventilation, air-conditioning, and electrical systems standards for a new residential construction project. Without these standards, a house is apt to run on the wrong voltage or be missing drainage pipes. Similarly, without IT architectural standards, organizationwide systems become yet additional islands of automation, akin to existing departmental solutions in that they are useful only to a limited segment of the business. (Chapter I-2 describes such an architecture.)

OBJECTIVES AND DELIVERABLES

The new management process contains six phases, each with a specific set of objectives and deliverables. As shown in Exhibit I-1-1, each phase of the management process generates a series of quickstrike opportunities and benefits analyses. The glue holding the process together is a tight system of program management activities. Combined, these three factors generate the creeping commitment necessary for the organization to ultimately buy into the program and implement the required systems capabilities. Exhibit I-1-1

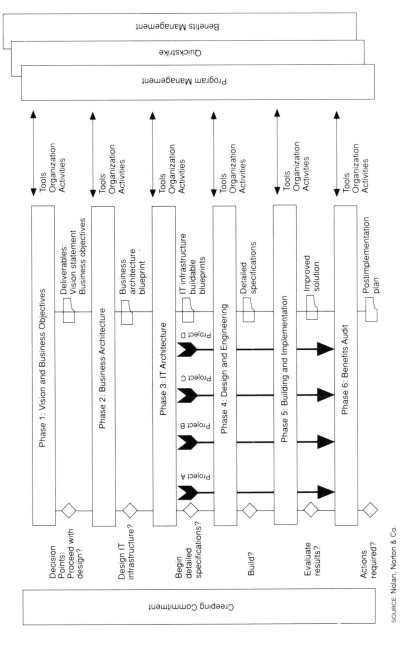

Exhibit I-1-1. The New Management Process

SOURCE: Nolan, Norton & Co.

embodies the managing principles previously discussed. The six phases, which are usually undertaken in sequential order, are described next.

Phase 1: Vision and Business Objectives. This phase is used to articulate the corporation's high-level business vision and strategic objectives. It is supported by precise, quantified performance targets. This phase of the management process includes a first pass at the business program, which is a statement of the objectives, scope, and goals of a specific organizationwide initiative and its supporting financial business case.

Phase 2: Business Architecture. This phase entails the identification and definition of the high-impact business processes supporting the business vision. It is the statement of a business model of the organization and serves as the foundation for the IT architecture (phase 3). The business architecture's specific deliverables include a map of the critical business processes as they currently exist and of the business process requirements of the future. Another critical deliverable is an initial plan—the improvement action plan—with key steps to achieving the new business architecture.

Phase 3: The IT Architecture. This phase develops the computing structure, beginning with an idealized top-down and bottom-up view of the information systems requirements to support the business process. This phase creates a blueprint for technology that enables the organization to conduct business in new ways with strategic potential.

The first step in formulating this architecture is baselining the architecture in place. Other important deliverables for this phase include the risk assessment (an evaluation of the risks inherent in the architectural choices made), a restatement of the business case that incorporates this new information, and the architectural migration strategy and plan. Phase 3 is an important phase for the identification of quickstrike initiatives. (See Chapter I-2 for guidelines on developing an enterprisewide IT architecture.)

Phase 4: Design and Engineering. This phase covers the translation of business and IT requirements into the guidelines and specifications critical to systems engineering and development efforts at the individual project level. Each broad organizationwide program may consist of several systems projects that must be managed independently. The design phase of the management process includes requirements definition, software evaluation and selection, conceptual design, and detailed design as its key deliverables.

Phase 5: Building and Implementation. This phase includes the coding, testing, documentation, piloting, training, installation, maintenance, and system migration activities involved in realizing an information system and propagating it throughout the business. The important deliverables for this phase are the developed system, the first implementation, and subsequent system migrations.

Phase 6: Benefits Audit. This phase entails the ongoing activities to measure performance improvements and program benefits and to ensure that

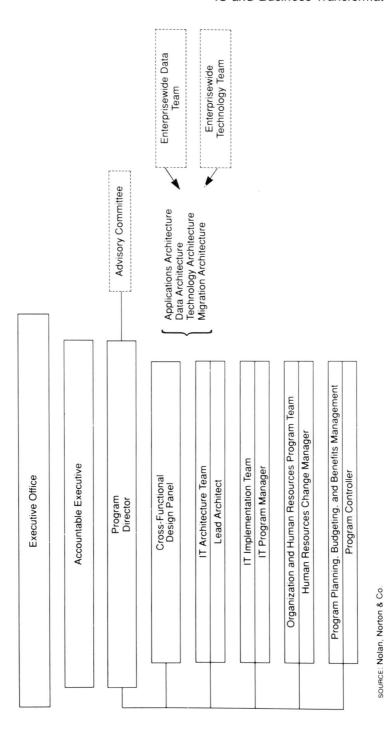

Executive Office

Accountable Executive

Program Director

Advisory Committee

Cross-Functional Design Panel

IT Architecture Team

Lead Architect

IT Implementation Team

IT Program Manager

Organization and Human Resources Program Team

Human Resources Change Manager

Program Planning, Budgeting, and Benefits Management

Program Controller

Applications Architecture
Data Architecture
Technology Architecture
Migration Architecture

Enterprisewide Data Team

Enterprisewide Technology Team

Exhibit I-1-2. The New Organization

SOURCE: Nolan, Norton & Co.

PARTICIPANTS / DELIVERABLES AND ACTIVITIES	Business Partners						IT Partners			Both
	Executive Office (content review)	Executive Steering Committee (process review)	Accountable Executive	Program Director	Advisory Committee	Cross-Functional Design Panel	IT Program Manager	IT Architecture Team	IT Implementation Team	Program Controller
Vision and Business Objectives	●	△	●	●	○	◑				
Business Architecture	△	△	△	●	○	●	◑	◑		◑
IT Architecture	▲	△	△	◑	○	◑	●	●		◑
Design	△	△	△	△●	○	●	●	◑	●	◑
Building and Implementation	△	△	△	△◑	○	△●	●	◑	●	◑
Benefits Audit	△	△	△	●	◑	◑	◑	◑	◑	●

● Primary responsibility for doing the work and leading all aspects of the activity

◑ Some participation in and responsibility for specific tasks within the activity

○ Peripheral involvement in the activity

△ Responsibility for reviewing the activity before going on to the next phase

▲ Contingent review only if business case changes

SOURCE: Nolan, Norton & Co.

Exhibit I-1-3. Overview of Roles and Responsibilities

continuous improvement is derived from the effort. Key deliverables for this phase are the benefits evaluation, system evaluation, and an identification of the lessons learned from the project. These lessons must be consolidated, project by project, to the broader program level to share the learning across projects and other similar transformational programs.

ROLES AND RESPONSIBILITIES

Each phase in the new management process is supported by a group of executives (see Exhibit I-1-2) charged with specific responsibilities to produce a detailed set of deliverables. The matrix in Exhibit I-1-3—which identifies the roles and responsibilities of these key individuals as well as new organization structure implications—highlights how this process differs from the traditional approaches.

Perhaps the most important ingredient in making this process work for the organization is well-orchestrated communication about the process throughout business and IS departments. Exposure to the new management process can be generated through executive awareness sessions, comprehensive documentation, training modules, and educational programs to train the trainers. These efforts support the new ways of accomplishing business, but require time and attention from both business and IT partners.

The ideal way to move forward with the new management process is to educate the organization and then to apply this process at the start of a new organizationwide initiative. Most corporations do not have that luxury, however, because they are already in the midst of undertaking several such initiatives simultaneously.

CONCLUSION

Companies can learn valuable lessons from incorporating this new management process, even in midstream. For example, the process can reveal whether staff members on critical programs understand what their roles are. It can also determine which key phases have been given short shrift or eliminated altogether.

Serious commitment at the highest level of the organization is the key to making the transformation process work, especially when the change involves reorchestrating the way in which units vital to the corporation work together. Traditional IT management must also accept the challenge and embrace this new management process to truly transform the organization.

I-2

IS Support of Strategic Objectives

Howard A. Curle, Jr.

IS DEPARTMENTS ARE being called on to justify expenditures for information technology. Corporate executives are asking pointed questions about how information technology supports the strategic business objectives of the corporation. A well-documented corporate IT architecture answers those questions by aligning IS projects, methodologies, and products with corporate business objectives.

An IT architecture is the infrastructure of technology that provides the foundation for automated business procedures and practices. Just as a city's infrastructure of roads, sewers, bridges, buildings, and public utilities provides the foundation on which the city lives and operates, the corporate technology infrastructure provides the automation foundation on which the corporation operates.

Each business organization has an IT architecture. Some lucky corporations have an elegantly crafted, well-documented, and cohesive IT architecture, and others muddle along in an anarchy of disjointed automation projects that sway and creak dangerously in the winds of business change. An IT architecture can be as simple as a list of approved and supported automation products or as complex as an interwoven structure of products, procedures, methodologies, and standards. Regardless of the structure, the IT architecture should be a vital part of the corporate business plan because it defines how the corporation will deploy technology on a strategic, long-term level to meet corporate business objectives.

TECHNOLOGY AND STRATEGY

The IT architecture is strategic in nature. Although it documents the current technology infrastructure, it also serves as a blueprint of the future technology direction of the corporation by:

- Examining technology directions beyond a two-year period.
- Providing technology migration planning.

- Joining technology products and directions with strategic corporate business objectives.

A corporate information technology architecture is different from an information technology architecture document. The corporate IT architecture is made up of corporate business objectives, the individual department automation plans that support those objectives, and the technology architecture necessary to support the automation plans. The IT architecture may not exist as a single document. One company may, for example, have a set of corporate business objectives, but each department may have an automation plan, with the IS group providing the information architecture document.

The technology architecture document explains the technology architecture component of the corporate IT architecture, and it changes fairly often to accommodate new technology. The corporate business objectives are the high-level goals of the corporation and should not change drastically from one year to the next. The automation plans, which outline an individual group's planned uses of technology to achieve corporate business objectives, are reviewed and changed on a yearly basis.

The technology document the IS department should provide ensures that there is a standard source of information about the various technology options that not only already exist in the organization but are available to solve the individual group's automation needs. When a specific department or function is developing an automation plan with the IS department, such a document imposes controls or checks on the automation planning process by preventing or avoiding such ineffective and inefficient practices as individual groups duplicating research or even purchasing an automation tool that already exists elsewhere in the organization. Exhibit I-2-1 shows the relationships between the corporate objectives and automation plans.

Many corporations use an automation plan that is tied to the yearly budget. The automation plan tells each segment of the organization what automation projects will be supported during that year and how many automation products they are authorized to purchase. The automation plan is tactical in nature, usually covering no more than two annual budget cycles. The automation plan may have a future trends section but usually does not extend into long-range planning.

The annual automation plan is part of the overall IT architecture in that the products and projects included in the automation plan must adhere to the standards, guidelines, and practices outlined in the architecture document. The IT architecture must be understood and supported by all employees in the corporation. It cannot be just an IS department document. Developing the architecture must be a team effort between senior management, the IS department, and the functional departments. Without a team effort to generate participant buy-in, the IT architecture will be reviled by many and used by none.

The overall IT architecture must include long-term corporate business objectives. These should be clearly defined by senior management and carefully detailed as part of the architecture. These strategic business objectives enable the architecture planners to identify specific automation technology

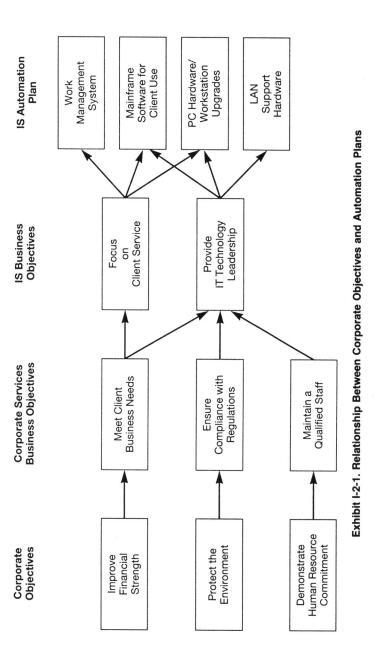

Exhibit I-2-1. Relationship Between Corporate Objectives and Automation Plans

that will support the company's business objectives and help avoid the pitfall of technology for the sake of technology.

For example, if a corporate business objective is to capture market share by increasing customer satisfaction, the planners might investigate technology to support a voice-activated inquiry and ordering system, bar-coding to improve inventory control, or videoconferencing to support customer meetings. Or, if a corporate business objective is to reduce administrative overhead by 10% and improve the accounts receivable function, the architecture planners might include technology to support an electronic document interchange (EDI) system for the purchasing and accounting departments. Again, technology decisions cannot be made in a vacuum; IT architecture planners must have corporate direction for their efforts.

The second step in developing a corporate IT architecture—that is, after the corporate business objectives have been identified—is to correlate specific areas of technology, both current and projected, with the specific long-term corporate business objectives. Each objective should have a list of the technology projects and products that will satisfy that objective. When that has been done, the work of building and documenting the technology infrastructure begins.

DOCUMENTING THE TECHNOLOGY INFRASTRUCTURE

The IT architecture document should describe the recommended principles, guidelines, and standards used within the company to support information technology. The document has many practical uses for supporting a business function. Continued use of the information in the document should provide an up-to-date and ever-expanding list of appropriate solutions to meet business problems. The document should be referenced when an employee:

- Hears about a technology but does not know what it is.
- Needs help in determining criteria for application platform placement.
- Needs to find a recommended software tool or utility to help in applications development.
- Has a transferred or new employee who needs a source of basic information about the information technology found in the department.
- Works with the IS professionals or vendors and wants to review the detailed technologies discussed in the meetings.
- Needs to know the standard hardware and software used in the company.
- Finds that the current technology is aging and needs to identify and plan for a replacement.
- Needs a desktop tool to perform a standard business function.
- Is preparing the department's automation plan and needs information about available technology and trends.

It is important to stress that the IT architecture document provides detailed but general information. As the complexity and specificity of a department's technology search or investigation increase, these users should work closely with the IS department to ensure proper integration and interpretation of the information contained in the document.

Several uses of the IT document should be considered inappropriate in most companies. The document should not be used as a handbook on how to acquire information technology. Purchasing procedures and departmental practices usually provide direction on and maintain control over budgeting and requisitioning requirements. Likewise, it should not be used as a justification for the acquisition of hardware or software. The IT document does not provide instruction on how to implement or integrate a particular technology in a business unit, and it is not a manual on how to use the technology following implementation. Product requirements, business unit procedures, and application function can require that similar information technology be used differently from department to department.

Blocks of technology are used to build the infrastructure document. Although the blocks can stand alone, in reality they are very much integrated because each complements and supports the other. These technology blocks should include current and planned technology implementation.

The following areas can make up the main categories of technology blocks:

- *Computer platforms.* Includes all the mainframe, midrange, and micro-computer platforms used in the enterprise.
- *Networks.* Includes the local, metropolitan, and wide area networks used in the enterprise.
- *Applications development.* Includes the tools, methodologies, and practices used to design, implement, and operate computer applications.
- *Data administration.* Includes the policies and practices for security, data integrity, disaster recovery, backup, and operational support.
- *Data management.* Includes the data base tools and structures used to build and maintain data base applications.
- *Desktop tools.* Includes the various word processors, spreadsheets, electronic communications, data entry, and other desktop tools that assist employees in doing their jobs.
- *Specialized technology.* Includes such tools as bar-coding, videoconferencing, and image processing.

Exhibit I-2-2 shows a sample structure for an IT architecture document.

Each of these building blocks must be defined in detail because the information is used as a guide for the purchase and implementation of the technology. For example, if the local area network (LAN) has been identified as the proper technology to achieve two strategic corporate objectives—improving customer service through local office automation and empowering local office employees through automation—the following types of information should be included in the LAN building block:

- Definition of a LAN (specific to the enterprise):
  —Geographical boundaries (where is it installed).
  —Administrative boundaries (who administers it).
  —Capacity boundaries (how many workstations).

- **Part I: Information Technology Architecture (1 document)**
- **Part II: Computer Platforms (5 documents)**
  - Introduction
  - Mainframe
  - Midrange
  - Personal computer
  - Network server
- **Part III: Networks (4 documents)**
  - Introduction
  - Local area
  - Metropolitan area
  - Wide area
- **Part IV: Applications Development Environments (5 documents)**
  - Introduction
  - . . . . for the mainframe
  - . . . . for the midrange
  - . . . . for the personal computer
  - . . . . for the network server
- **Part V: Data Administration (1 document)**

- **Part VI: Data Management (5 documents)**
  - Introduction
  - . . . . for the mainframe
  - . . . . for the midrange
  - . . . . for the personal computer
  - . . . . for the network server
- **Part VII: Desktop Tools (5 documents)**
  - Introduction
  - . . . . for the mainframe
  - . . . . for the midrange
  - . . . . for the personal computer
  - . . . . for the network server
- **Part VIII: Specialized Technologies (5 documents)**
  - Image processing
  - Bar-coding
  - Multimedia
  - Automated call distribution
  - Videoconferencing
- **APPENDIXES: (2 documents)**
  - Glossary
  - Product lists

Exhibit I-2-2. IT Architecture Document Structure

- Definition of LAN applications approved for implementation, including information about:
  —Document processing.
  —Electronic mail.
  —Local customer data base.
  —Local office spreadsheets.
- Corporate architectural considerations, such as information about:
  —Functional specifications for LAN hardware components, including server configuration (processor size, speed, and memory), workstation configurations, network interface card specifications, wiring specifications, and UPS specifications.
  —Functional specifications for LAN software components, including network operating system (NOS) specifications, approved NOS parameters and configurations, and approved workstation configurations.
  —Approved products that meet the functional specifications, including server hardware and software, workstation hardware and software, network interface cards, LAN wiring components, and application software.

> —Future corporate business trends or technical trends that may impact LAN implementation or require product migration, including processor migration, NOS migration, wide area network (WAN) connection requirements, and centralized LAN management.

- Full life cycle costs for implementing a LAN, including such information as:
  - —Initial purchase costs.
  - —Implementation costs.
  - —Training costs.
  - —Maintenance and upgrade costs.
- LAN implementation considerations that encompass such information as:
  - —Hours of operation and support.
  - —Application mix.
  - —Node naming conventions (for WAN compatibility).
  - —Capacity planning.
  - —Network tuning.
  - —Network security.
  - —Disaster recovery.
- Human resources considerations, which include information about:
  - —Network administrator selection.
  - —Network administrator training.
  - —Application training.

Exhibit I-2-3 shows a sample IT architecture document chapter on LANs.

Blocks similar to this could be constructed for mainframe, midrange, and microcomputer platforms, programming languages, data bases, WANs, word processing programs, EDI, bar-coding, videoconferencing, and any current or planned technology that is part of the organization's IT architecture. The list of topics is as extensive as the number of technology areas available to support strategic business objectives. However, each topic should contain similar types of information; for example, considerations for costs, training, implementation, integration, enhancements, and maintenance should be addressed in addition to the basic technology information provided.

Because the list of topics is so extensive and the potential for a very large document is high, the IT architecture document must have a detailed table of contents, index, and glossary. It is also helpful to include decision tables in the beginning of each technology section. For example, in the network technology section, a decision table would say: "If you need corporatewide distribution of data, see the Wide Area Network chapter" or, "If you need local or departmental distribution of data, see the Local Area Network chapter." It must be easy to navigate within the architecture document if it is going to be used by many people. A common format must be used by the individuals writing the document to make it consistent and easy to read. Having a common format also reduces the amount of time spent correcting style differences when the document reaches the review stage.

Part III-Chapter 2: Local Area Networks
Table of Contents

Exhibit I-2-3. Sample Document Chapter

Exhibit I-2-3. (cont'd)

REVIEWING THE DOCUMENT

After the IT architecture document has been drafted, including technology specifications, migration plans, and implementation considerations, the document must be marketed to the corporation. This involves developing an overall marketing plan that includes the client community in the approval process. Too many well-written and technically correct IS documents have failed miserably because the client community was not involved, did not buy in to the process, and resented having to accept another IS mandate. The architecture must be marketed to the clients as their tool to help them satisfy their goals and objectives.

As each section of the architecture document is completed in draft form, it should be routed to an architectural review board for technical and business review. Each architectural review board should consist of no more than a dozen IS and client department personnel and should concentrate on a specific technology area. Members of the review boards should be selected because of their potential involvement with or expertise in the particular technology area. Client personnel are included on the review boards because this is a corporate-level process that requires the active involvement of all concerned corporate citizens if it is to succeed. The architectural review board should review the document for technical accuracy and content, not writing style. The common format used for the document should reduce style contention. The review process should involve a formal routing procedure and established due dates.

After the reviewers have completed their evaluation, the document should be approved for publication by the IS department management team. The management team and the entire IS department must support and follow the IT architecture document, if it is to be accepted by the client community. Senior corporate managers must also support the document. Without their support, the technology directions and standards listed in the document will be ignored. Distribution of the document can take many forms, from paper distribution to online electronic distribution.

CONCLUSION

The IT architecture cannot be set in concrete. The document will be under constant revision as business and technology needs change. The IS department must ensure that the architectural review boards and the client community have a mechanism by which they can submit changes and suggestions to the IT architecture group. Two-way communications are vital, with the clients talking to the architecture group and the group getting out of the IS ivory tower to talk to the clients. A revision cycle should review each technology section at least once a year.

The IT architecture document must be a resource and common reference for the entire corporation. There should be little confusion as to what technology directions have been set to meet corporate business objectives. When clients have a technology question, they should be able to use the index or the table of contents in the document and follow the path to the best solution for their technology needs.

The architecture will change, but different sections will change at different rates. Business objectives and the technology areas tied to those objectives should change very slowly. Technology specifications will change at a somewhat faster rate as technology changes, and the product sets will change the fastest of all. For that reason, migration planning must be included in the product set sections of the architecture.

Tactical automation plans and strategic information technology architectures must be joint ventures between senior management, client departments, and the IS department. No one group has all the answers to a corporation's business problems. But when all parties work together to establish a blueprint, automation solutions to business problems become carefully charted journeys to excellence rather than unplanned adventures to nowhere.

Section II
Management Issues

COMPANIES THAT ARE REENGINEERING their businesses to be more responsive to competitive and other outside pressures are relying on information technology to support their reengineering efforts in almost every instance. IS management, in turn, is having to look inward to determine what changes are necessary within the IS function so that it can continue to be supportive of the corporate effort.

Chapter II-1, "Information Engineering and Business Strategy," describes a way of improving customer support through chain-based management, an information engineering strategy that directly supports the business strategy. This chapter explains how to augment information engineering to more closely conform to the needs of the value-chain approach that drives many business restructuring efforts.

Chapter II-2, "Negligence, Litigation, and Responsibility for Information Security," examines IS management's role in establishing and managing an information security program. This chapter transcends the usual material on information security by informing IS readers of the consequences of negligence, the impact it can have on the information security program's effectiveness, and the potential for lawsuits.

Organizations and their managers may be successfully sued by those who have suffered damages as a result of the failure of an information system to ensure—within reason—the confidentiality, integrity, or availability of the information it contains. Chapter II-2 is intended to help IS managers understand and fulfill their legal obligation to provide for reasonable information security, by pointing out possible consequences of failure to provide such security. IS security practitioners can work effectively with in-house or external legal counsel to minimize exposure to litigation.

II-1

Information Engineering and Business Strategy

Mac Clark

MANY LEADING COMPANIES have launched large-scale efforts to deliver greater customer value by reengineering their businesses on the basis of value-chain logic. Although generally successful, many such initiatives have encountered delays and difficulties that have far-reaching implications for the information strategies that support them. This chapter suggests a way IS managers can create customer value more effectively by building an information chain–based approach paralleling that of the value-chain concept. Specifically, the chapter discusses ways of augmenting information engineering to more closely conform to the needs of the value-chain logic that drives many restructuring efforts. These methods permit IS and senior managers to more effectively resolve organizational dysfunctions and to create rewards and incentives that promote high performance.

VALUE CHAIN–BASED MANAGEMENT

Senior managers can and should play an influential role in implementing business process modifications based on the value chain, a concept espoused by many business executives and detailed in the book *Competitive Strategy* by Michael Porter of the Harvard Business School. The value chain helps managers develop a clear analytic framework for understanding the value-generating operations within their business activities. A typical value-chain schematic is shown in Exhibit II-1-1.

Using value chain–based logic, many companies have pursued management initiatives to increase their competitiveness by making fundamental changes in how they create value for their customers. Business process reengineering is a way of improving operations that is consistent with value-chain logic. Reengineering efforts seek to eliminate those activities and tasks that add little value to the firm's output of goods or services. This reengineering takes the classical form of streamlining functions, sharply reducing levels of management, and even outright consolidation of previously autonomous operating units. More notably, reengineering includes process

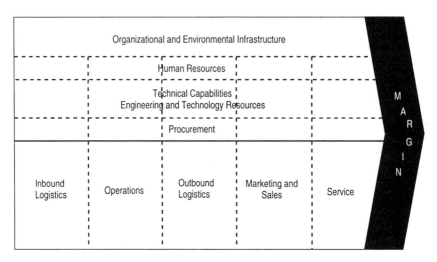

Exhibit II-1-1. Sample Value-Chain Schematic

reorganizations that emphasize effective information flows and tight functional integration of the various organizational units.

Organizational Resistance

Some companies discover that these changes can be inordinately difficult to bring about. Organizational resistance and the inherent limitations of information systems are frequently cited as barriers to progress. There is little wonder that organizational resistance springs up; middle managers do not want to lose their jobs or become marginalized.

Overcoming organizational resistance requires skillful senior managers and the selection of effective incentives with appropriate performance measures to validate these incentives. This is a familiar problem, involving such issues as job security, organizational politics, human relations, as well as each individual's motivation, dignity, and sense of worth. Senior managers with backgrounds in solving such problems in traditional settings can also find ways to solve them within value chain–based initiatives.

The limitations of information systems are unfortunately far less tractable because the technical hurdles are generally higher than the level of organizational talent and experience. Outside consultants can usually boost organizational resources temporarily, but eventually the job must be shouldered in large part by the organization itself.

In this situation, it is vitally important that senior managers depart from traditional thinking about information resources. Senior managers must become deeply involved in the specification, design, and application of these resources by managers throughout the organization. Not all projects spawned by the various initiatives will succeed, yet every effort consumes resources, the most precious of which is calendar time. If only for this reason, senior managers must involve themselves in these efforts. In the global market, the never-ending race cannot be won by those who tarry; every possible effort must be made to optimize calendar time in achieving quality performance.

Problems in Value-Chain Logic

Value-chain logic forces an organization to examine its activities to determine which ones contribute most to gaining a desirable advantage over its competitors. Managers eliminate activities that add little or no value for stakeholders; new activities that increase customer values are created. These changes often reach into the heart of the product or service offered and result in fundamental redesign.

Although information systems sometimes need little apparent modification to fit the new order of the day, the implementation of the modifications can be a demoralizing experience. This happens because information flows and the mechanisms that support them are incapable of the level of integration required to support true value chain–based functional capabilities.

For example, use of just-in-time manufacturing methods and the concomitant reduction of inventory levels, may require many more organizational players than just the inventory department and the production scheduler. This kind of cross-department decision making requires new views of data that simply are not feasible through the traditional online functions and batch reports.

IS specialists generally have little authority to diagnose and resolve these issues, because these are fundamentally issues of organizational design and specific organizational behavior. Although the IS specialists can modify existing information systems to meet functional requirements, only senior management can troubleshoot the organizational dysfunctions and eliminate them.

GUIDELINES AND METHODS: INFORMATION ENGINEERING

Information engineering is a powerful tool that IS managers can use to achieve greater levels of competitive advantage. Information engineering allows managers to identify the collection of high-level objectives, goals, strategies, and performance measures that support the organizational mission.

Senior managers can clearly specify each of these strategic planning elements within the information engineering framework. With these specifications in view, IS specialists can then more effectively create information architectures that support each one of these elements. Information engineering is an established methodology, and in fact, several automated tools exist that support it.

Value-chain logic cannot be spanned by information engineering alone. Because value-chain logic demands more extensive business process reorganizations, it becomes increasingly difficult to apply information engineering in its pure form. The remainder of this chapter suggests a modified information engineering approach.

The Information Chain

To begin, the notion of information chains is added to the basic elements of the information engineering approach. The information-chain concept parallels that of the value chain. In fact, for every component of the value chain, at least one information chain exists to support it.

Such a chain may begin with a marketing forecast. The forecast leads to a sales plan, from which managers develop a production plan, and thence to a series of decisions about purchases, labor force commitments, and finally to a series of sales results. The sales results are eventually quantified as "Actuals" in a sales report, and senior managers can assess the validity of the original marketing forecast in light of these actual results. Exhibit II-1-2 shows how this series of events fits into the value chain.

Unfortunately, most information systems cannot support the association of specific plans and observed results. That is, they cannot close the information chain. Although these systems are excellent at processing transactions, they lack the capability to trace the flow of events, materials, information, and the decisions managers make about them.

The transaction processing focus is an intrinsic limitation, but it is not the only one. Another limitation is the overwhelming emphasis most organizations place on financial results. When organizations stress financially ori-

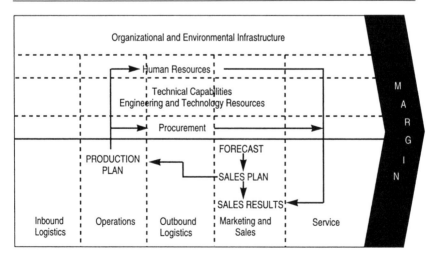

Exhibit II-1-2. How the Information Chain Fits into the Value Chain

ented performance measures, they tend to obscure or confuse the tracking of more fundamental causes of performance successes or failures. New accounting methods like activity-based costing are an improvement, but they still stress financial measures. Creating customer value is a tough proposition without a focus on traceability.

Traceability of Cause and Effect

Traceability of cause and effect is a basic requirement in the transition to competing on the basis of value-chain logic. Traceability is important in solving problems of delivering goods to customers on time, because this performance measure is fundamental to perceived value in the marketplace. In this area, most information systems can provide a quantification of service levels, but few provide the mechanisms to determine why specific measurements were observed.

For example, many steel service centers have informative systems that can accurately report how many days it took to deliver a quantity of steel to a customer, but few such systems provide management insight into why some deliveries were late. The diagram in Exhibit II-1-3 shows an information chain relevant to on-time delivery. The measure performance requires feedback from every link in the chain.

Without this information feedback, senior managers cannot be certain that their efforts to gain competitive advantage are successful. Even if delivery times improve, it is not clear whether this improvement was a result of faster delivery of raw materials from suppliers or higher levels of performance

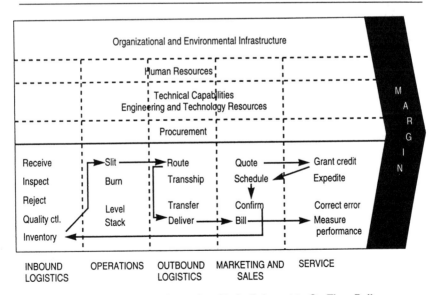

Exhibit II-1-3. Sample Information Chain Relevant to On-Time Delivery

from the organization. Conversely, were more orders delivered late because salespeople made optimistic delivery promises that no organization could fulfill? Or did the shop-floor manager perform poorly in scheduling production operations, thus creating a cascade of delays in order fulfillment?

Most systems based on additional design approaches will eventually fail to answer such questions when senior managers push ahead with value chain–based competition. These system failures exacerbate those caused by poor organizational cooperation; good information is lacking just when the departments need it most. Traditional technology architectures and component selections rarely anticipate such decision-making needs, so they respond poorly.

To deal effectively with these problems, senior managers must know and understand the processes on which they base their success, especially the information processes. For initiatives that pursue value-chain logic, operating results are the consequences of decisions of others as well as ourselves.

Priorities naturally differ across operating departments and units. What may be a critical customer service priority for one department could be an irritating annoyance for another. While such disparities are not new (there are many business school cases on resolving just such conflicts), value-chain logic makes these situations increasingly more frequent and far more important to solve effectively. For the information strategist, resolving these issues imposes a need for clear vision—of what cooperation means and of what the new organization must be.

The Value-Chain Architecture

The key benefit of value-chain logic is that it clarifies the relationship of internal operations to events visible to the company's customers and critical stakeholders. Information engineering, with a few methodological improvements, can help clarify the corresponding information relationships through which the company creates those events. For example, the function-entity matrices that contrast business function against data can be useful in finding the point of sensitivity and leverage in performance.

Furthermore, data flow diagrams can be used to identify organizational units that are value-chain participants, and in some cases it is possible to derive specific event sequences that highlight opportunities for improved performance. For example, every data store in a diagram depicting work flow in an order-fulfillment process is an opportunity for creating a faster, automated response. Similarly, every exception that triggers a management decision is an opportunity to provide electronically the data needed to advance the decision to completion without having long delays to interrogate manually maintained records.

By making the information resource conform to the value chain it supports, it is thus made to mirror the sequence of events, operations, and functions that create the values that are visible to customers. Business reengineering promotes harmony between customer values and competitive effectiveness. Information engineering, properly augmented, extends this harmony to the organizational functions themselves.

CONCLUSION

Most modern business applications are geared to perform transaction processing and ignore the value-chain requirements of global competition. Too often, a senior manager seeking to reach critical business decisions will find the necessary information locked tightly within the company's computerized data base. To solve this problem, information specialists have created a class of systems: executive information systems.

This solution is regrettably too narrow. It is vitally important that executives have such information at their fingertips, but even more important is giving analogous information to the line managers who must make the restructured business processes work.

Unless line managers can use unified, complete, and responsive information chains, they will be unable to serve the organization's wider purpose. Potential problems to look for in an information chain—that is, missing links in the chain—are as follows:

- Isolated standalone systems.
- Departments that do not link to information chains created by other departments.
- Departments that create information no others use.
- Undocumented departmental decision processes.
- Ill-defined or inconsistent performance measures.

Unless senior management can create a system of measures and rewards to motivate cooperative supportive behavior, value-chain logic cannot easily succeed. The information-chain approach can help senior and middle managers make the restructured business processes work better by tracing the path of information and events involved in the value-creating activities.

II-2

Negligence, Litigation, and Responsibility for Information Security

Peter C. Gardiner

UNDER THE STANDARD of due care, managers and their organizations have a duty to provide for information security even though they may not be aware they have such obligations. These obligations arise from the portion of US common law that deals with issues of negligence (i.e., the law of torts). If managers take actions that leave their information systems unreasonably insecure, or if they fail to take actions to make their information systems reasonably secure and as a result someone suffers damages when those systems are penetrated, the managers and their organization may be sued.

Information security is still largely an unknown entity to most people, including lawyers. Managers can and often do ignore sound advice offered by information security professionals for various reasons. In the past, when the confidentiality, integrity, or availability of an organization's information systems was breached and damages occurred, the majority of damages were internal and were simply absorbed by the organization. However, information systems and their services now reach far beyond the boundaries of the organization providing them. They are relied on by more people outside the organizations providing the services. These systems affect the lives, livelihood, property, and privacy of more and more individuals.

As a result, a growing number of users and third-party nonusers are being exposed to and are now actually experiencing damages as a result of failures of information security in information systems. For example, a company that specializes in keeping and reporting on consumer credit ratings may experience a breach of information security as a result of negligence. The individual damaged in such instances could be the person being reported on, who is neither the keeper of the credit reports nor the person seeking the credit report. Because these individuals are outside organizational boundaries, they are under no obligation to simply absorb damages. Instead, they may turn to litigation. Therefore, managers must proactively provide reasonable information security for their information systems.

This chapter presents an overview of the fundamentals of negligence and suggests ways that negligence may form the basis for lawsuits when information security has been breached. Basic concepts are presented from a nonlegal point of view; this chapter is not intended as a comprehensive, legal presentation. Rather, the intent is to inform the security professional about the concepts of negligence and the ways an understanding of these concepts may help owners and operators of information systems develop a standard of due care.

THE LAW OF TORTS

Simply stated, a tort is an action that violates the civil duty people have to one another. Negligence is one type of tort. The law of torts makes courts the decision maker for private disputes when the negligent actions of one person injure another person. The court decisions are designed to find out who was wrong and then to correct the wrong.

Once courts entered into disputes between individuals, rules were developed to help standardize court proceedings and to help different courts reach similar decisions in similar situations. One of the rules dealt with the concept of liability. In its simplest terms, liability means responsibility. To say a person is liable is the same as saying a person is responsible or can be held responsible. If a person is liable, that person has tort liability. There are three possible ways a person can acquire tort liability:

- By doing something intended to cause harm.
- Through negligent conduct that creates an unreasonable risk of unintentionally causing harm.
- Through conduct subject to strict liability, without intent or negligence, to the extent that it has survived from the early law or has been reestablished by modern ideas of policy.

In this chapter, the focus is on negligent conduct in which, by failing to provide for reasonable security in their information systems, managers and organizations can be held liable and may be sued when their systems are breached and damages occur.

NEGLIGENCE

If someone has engaged in negligent conduct and has caused harm or damages to another, that person can be charged in court by the person harmed. The person bringing the charge of negligence is called the plaintiff; the person being charged is called the defendant. In a court setting, the word *negligence* is used to describe the conduct of the defendant.

A legal charge of negligence cannot be based solely on negligent conduct. Negligent conduct by one person may create a risk of harm to others; if no one is actually harmed, however, a charge of negligence will not stand up in court. A plaintiff charging negligence must prove the existence of each of the following five elements of negligence to win a court case:

- *Duty*. A person must act, or may not fail to act, in a way that prevents exposing others or their property to an unreasonable risk of harm.
- *Breach of duty*. This occurs when a person fails to act in ways that meet his or her duty.
- *Cause*. Cause is established by determining whether the conduct of an individual (i.e., the defendant) has resulted in or caused the damages suffered by another (i.e., the plaintiff).
- *Proximate cause*. Proximate cause (sometimes called natural cause) defines the limits in tracing the link between a given cause and its claimed effect. When the link between cause and effect cannot be traced, liability stops.
- *Damages*. These are the actual losses suffered by one person (i.e., the plaintiff) when injured as a result of the negligent acts of another (i.e., the defendant).

Although many people are not aware of it, everyone has the duty to act (or not fail to act) in a way that will not expose others or their property to an unreasonable risk of harm. In other words, everyone must conform to a certain standard of conduct. Managers of information systems have a common-law duty (as opposed to a contractual duty) to prevent exposing those who use these systems to an unreasonable risk of harm.

BREACH OF DUTY

Negligence may be charged when a person has a duty to another and breaches that duty. Interestingly enough, a defendant may engage in negligent behavior but not be liable if there was no duty to the plaintiff. To successfully charge negligence with respect to duty and breach of duty, a defendant must have a duty to the plaintiff and then have breached that duty.

Unfortunately, it is not simple to determine when one person has a duty to another. Several factors are involved:

- Whether the harm that occurs could be reasonably foreseen.
- What a reasonable and prudent person would do in similar circumstances.
- Sufficient probability that harm will occur as the result of a particular act, such that a reasonable person would take action to avoid it.
- Balancing anticipated harm with the expense and inconvenience of reducing the anticipated harm.
- The standard of due care.

Foreseeability

In the definition of negligence, a person is obliged to avoid exposing others or their property to unreasonable risks of harm but not all risks of harm. One of the key tests to determine whether a risk is reasonable or unreasonable is whether or not the resulting harm could have been anticipated. If the harm that occurs to one person as a result of the acts of another could not reasonably have been anticipated, there is no liability for that harm. On the other hand, if the harm could have been reasonably anticipated, there is liability.

In information systems, there are various well-identified threats that can result in failures of data confidentiality, integrity, and availability, which in turn could cause damages to people and organizations. Some organizations, including the American Bar Association and the National Center for Computer Crime Data, publish such information periodically. For example, according to some estimates, between 20% and 25% of information security breaches are caused by insiders (i.e., disgruntled or dishonest employees). About 3% to 5% are caused by outside hackers. There are published accounts of what happens when an information system is attacked by either of these threats. If a reasonable and prudent person would foresee these threats, anticipate how these threats might expose others to harm, and therefore act to establish countermeasures to reduce an information system's vulnerability to them, so must a manager of information systems.

Reasonable and Prudent Person

The courts have insisted that the reasonable and prudent person is a hypothetical person of ordinary prudence, not an overly cautious individual who has no human frailties and is constantly preoccupied with the idea that danger may be lurking in every direction at any time. This hypothetical nature is important. In a case, jurors must not be asked what they would do but what they think this hypothetical person would do under the circumstances, which is always a judgment call left entirely up to the jury. If a jury decides that a person acting reasonably and prudently would have acted as the defendant did, the defendant is not liable for harm. If, on the other hand, the jury decides that a person acting reasonably and prudently would not have acted as the defendant did, the defendant is liable for harm.

Probability

Foreseeability is not determined by probability. One way defendants have attempted to show that harm is not foreseeable is to argue that it was a low-probability event and therefore was not foreseeable. The argument is that if the harm that occurs to a person is the result of an unusual, extraordinary, and improbable occurrence, there is no way that a person acting reasonably and prudently could have anticipated that harm.

It is true that there is no liability when the harm that occurs is unusual, extraordinary, and improbable. However, improbable does not just mean that the probability of the harm occurring is less than the probability of the harm not occurring. In fact, courts take the position that if the probability of harm is sufficiently serious that an ordinary person would take precautions to avoid it, failure to do so is negligence. If a jury concludes that a reasonable and prudent person in similar circumstances would anticipate harm and act accordingly and the defendant did not so act, the defendant will most likely lose, regardless of the probabilities involved.

The implication for information security is clear. A manager may avoid acting to improve information security because a risk analysis shows that the known threats are all of low probability, the resulting annual loss estimates are low, and therefore the proposed countermeasures are not cost-effective. Although this is a reasonable position to take from an economic perspective, it is not a sound position from a legal perspective.

For example, a risk analysis identifies a threat in which a disgruntled employee might gain unauthorized access to confidential personnel data and release it publicly to embarrass the company. The risk analysis may show this threat has a probability of 0.001 for a given year. Management decides to save the expenses associated with installing countermeasures to protect against this low-probability threat. If this threat occurs and employees are damaged by the release of confidential data, a lawsuit charging negligence is likely. During the trial, the court will not be interested in management's rationale that countermeasures were not needed because the threat was of low probability. The court will make its decision on the basis of the actions of the reasonable and prudent person in similar circumstances, not the balance of probabilities.

Balancing Public Use, Harm, and Safety

The courts have recognized that everything people use cannot be made absolutely safe. In many settings, the benefits enjoyed by people occur because they are able to use technology and machines that can inherently and foreseeably cause harm. The use of technology is permitted because the benefits gained are large and the potential harm is small. However, as the potential for harm increases and begins to outweigh the benefits of use, the public has a right to demand that a technology be made safer.

A balancing act occurs in the courts between beneficial use, harm, and safety. Courts do not require that a technology be made absolutely safe. No court will require safety measures that are no expensive and inconvenient that they reduce the benefits of using the technology out of proportion to the harms that might occur without such efforts. In each case, the test for the balance between the public benefit, the anticipated harm to the public, and the expense and inconvenience of making something safer is what the reasonable and prudent person would do in similar circumstances. The bottom line is that an organization's budget is not the determining factor in whether or not money should be spent to make something safer.

In information security settings, managers often defer expenditures for countermeasures, claiming that the recommended countermeasures cost too much. However, the results of a financial analysis should be only one of many factors considered in deciding whether or not to implement certain countermeasures. The decision should also balance the benefits gained with the potential for harm to the public. In fact, many information security countermeasures are relatively inexpensive when viewed with respect to the public good.

For example, a large vendor of microcomputer software examines the costs of installing an antivirus countermeasure to make sure that all software packages shipped are free of viruses and decides it is too expensive. A virus then infects the company computer used to make the master software disk, which is then used to make all copies for shipping. Every software program shipped then has the virus. Every user who purchases the program, uses it, and suffers damages from the virus may have a basis for suing the software vendor for negligence.

Standard of Due Care

In helping to enhance the understanding of what duty one person may have to another, the courts have developed the concept of a standard of due care. In effect, this standard dictates what a person must know and what care a person must exercise with respect to another person. An individual cannot escape liability just because ignorance is claimed. Under the standard of due care, a defendant may not be able to claim ignorance; there are certain things defendants simply must do whether they know it or not. The standard of due care relates back to what the reasonable and prudent person would do in similar circumstances.

One way defendants attempt to defend against a charge of failing to meet the standard of due care is to claim that what was done in the defendant's organization is exactly what everyone else in the same industry is doing under similar circumstances. This does not hold up in court. Courts have taken the position that industry practice may not be the most effective way to make something safe, and when that is the case, there is a duty to adopt a more effective way if the technology is available, could be known, and would be adopted by a reasonable and prudent person. Expert evidence may be sufficient to prove a better way even if the industry is not using it. In essence, it is possible to be held to a standard of care that should be used in any industry, even if no one is using it at the time.

This aspect of duty could be particularly troubling for information security, because it basically says that some countermeasure may be insufficient. For example, user-generated passwords are widely used in systems as a means of access control. However, there are lists containing 600 to 800 common passwords that, it is claimed, can access a high percentage of systems in the US. It is also widely argued that as a countermeasure to unauthorized access, use of passwords by themselves is now an obsolete countermeasure. Many experts recommend the use of any two of the three major methods available for providing access control: passwords, handheld tokens, and biometrics. If unauthorized access attempts are foreseeable (which they are) and the only countermeasure in place is a system that allows users to generate their own static passwords, and better technologies are available that are not excessive in cost or inconvenience, the door to a negligence charge is wide open when damages occur.

CAUSE, PROXIMATE CAUSE, AND DAMAGES

Sometimes called cause in fact, cause is the element in negligence that determines whether the conduct of the defendant has caused the plaintiff's damages. When negligence is charged, it is insufficient in a court of law for the defendant to claim that the damages would have occurred even if the defendant had not been negligent. On the other hand, the mere fact that an act by the defendant could have caused injury is not sufficient. In addition, there are situations in which there could be multiple causes (i.e., concurrent causes) of damages.

In information security, the focus is on whether a breach of security was actually the direct cause of a plaintiff's damages. If, for example, a prime contractor's information system was breached and proprietary information was released about a subcontractor's product, which immediately upon its release caused most of the subcontractor's other clients to cancel orders for that product, the subcontractor might charge negligence and initiate litigation.

Intervening Events. Most courts take the position that there must be practical limits on how far to go in attempts to establish a link between a given cause and a claimed effect. The real challenge involves deciding how to take into account intervening acts (i.e., of other people or of nature) that occur after the original negligent act and before damages occur to a defendant. The more intervening acts, the harder it is to show that the effects were caused by an original negligent act. In addition, effects may be distant in time or place from an original negligent act asserted to be the cause.

Courts look for cause and effect only within the scope of ordinary human understanding. Every person is responsible for damages that are the proximate results of his or her own acts. When courts cannot trace the link between cause and effect any further, liability stops.

This concept of proximate cause is important because it involves a decision as to where the limits to liability end. In information security, proximate cause is important because in many situations in which countermeasures are absent or inadequate, there may be many intervening acts and large gaps between the time of the security breach and the time the plaintiff suffers damages. The ability to trace and connect the link between the original negligent act and the damages that occur varies from case to case.

For example, a subcontractor's clients cancel orders for a product after a leak of proprietary information about the subcontractor's products. The case may not be so clear, however, if the cancellations had occurred 10 months after the release of the information and all the clients were overseas, and furthermore if there were intervening events (e.g., announcements about new products that compete successfully with the subcontactor's products or a slowdown in the international economy). In some cases, it is not simple to determine whether the defendant's action (or lack of it) was the proximate cause of the plaintiff's damages.

Finally, a plaintiff charging negligence must prove the existence of damages. Damages are the actual losses that the plaintiff suffers as a result of the negligent act of the defendant. Even if the defendant has committed negligent acts, the defendant cannot be held liable for negligence if the plaintiff was not harmed. In other words, without damages, there is no case for negligence.

ADDITIONAL LEGAL CONCEPTS AFFECTING LITIGATION

There are three additional legal concepts that, together with the concepts of negligence, should alert information security managers to the potential for litigation. These concepts are summarized as follows:

- *Negligence per se.* A violation of a statute or regulation is negligence as a matter of law when the violation results in injury to a person or persons protected by the legislation and when the harm is of the kind that the statute or regulation was passed to prevent. Violating the statute is conclusive evidence of negligence and is called negligence per se.
- *Res ipsa loquitur (i.e., the thing speaks for itself).* This concept allows a jury to consider the circumstances of a given case and, in the absence of a satisfactory explanation by a defendant, conclude that an accident occurred from the defendant's negligence provided that:
  —The accident was one that ordinarily does not occur without someone's negligence.
  —the accident was caused by something within the exclusive control of the defendant.
  —The plaintiff did not voluntarily act or contribute to causing the accident.
- *Respondeat superior.* This doctrine states that employers are liable for the negligence of their employees when the employees are acting in the scope of their jobs, regardless of what employers do to prevent such negligent acts.

Negligence Per Se

In negligence per se, all that needs to be proved is that a violation of statute occurred. If a statute or municipal ordinance, for example, imposes a specific duty on a person for the protection or benefit of others, neglecting to perform the duty makes that person liable to anyone who is injured as a result of that neglect. In general, "a violation of a statute or regulation constitutes negligence as a matter of law when the violation results in injury to a member of the class of persons intended to be protected by the legislation and when the harm is of the kind that the statute or regulation was enacted to prevent" (*Stachniewicz v. Mar-Cam Corp.*, 259 Or. 583, 488 P.2d 436 [Or. 1971]). Duty in such instances is imposed by statute so that proof of violating the statute is conclusive evidence of negligence, which is called negligence per se.

This is of direct interest to the IS manager because so many state statutes have now been passed in addition to federal statutes with respect to computer and high-technology crime. Moreover, there are now various statutes that deal with privacy of information. Any number of negligent actions by people in an organization can lead to violations of privacy. For example, some companies institute the practice of saving paper by using both sides of paper for printing output. There have been instances when output has been printed on paper containing employee payroll information on the reverse side. Another violation of privacy may occur if computer terminals face the doors in offices so that passersby can look in and view another employee's payroll information on the screen. Furthermore, access control systems are often bypassed during the morning rush to begin work because there are so many people trying to gain access simultaneously that it would be very time-consuming to check each one individually.

Res Ipsa Loquitur

In some instances, it may not be possible to clearly link someone's damages or injury directly to another's negligent act. It may even be impossible to provide any direct evidence about what has caused the damage. In such cases, res ipsa loquitur may be used to construct a causal link between a defendant's inferred act and a plaintiff's actual damages. Res ipsa loquitur is used only to make inferences from events that cannot be explained otherwise. In general, it permits a jury to consider the circumstances of a given case and, in the absence of a satisfactory explanation by a defendant, conclude that an accident occurred from the defendant's negligence.

In information systems, for example, res ipsa loquitur may be applicable in security breaches in which a file containing previously correct information about someone is discovered to have been altered to show incorrect data. The file has existed exclusively within a company's information system, and only the company's employees can access it. The changes made to the data subsequently damage that person. There is an audit trail showing that company employees accessed that file but that there have been no other access attempts. In such a situation, res ipsa loquitur might be used to try to link the damages to negligent acts of the company or its employees.

Respondeat Superior

Sometimes called imputed negligence or vicarious liability, *respondeat superior* means to ask the higher level to be answerable. Under this doctrine, an employer is liable for the negligence of employees committed while they were acting in the scope of their job. This is an especially troublesome doctrine because an organization that played no part in an employee's negligent act, did nothing to encourage the negligent act, and in fact may have taken precautions to prevent the negligent act nevertheless becomes a defendant charged with negligence just as if the organization had committed the negligent act itself. Employers cannot protect themselves from liability even if they impose safety rules or instruct their employees in expected behavior on the job, no matter how specific and detailed their orders may be.

For example, employees in an IS department violate specific written orders of the organization that state that no external modems are ever to be used. They connect modems to their personal computers and leave them on 24 hours a day so that they can dial in from home at any time and access the mainframe at the office. As a result, a hacker breaks into the mainframe and causes damages to a third party outside the organization when information about the third party is compromised. The third party could charge negligence and hold the employer liable under respondeat superior regardless of what the written orders were.

IMPLICATIONS FOR INFORMATION SECURITY

Once most information security professionals understand negligence and the three related legal doctrines presented in the preceding section, they react with great concern. It is relatively easy for them to see that if a person suffers damage as a result of a security breach in an information system that has inadequate countermeasures, the organization is vulnerable to negligence litigation, which can be costly.

It can be argued that the entire purpose underlying information security is to protect the confidentiality, integrity, and availability of information. The managers and employees who provide information systems and their services to users have a duty to prevent others or their property from being exposed to unreasonable risks of harm. This duty is unavoidable. The exact duty with respect to confidentiality, integrity, and availability is still evolving in the courts; when these duties are required by contract or by statute, however, they are clear.

For example, when a company advertises the secure characteristics of its information services, it will be held to the standard it advertises. Absent contracts, statutes, and advertisements, the duty with respect to availability, integrity, and confidentiality may well be defined through lawsuits brought into the court system. If a company is to rely on the integrity of its information without the proper information security safeguards in place to ensure integrity, it is an invitation for anyone who has been damaged by the lack of integrity to sue for negligence for failure to exercise the standard of due care.

As more people experience information system–related damages, it is likely that more negligence litigation will occur. One key to proving breach of duty in negligence cases is to show that insufficient countermeasures are in place for threats that are foreseeable. Many threats are now well-known.

For example, the National Center for Computer Crime Data published a document summarizing computer crime and information system crime statistics. This report shows the number of computer crimes in various jurisdictions, the demographic makeup of the computer criminals, and average losses. The national media have presented extensive coverage on some of the more newsworthy threats: viruses, hackers, and worms, which account for an estimated 2% to 5% of the threats to information security. Yet, as shown in Exhibit II-2-1, employee accidents and error account for 55% of known threats; dishonest or disgruntled employees account for 25%; and natural disasters, fire, floods, and earthquakes account for 20%. Although these represent a vastly higher percentage of known security threats, they receive little attention beyond information security literature.

Threat analyses are usually published along with recommended countermeasures and consequently are known and therefore foreseeable. When

Threat	Known Threats (%)
Accidents and Errors	55
Employee Dishonesty	15
Employee Revenge	10
Fire	15
Flood Damage	3
Earthquakes and Other Natural Disasters	2

Note:
This list does not include an estimate of the threat from hackers and outsiders, which many estimate at ranging from 2% to 5%.

SOURCE: Executive Information Network, as reproduced in *Commitment to Security, The Second Statistical Report of the National Center for Computer Crime Data* (Santa Cruz CA: National Center for Computer Crime Data, 1989).

Exhibit II-2-1. Information Security Threats

---

available countermeasures are not in place against foreseeable threats and a person is damaged as a result, litigation is increasingly likely to occur.

Unfortunately, many of the available countermeasures against known threats are simply not used. Security measures range from the simple (e.g., changing the vendor-supplied password for a mainframe user) to the complex (e.g., encryption on a voice and data network). If currently available countermeasures are known and not used against threats that are foreseeable, it would appear that organizations simply hope that no one is damaged as a result of negligent acts.

Although the law is still evolving with respect to civil litigation over information system–related losses, it seems reasonable to suggest that the standard of due care will remain the same as in other negligence cases: What would the reasonable and prudent person have done in similar circumstances? If a reasonable and prudent person would have foreseen the threat and placed a known countermeasure in place regardless of what the current industry practices are, that may be the context in which a system's negligence will be judged.

IS-Related Damages

With respect to information system–related losses resulting from breaches of security, there are two main kinds of damage that may occur, either individually or in combination. Damages can be direct (which are easy to identify and count) or indirect (which are much more difficult to assess). For example, damages that are measured in terms of immediate client loss could be considered direct. However, as news about the loss of clients spreads, other potential clients may simply shop for services elsewhere. These would be considered indirect damages.

Direct and indirect damages can involve loss of money, loss of goods, disruption of service, loss of system integrity, loss of confidentiality, loss of opportunities, and loss of reputation. For example, more and more transactions among vendors and clients are being done through the use of electronic data interchange (EDI) and faxes, which use neither encryption nor authentication to verify information or orders. Significant damages can occur when legitimate organizations are impersonated by others issuing false information or orders for materials or services.

HEADING OFF NEGLIGENCE LAWSUITS

One of the emerging tasks of IS managers is to avoid lawsuits charging negligence. In other industries, notably in the manufacturing industry, product liability lawsuits arising as a result of negligence are teaching managers and organizations an expensive lesson: lawsuits charging negligence cannot be fended off by simply ignoring them. Some proactive measures are required.

The organization should assemble a team to design and develop an information security program and recovery plans and to recommend appropriate insurance covering lawsuits. The security program and the recovery plans must then be implemented. Although taking these proactive steps will not necessarily prevent an organization from being charged with negligence lawsuits, they can reduce the organization's risk of losing such lawsuits. Exhibit II-2-2 summarizes the steps.

Assembling an Information Security Team

A team must be assembled to design and implement a systematic information security program. This team should be interdisciplinary; not only must engineering, management, and human resources experts be involved, but attorneys must participate from the start. Attorneys bring a unique and important perspective to the program because they do not argue for effective engineering or human factors or for cost-effective solutions. Rather, they

---

Step 1: Assemble an information security team:
- Appoint attorneys and interdisciplinary members.
- Charter the team to design and implement an information security program.

Step 2: The team designs the information security program, which:
- Identifies foreseeable threats and countermeasures for those threats.
- Identifies standards of due care and the organization's duties to users (including those required by statute).
- Identifies the countermeasures for those threats identified, according to what a reasonable and prudent person in similar circumstances would implement.

Step 3: The team develops recovery plans and makes insurance recommendations.

Step 4: The organization implements the security program.

Exhibit II-2-2. Steps to Avoid Negligence Lawsuits

argue for preventive legal actions that will make it difficult for anyone to prove negligence in court.

Designing the Program

The information security program should contain several components. First, it must identify foreseeable threats as well as countermeasures for those threats. Second, it must identify the standards of due care and the organization's duties to its users, including those required by statute. These duties should be identified at the start of the project and updated periodically. Finally, the program must make recommendations on implementing the countermeasures for those threats that have been identified.

Because risk cannot be reduced to zero, the organization must be prepared to argue that it acted as a reasonable and prudent person would act in similar circumstances. The organization must be prepared to argue that its countermeasures are on the correct side of the balance between a duty to provide for the public good and the cost and inconvenience of these countermeasures.

Developing Recovery Plans and Obtaining Insurance

An effective information security program identifies the organization's duties and the proper safeguards; however, implementing these safeguards is not enough. Under the doctrine of respondeat superior, a negligent act of one employee in the course of his or her duties can expose the organization to a charge of negligence. Therefore, it may be insufficient if the program puts in place information security precautions, policy precautions, hardware and software precautions, education and training awareness precautions, precautions in advertising, and precautions through testing and control. Negligent acts may still occur and cause damages.

In operational settings, where it is simply impossible to eliminate every negligent act that may cause damages, the ultimate strategy is to develop recovery plans and obtain insurance as part of the lawsuit avoidance program. Although recovery plans do not necessarily alleviate threats to information systems, they can minimize or mitigate resulting damages. For example, if viruses circumvent antivirus programs and wipe out a hard disk, a complete virus-free backup can permit recovery without interruption to a user.

As a last resort, an organization should consider obtaining lawsuit insurance. Most manufacturers, doctors, and other professionals have had to turn to insurance companies to cushion the blow of civil lawsuits charging negligence.

CONCLUSION

Currently, there is considerable debate over whether charges of negligence will result in a significant amount of litigation over information system–related losses. Some believe that an explosion of litigation is inevitable. Others feel that it will be hard to prove the elements of negligence in court, particularly with respect to proximate cause. In addition, some argue that the joining of information technology, information security, and negligence is so foreign to most users, attorneys, and courts that it will be a long time before such cases are filed.

For the moment, it appears too early to tell which path negligence litigation will take in information system–related losses. Some cases may make their way into the court system and draw considerable attention in the process. In addition, the risk that such cases will be filed may be increasing.

There are two implications for IS managers with respect to the potential for litigation over information system–related losses resulting from negligent acts. First, the potential for negligence litigation is another arrow in the quiver of IS managers as they attempt to persuade line managers to take the proper action to secure their information system against foreseeable threats.

Second, regardless of the current state of affairs with respect to civil litigation charging negligence, it seems prudent to act as though such litigation were a highly likely scenario that should be strategically planned for. If a high volume of lawsuits does not emerge, the worst that could happen to an organization is that it spends more than it otherwise would have on information security. If so, from a security perspective, it could be argued the organization has done the right thing for the wrong reason.

If, on the other hand, lawsuits do become more common, the organization will probably have spent less on increasing information security than it otherwise might have lost in court without it. In either event, the organization will have increased the confidentiality, integrity, and availability of its information and at the same time will have protected itself from an emerging epidemic of negligence lawsuits.

Section III
Leveraging Technology

TAKING FULL ADVANTAGE of promising technology is a prime responsibility of IS management. That means much more than implementing technology that someone else has chosen. It means, among other things, that the IS management team must be alert to opportunities for using new technology in fields traditionally void of technology application. The chapters in this section are dedicated to the application of technology to one of the most pervasive and costly problems facing business today—what to do with the wealth of information that is not in machine-readable form.

The use of optical disk technology to link computer data and documents is creating a major market because it gives an excellent return on investment as well as providing a unique way to access information, reduce costs, and improve productivity. Chapter III-1, "Technology for Document Management Systems," describes the application of optical disk technology in a typical organization and illustrates a process to integrate data and image documents.

Imaging technology provides organizations with significant opportunities for reengineering work processes and streamlining routine operations through work flow automation. Implementation of an imaging system requires proper planning by IS management to ensure that these expectations are realized. Chapter III-2, "Planning for Document Management Systems," defines issues ranging from organizational obstacles to technical and performance considerations, including network operating systems, LAN-based versus mainframe-based implementation, and development tools.

III-1

Technology for Document Management Systems

Mason Grigsby

PAPER FILES AND COMPUTER OUTPUT continue to function as separate systems, with little or no link between the media. The growing demand for immediate information access and response highlights the main problem with each of these methods of independently storing and retrieving information. In most business systems, both these sources must be accessed to respond properly to a request for information.

Because of the many advantages of digitally storing documents on optical disk, optical disk–based systems are becoming an integral component in office automation. This chapter outlines the basic design and practical uses of two applications for digital optical systems:

- *Document images.* Paper documents that are received from outside the organization and now stored offline in file cabinets.
- *Computer data.* Computer page data that is stored magnetically online or offline on paper, computer-output microfilm (COM), or magnetic tape.

These two applications are regarded as major ways to leverage technology in the office. Document image application systems are used for the storage and retrieval of scanned paper documents, and computer data application systems are used to store and retrieve ASCII output.

Optical disk–based systems bridge the gap between existing paper document files and computer output data. The ability to create electronic images of paper files and combine them with computer output on optical disks allows the integration of these documents types into other mainstream office automation systems.

Document image and data application systems use digital optical disks for the storage and retrieval of paper documents and computer output. Image systems have the ability to digitally capture images of paper documents with a document-digitizer scanner; store the image on the optical disk; index and retrieve the image using application-specific indexing and retrieval software; and display, print, or transmit the retrieved images to a user location.

Data systems similarly provide access to computer output now stored on paper, magnetic disk, magnetic tape, or COM; however, the process to cre-

	Image Documents Capacity per Disk	Data Documents Capacity per Disk
5¼-in. optical disk (940M bytes)	16,000 pages	650,000 pages
12-in. optical disk (5.6G bytes)	140,000 pages	4,600,000 pages

Compressed image page = 50K bytes (bit-mapped)
Compressed data page = 2K bytes (ASCII)

Exhibit III-1-1. Differences Between Data and Image Storage on Optical Disk

---

ate the index and optical data record is totally automated. The print spool file is automatically downloaded to the optical disk auxiliary processor, and the page output data is written to optical disk for subsequent retrieval by terminals connected to a host or network microcomputers.

Exhibit III-1-1 illustrates the differences in storing bit-mapped image documents and computer (ASCII) data output. The methods of storing and accessing these two data types evolved as independent solutions to what is actually a central, information-file problem. A brief explanation of the information process and document types is important to understanding how these optical application systems evolved.

EXTERNAL SOURCE DOCUMENTS

Paper documents are a major management concern. These incoming (i.e., created outside the organization) source documents cause filing requirements to grow by 25% to 30% per year. Other reasons fueling interest in digital optical systems to handle this paper storage problem are:

- *The ubiquity of paper documents in the office.* Paper is not going to disappear in the near future. Currently, less than 2% of all corporate data is in digital form, yet customer service increasingly requires fast document retrieval.
- *Labor costs.* The cost of retaining personnel for filing and retrieving paper documents is becoming prohibitive.
- *The demand for instant retrieval of information.* The storage and retrieval of external documents is becoming mandatory for corporate decision making and for handling customer service and collection functions.
- *Growing competition.* In addition to operating cost reduction potential, optical systems frequently have strategic significance.

INTERNALLY GENERATED COMPUTER DATA

Online systems, in most cases, contain only 60 to 90 days' worth of data. The reason is the high cost of direct access magnetic storage. A major alternative to online storage for active-use data is COM. COM is an important productivity tool for managing the billions of pages of data being generated from computer systems. Despite the popularity of COM (34% of all computer print files are output to COM), the work environment is not always conducive to its use. Paper therefore remains the primary storage medium for most of the computer data that must be referred to continually.

An extended online capability reduces or eliminates COM and paper and provides faster retrieval of information. The need to keep data in electronic form for extended periods for audits and historical purposes has led to large magnetic tape libraries. However, access to tape library information is also relatively slow and inefficient. In the current information environment, these offline microfiche, paper, or magnetic tape systems are not integrated into the computer information transaction cycle. They are separate storage media with separate retrieval processes. The lack of integration of computer data, COM, and printed paper reports creates an extended information search process that is usually measured in hours or even days. A major reason for implementing optical information systems in daily operations is to achieve basic productivity improvements and to reduce costs.

BENEFITS OF DIGITAL OPTICAL INFORMATION SYSTEMS

A combination of optical disks for image and data storage, retrieval software for index data management, and transmission of images or data to remote locations provides a system that has great strategic potential.

Exhibit III-1-2 illustrates an optical data system for capturing, storing, and retrieving page-oriented computer output. Exhibit III-1-3 illustrates an optical image system. This system consists of a document-digitizer scanner, optical disks, a server, indexing and image retrieval software, a bit-map,

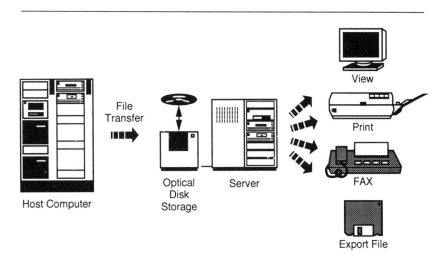

Exhibit III-1-2. An Optical Data System

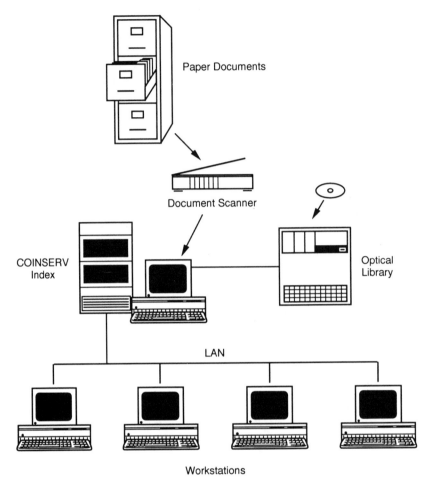

Exhibit III-1-3. An Optical Image System and the Conversion of Paper Documents

high-resolution monitor, and a laser printer. These systems are modular and can be expanded into larger, enterprise-level document image and data management systems with multiple workstations and optical disk storage libraries.

Optical Data Systems

An optical data system enables users to access frequently needed computer-based information (i.e., corporate reports, statements, transaction data, customer-history files) in a rapid, cost-effective, and efficient manner.

These systems replace computer printouts, COM, and archival magnetic tape storage, as well as reducing reliance on magnetic disk storage. They allow data to stay online, providing quick delivery of current as well as historical computer records at low cost. The term applied to this class of system is COLD (computer output to laser disk).

Exhibit III-1-2 illustrates the process of moving output data from a host system, extracting the relevant index fields, and writing the data to the optical disk. Features of this system include a capability to overlay forms and to display 132-character report formats on the system's workstations.

The benefits of optical data systems include the following:

- Optical data systems provide extremely fast access to information (i.e., 2 to 10 seconds), resulting in reduced labor costs (e.g., research, filing, and hard-copy reproduction) and faster customer service capability. Productivity is improved by 50% or more.

- Data is stored in printed-page format on high-density optical disks with storage capacities of 600,000 pages (on 5¼-in. disks) to 5 million pages (on 12-in. disks). Because the data on optical disk media is machine readable, it can easily be restored to the host computer for post-processing or special ad-hoc reporting.

- The multilevel cross-reference index can be structured to allow retrieval of data by any desired field (e.g., invoice number, customer number, customer name, or date). This significantly increases the number of transactions an employee can handle. Productivity is 3 to 10 times faster than with microfiche.

- Users can annotate the formatted page data with information that may be relevant to a transaction. The additional information is stored electronically as a note and tagged to the corresponding data page, thereby providing a complete audit trail of all file-access transactions.

- The cost of computer output microfiche and computer paper is eliminated.

- An enterprisewide repository can be created with little or no change to existing mainframe or network systems.

The major benefit is that these systems are now capable of providing an enterprisewide data repository with distribution and access from microcomputers on a local area network, remote terminals on a wide are network, and terminals connected to a host. Fast access to optically stored data is possible because the index to the output data is stored on magnetic disk with the exact optical disk page location. This index also provides access to documents across multiple optical media and allows the optical disk jukebox library to efficiently manage disk exchanges.

Image Systems

Converting externally generated paper source documents to a digital record requires creating document-digitized images with a bit-map scanner and keying the cross-reference index data into the magnetic data base. This scanning process is the key difference between optical data systems and image systems, which must be converted to digital form (see Chapter III-2).

Exhibit III-1-3 illustrates the document-conversion procedure. The systems flow begins with receipt of external source documents. The paper is scanned, index files are keyed, the image is written to the optical disk, and an optical disk address is automatically assigned to each document. This address is then incorporated into the online magnetic index, thus linking the scanned page to the index. Because there are often long-term legal or audit requirements for storing paper documents, this system must be capable of accessing the index for as many as five to seven years. The capability to manage large, magnetic disk–index data bases is therefore key to optical systems.

The document management software controls the index data that is located on the magnetic disk and the retrieval of the images stored on the optical disks. The software provides direct access to an unlimited number of images (documents). This combination of magnetic data base indexing and optical-image retrieval provides an access time of 4 to 20 seconds to any document image in the file. (The longer search times are attributable to the need to exchange optical disk platters in a jukebox.) Access from a spinning optical disk is usually less than 10 seconds and often less than 5 seconds.

DATA AND IMAGE INTEGRATION

An integrated optical information system includes optical disks for image and data storage, client/server capabilities, and software for index data management. Such an integrated system can offer enterprisewide electronic distribution of images and data and can provide great strategic potential.

This integrated optical information system provides a magnetic data base that contains all of the common index data necessary to link the computer output with the related source-document scanned image. For example, a computer-generated customer statement can be automatically tied to all the supporting source documents (e.g., the credit application, credit card drafts, and customer correspondence), or a computer-generated invoice may be linked to the source documents (e.g., purchase order and signed delivery document).

Client/Server–Based Systems. Although numerous optical information systems are on the market, the most popular are client/server–based systems, which feature a powerful dedicated server and low implementation cost. These combined data and image management systems consist of the following components:

- Removable write-once, read-many (WORM) digital optical disks with a storage capacity from 650M bytes per disk to more than 8G bytes per disk.
- A document digitizer scanner that captures documents and graphics (i.e., signatures, logos, diagrams, pictures) and is a high-speed bit-map scanner or a combined optical-character-recognition/bit-map scanner.

- A laser printer for hard-copy reproduction of documents.
- Application software and data base management systems for indexing and retrieval and management of the document images and computer data contained on the optical disks.
- A server for controlling the document management functions of capture (i.e., scanning paper and downloading data from a host computer), indexing, retrieval, sequencing, printing, and electronic distribution.
- An optical disk library unit (i.e., jukebox) for expanded online optical disk capacity. These jukeboxes can provide more than 3T bytes of storage.
- Local or wide area networks for access by multiple workstations.

CONCLUSION

The growing problem of managing paper and providing longer-term access to all forms of information is precisely why there is a need for document storage and retrieval systems that capture external documents, create retrievable digitized images, and link them with mainframe computer output. These digital document image and data systems can be used for both departmental and companywide applications.

Optical information systems can add significant value to existing applications, cut the cost of operations, increase productivity, improve customer service capability, and improve cash flow by speeding the collection process. The net result can be a significant competitive advantage. The next chapter discusses some of the issues that must be addressed in implementing document management systems, especially the work flow and network impact of these new imaging technologies.

III-2

Planning for Document Management Systems

Nathan J. Muller

===

===

EARLY DOCUMENT IMAGING solutions were aimed at large companies with intensive document-handling requirements. These high-end solutions were usually based on turnkey mainframe or minicomputer systems and were expensive. With improvements in technology, imaging systems are becoming more affordable and available at a range of levels, from host based to standalone. Imaging systems running on local area networks (LANs) are attracting businesses with promises of speeding up business processes and cost savings.

If properly deployed, the benefits of imaging systems include better document control as well as reduced processing time, storage space, and clerical support. These benefits logically lead to improved customer service, which is of strategic importance to most businesses.

If a department or work group spends 20% of its time handling paper documents, or its paper volume is steadily increasing, a document imaging system may be justified. Another justification for an imaging system comes as a result of the significant time-value of certain transactions.

ORGANIZATIONAL ISSUES

Department managers are often forced into adopting a defensive posture, because a new way of doing work usually means that they must give up something, whether it is resources (in the form of budget and staff), power and prestige, or control of various operations. Perhaps as important, they see themselves as having to sacrifice an operating philosophy that they have invested considerable time and effort to construct and maintain throughout much of their tenure. These so-called soft issues of managers' feelings and perceptions must be addressed to ensure success with the hard issues of the technical requirements of implementing an imaging system.

Few companies have the advantage of implementing an imaging system without consideration for an entrenched base of potential users. In fact, most imaging systems are run by the same employees that used the outmoded practices and procedure being replaced. Planning is best undertaken using a team approach that gives all parties concerned a chance to buy into the new system. Not only should IS and senior management be included in the planning process, but representatives from records management and the various business units should participate as well.

The planning process should include the articulation of organizational goals that the move to imaging is intended to achieve, outlining anticipated costs and benefits. This stage of the planning process is also intended to address the most critical concern of the participants: how they will be affected by the change. Once the organizational goals are known, they become the new parameters within which the participants can shape their future.

This participative approach facilitates cooperation and has the effect of spreading ownership of the solution among all participants. A solution dictated by senior management often engenders resistance. With the participative approach, the participants have a stake in the outcome of the project: success brings the rewards associated with a stable work environment and a shared vision of the future; failure brings the liabilities associated with a tumultuous work environment. Although participative planning takes more time, its effects are often more immediate and long-lasting than imposed solutions, which are frequently resisted and short-lived.

DETERMINING THE APPLICATIONS

If managers resist change, they are not always protecting their own turf against encroachment. Resistance may mean that the operations they control are really not suitable for imaging technology. The best applications for imaging technology are those in which:

- The relationship of information to business success is understood and the need for improvement in terms of timely access to information is clear.
- The work flow lends itself to automation. Any routine task that involves standard forms, such as loan and insurance claims processing, is a candidate for computerized document imaging.
- The amount of paper handling can be significantly reduced, thereby minimizing clerical staff, filing errors, and duplication of work.
- A significant positive return on investment is likely, not only in dollars, but in productivity efficiencies that streamline work processes and improve customer service.

Identifying the true cause of resistance to change can greatly improve the success of an imaging system implementation; the selection of appropriate applications also increases the chance of success with imaging. Resistance may be overcome by phasing in the document imaging system and choosing a work process that will not jeopardize mission-critical functions and place the company at risk in case of early implementation mistakes. When the application has been fine-tuned, the document imaging system may be extended to other work processes.

UNDERSTANDING PROCESS AND WORK FLOW REQUIREMENTS

Document imaging appeals to corporate executives because it offers opportunities to improve customer service while reducing operating costs. It appeals to IS management and technical professionals because it incorporates many areas of technology in innovative and productive ways. However, implementation requires thorough planning to ensure that these expectations are realized.

The success of document imaging often hinges on the extent to which business processes and work flow can be understood. The most obvious way to understand work flow is to learn how people do their jobs and to solicit their input on how work and processes can be improved. If there are procedural problems, they must be hashed out among all participants early on so that work flow can be properly scripted for automation.

Various departmental processes should be mapped out and scripted well ahead of the imaging system's implementation. Among the problems that often come to light are processes that result in duplications of effort, employees working at cross-purposes, and situations that produce unnecessary paperwork and filing requirements.

The key planning effort that must be performed before implementing an imaging system is an evaluation of document processing needs. At minimum, the following tasks should be performed:

- Listing all documents that are currently being processed by the business.
- Determining how many of each type of document arrives at each business location daily, weekly, monthly, and yearly.
- Finding out who provides the data in the documents, how the data is used, and what information systems or applications currently use the data provided in the documents.
- When a document is retrieved, establishing what information contained in it is most frequently used.
- For each document, determining appropriate index fields.
- Preparing a flowchart for each type of document, identifying the path it follows when it is received in the office, the stops it makes, what happens at each stop, and what alternative paths exist.

Imaging and Reengineering. Most companies change both their structure and function. In fact, change is looked upon as beneficial because it keeps the organization in step with and adaptive to changing customer needs and market directions. To ensure its effective implementation, imaging also requires this kind of self-examination. After all, automating an inefficient process only wastes corporate resources.

When viewed in this way, imaging can become a catalyst for business reengineering. Instead of merely automating inefficient processes, reengineering entails the restructuring of fundamental business processes before they are automated. The result is tightly coupled synergies between IS and various business processes to achieve efficiency and productivity gains. In the case of imaging systems, automating and managing work flow results in the streamlined processing of documents, speedier distribution of information to the right people, and greater productivity from the people who use the information. In turn, corporate responsiveness to a variety of external stimuli is improved.

LEVELS OF PROCESS REORGANIZATION

If the goal of imaging is only to overlay the technology on the existing organization, the benefits of investing in the technology will be minimal. There are several levels of technology implementation that merit consideration, categorized by increasing levels of process reorganization.

Pilot Projects. Set up for limited use at a single location, these projects usually have little value because instead of fostering commitment, they promote a wait-and-see attitude that more often than not guarantees failure. Pilot projects do have value in one respect, however, and that is in testing assumptions before a departmental or enterprisewide implementation.

Internal Integration. In helping to move information between processes, this method may yield significant benefits. However, if existing processes are not made more efficient first, long-term gains will be limited and return on investment delayed.

Process Redesign. This method restructures an entire organization or discrete departmental process to take advantage of imaging technology. Although this method can produce noteworthy improvements in efficiency, it can also be difficult and time-consuming to execute.

Network Engineering. This method extends the reorganization process to locations outside the company's main location. It can produce enterprise-wide benefits, but it is also difficult to implement.

To properly implement a technology at the right level of process reorganization requires that companies strive to understand their business processes, which is not as easy as it sounds because it involves a commitment of staff effort and time. It may be more effective to have a consultant evaluate various business processes and work flows, or to use the professional services of an imaging system vendor. An objective and accurate assessment can thus be rendered that, in turn, helps ensure that the investment in corporate resources can be targeted wisely. Alternatively, an evaluation of business processes and work flows can be performed internally, either with third-party assistance or follow-up review to validate (or invalidate) the conclusions. Considering the high cost of imaging system implementation, these extended measures may be warranted.

LEVELS OF IMPLEMENTATION: LAN-BASED VERSUS MAINFRAME

One of the major decisions that must be addressed early on is whether to implement imaging at the microcomputer level in conjunction with the organization's LANs, or at the minicomputer or mainframe level. Economics favor the former approach, because this solution takes advantage of the installed base of personal computers, which also provides more implementation flexibility and scalability than either the minicomputer or mainframe solutions. All that is required (at incremental cost) are the proper software and peripherals. If an organization has implemented cooperative processing, however, it can use its mainframe or minicomputer for image data bases and add LAN-based server functions.

With proprietary imaging systems, the vendor usually provides a host gateway that runs on the imaging server. With LAN-based systems, the host gateway can be implemented through a communications server or at the personal computer. A LAN-based host gateway therefore provides a more flexible, higher-performance solution.

LANs are well suited for work flow image applications because they are able to support the transfer of images between all nodes—workstations, scanners, storage devices, and printers. LANs also allow for greater flexibility in host access because users have a variety of gateways and terminal emulators from which to choose.

LANs can give remote users access to both the document image index and the images themselves. Usually, remote users are able to review the documents in the image index and select images for retrieval by facsimile transmission. Any office with a modem-equipped personal computer or fax machine is a potential imaging location even though it may not be attached locally.

PERFORMANCE TUNING OPPORTUNITIES

LANs also provide more opportunities for performance tuning. Using LAN management systems, analysis tools, and utilities, the manager can accurately measure performance and take immediate steps to make improvements, such as segmenting the network into subnets, caching images, using compression techniques, and adding higher-performance peripherals. Because performance demands may vary daily, the ability to respond quickly constitutes a key benefit of LAN-based imaging systems over mainframe-based systems.

Subnetworks. Performance on the main imaging network can be maintained by putting resource-intensive services (e.g., scanning, printing, and faxing) on subnetworks. These subnets can be selectively isolated from the rest of the network using bridges or routers. Such an arrangement would allow a large accounts payable department, for example, to scan 10,000 invoices a day without bogging down the main network where users are trying to retrieve data. Scanned images are stored on disk and registered in the image system index by means of a batch process.

Caching Images. Performance can also be increased by caching images, which is also known as "prefetching." This method involves moving images from optical media, where images are permanently stored, to magnetic media, which provide a faster access time for work flow operations. Caching is implemented on the basis of an understanding of which images are likely to be required next. This technique is effective in work flow applications in which queues of images must be worked on. The vendor's storage management utilities are used to implement image caching.

The storage media also affects image system performance. Generally, magnetic storage offers much higher performance than optical drives, although optical disks are used as a permanent image storage repository because of their high capacity. With LAN-based servers, which can provide tens of gigabytes of online storage, the selection of storage media should be based on the cost benefits of the storage alternatives and not necessarily on technical feasibility.

Compression Techniques. Data compression algorithms have long been a part of modem communications. Vendors have been adding data compression to bridges and routers as well to improve throughput between LANs. File transfer software that implements data compression across operating systems is also available, allowing images to be compressed under IBM's MVS, for example, and decompressed under MS-DOS.

ROLE OF NETWORK OPERATING SYSTEMS

The degree to which the imaging software is integrated with the network operating system can have a significant impact on the performance of critical imaging components, such as scanner and printer drivers, optical subsystem drivers, and data base interfaces. The network operating system controls server operation and essentially provides the framework for communications over the entire LAN. The operating system comprises many modules that are responsible for recognizing users, associating their identities with access privileges, and routing their requests. As such, the operating system determines the server configuration, including the microprocessor type, the amount of accessible memory, and hard disk storage. Many of the components of imaging systems, such as scanners, printers, and monitors, are already in common use for other applications. Imaging vendors have recognized the need for drivers to be included in their systems for these components.

Most LAN-based imaging systems use NetBIOS, a transport-layer programming interface, to communicate between the client workstations and image servers over the network. At the NetBIOS level, there is no distinction between the server and the client. The two types of computers communicate by sending small messages called datagrams. Because NetBIOS is a high-level specification, the imaging system that uses it can operate similarly across different network operating systems, although it usually operates more slowly than an imaging system that uses native network protocols, such as NetWare's SPX/IPX and Banyan's VINES IP.

Not all imaging vendors support NetBIOS or native LAN protocols, however. Hewlett-Packard Co. offers UNIX-based systems that support TCP/IP. Microsoft Corp. and Novell, Inc., have developed driver standards that allow multiple protocols to operate on the same LAN and use the same network interface card to communicate with an attached workstation.

TOPOLOGY CONSIDERATIONS

Most office technologies are brought in to solve specific business problems. If the solution is successful and it can be applied elsewhere, the technology spreads to other departments. The same is true of imaging.

Because the great bulk of paper that enters departments or work groups never leaves, it is recommended that when planning an imaging system, a departmental topology be designed with emphasis on work flow, rather than on a central repository to be accessed by all departments. This is because performance will diminish when too many users try to access the relatively limited number of mainframe ports. Work flow operations depend on instant access to stored images. This is best achieved by LAN-based image systems or dedicated host-based systems.

IMPACT ON EXISTING LANS

It is also important to assess how the imaging system deployment will impact existing local area and wide area networks (WANs). Because data files are very large, careful planning is necessary to avoid impeding the flow of traffic. The cost and method of adding extra bandwidth must be considered. Among the methods for improving the flow of traffic on LANs are:

- Taking advantage of ubiquitous twisted-pair wiring to add more bandwidth. Fiber backbones can be used if necessary to connect LANs within a building or campus environment.
- Segmenting existing LANs so that image traffice is separated from other applications. Segmenting overgrown LANs into smaller subnets through the use of bridges and routers can improve overall network performance and facilitate management.
- Making use of data compression to minimize the traffic that must traverse the LAN. Because of their size, image files lend themselves to high compression ratios.

To integrate standard data and images on the same Ethernet, there are several issues that must be addressed, including packet size. Ethernet users must contend for network access, which means a station that has packets (i.e., messages broken into fixed lengths) to send must first check to see whether the transmission medium is available. If it is available, the station transmits a packet. The maximum packet size for Ethernet is 1,500 bytes. Larger packet sizes allow the network to approach the theoretical maximum throughput of the network, which is 10Mb/s.

Although it is possible to use packets larger than 1,500 bytes to improve image-transmission performance on LANs, implementing nonstandard packet sizes has several implications. Because larger packet sizes violate the standard, steps must be taken to ensure that this violation does not negatively affect other network hardware and software designed to the standard. This can be accomplished by ensuring that network interface boards on all network stations have enough buffer memory to support nonstandard packets. Such interface boards are usually expensive, however. If adjacent networks are not configured to support larger packet sizes, internetworking can become more complex. This is because a packet-restructuring function must exist at network interface points. In addition, because of the increased processing that must be done, network performance may degrade.

PERFORMANCE BOTTLENECKS

Although the source of performance bottlenecks can be any one of the many system components, in an imaging system the I/O devices are usually the culprits. Jukebox (a data base server that stores information on multiple optical disks) robotics and disk spin-up and spin-down time can constitute a serious bottleneck. The situation worsens when a few large documents, stored across multiple optical platters, are requested at the same time.

There are several ways to alleviate this problem. The first entails prefetching the images through work flow software. This allows the system to batch-retrieve images overnight when the system is used the least.

A second solution is to employ an optical-storage manager that writes to a single optical disk all the images that belong to one folder. This prevents the folder from being fragmented over multiple optical disks in case it grows.

Another method is to implement a hierarchical data-storage scheme. This involves understanding the use and life cycle of a document. For example, when a document is in the active part of its life cycle, it is stored on magnetic storage, which has fast retrieval capabilities. When the document becomes inactive, it should be automatically moved to optical media in a jukebox. When the document is archived, it should be moved to an archive medium, like helical scan tape. A document should be able to move back and forth through this hierarchy.

Dedicated versus Shared Network. The planning of a computerized document imaging system becomes quite difficult when there are other types of data flowing on the network, so it becomes necessary to condider whether a dedicated imaging network or a shared network is better. The main issues are the predictability of the traffic pattern and the performance required. Transmitting mixed data types across a network does not necessarily cause problems, but performance optimization becomes a requirement and may entail some compromises.

Although due consideration should be given to mixed use of the network, image-intensive production environments, such as a claims-processing application, usually require dedicated networks. In these cases, network parameters can be tuned to optimize performance for predictable traffic patterns.

In striving to make images just another resource available at the desktop, device I/O and network speeds must advance to where frame-size optimization decreases in importance. Multimedia data—images, data, voice, text— can then traverse the network without degradation. A pilot image network can be segmented from the production network to test all these assumptions.

IMPACT ON EXISTING WANs

When imaging applications are added to existing private networks or public network services, the benefits are even more pronounced because the imaging system provides an enterprisewide solution to the paper-processing problem. Because imaging poses a potential congestion problem on existing facilities and services, methods for improving the flow of traffic on WANs must be considered. Among the most common solutions to the problem of congestion are:

- Taking advantage of new high-capacity digital services, such as frame relay and SMDS, which run over T1 and T3 facilities.
- Considering integrated services digital network (ISDN) high-capacity channels for dial-up bandwidth. This option can relieve congestion during peak traffic periods. The user pays only for the amount of bandwidth used and for the period it is used, just as with an ordinary phone call.
- Using compression-equipped bridges and routers to minimize traffic on the WAN. Four-to-one compression applied to a 384K b/s Fractional T1 line yields the throughput of a T1 line, but at much less cost than a T1 line.
- Using routers that have the capability to automatically reroute traffic around failed links and balance the traffic load across multiple paths.
- Making use of traffic-reduction techniques (e.g., large packet) in conjunction with burst-mode technologies to minimize acknowledgment messages that can waste bandwidth.

The last item deserves elaboration. Novell's IPX protocol, for example, breaks down the data into 512-byte packets for transmission over the WAN and usually requires acknowledgment of each packet. As a result, a lot of traffic can build up on the links quickly. Using a router that employs large-packet technology can greatly reduce the amount of traffic on the links by bundling together 512-byte packets into a single 4,096-byte packet. With fewer packets traversing the link, there are fewer acknowledgments. With fewer acknowledgments, there is also less delay. Novell's packet-burst technology complements the large-packet solution by allowing more packets to be sent out with one acknowledgment—the equivalent of shipping a freight train of information instead of just a freight car.

DEVELOPMENT TOOLS

For companies that want to integate imaging systems with existing applications and data bases, the two key concerns are the capabilities of the imaging system's development tools and how well they fit organizational requirements. Addressing these concerns requires an assessment of the development tools the organization currently uses; the supporting components of the development environment that allow for application testing and debugging are critical to successful imaging implementations.

Essentially, there are two choices of development tools: script-based and object-based. Script-based languages offer high-level support for indexing and work flow processes. Large, complex imaging systems have been built using script-based tools. Many smaller vendors of document imaging systems (and multimedia systems) also use script-based languages.

Object-oriented tools are popular in the Windows client/server environment. Generally, these tools do not require the same level of programming expertise as script-based development tools. Objects are discrete modules of code and data with distinct functions. They can be used to customize existing applications or separately modified to speed applications development. The use of objects also reduces production costs and simplifies maintenance. Object technology also promotes application code reusability, interoperability, and portability, in turn improving the overall reliability of distributed programs.

CONCLUSION

Despite the large investments companies have made in office technologies over the years, productivity gains have been hampered by the huge quantity of paper these technologies have produced. Imaging technology addresses the paper problem. Furthermore, implementing imaging systems can provide significant opportunities for reengineering work processes and streamlining routinized operations through work flow automation.

Computerized document imaging has already become indispensable at many companies in which paper storage has become a problem. The benefits of implementing imaging systems include better document control, faster retrieval, and multiuser access. These benefits can improve the overall responsiveness of the enterprise to a variety of external stimuli, particularly the needs of customers.

IS managers, with their computer expertise and accumulated knowledge in supporting mission-critical applications, can help others understand how technology can improve business processes and work flow dynamics. IS can also play a privotal role in selecting the right applications for image processing and in encouraging a participative approach to planning, which goes a long way toward overcoming resistance to change.

Section IV
Human Resources Management

MENTORING IS RAPIDLY BEING RECOGNIZED as a legitimate management development tool. Some astute aspiring employees have been using an informal mentoring process for years. Organizations are now recognizing and formalizing the mentoring process as part of an organized management development process.

Unfortunately, IS managers and their subordinates have been slow to become involved in the practice. Chapter IV-1 describes the nature of and the different types of mentoring relationships. The chapter also offers some practical guidelines and advice for participation in the process, whether as a formal exercise endorsed and supported by the organization or as an informal exercise in which participants grow a relationship that best meets each other's career needs.

IV-1
Mentoring

Stewart L. Stokes, Jr.

MENTORING IS THE PROCESS whereby experienced people in an organization formally and informally help their (usually) less-experienced colleagues navigate the culture and politics of the organization and its departments. Mentoring is a way of organizational life, well understood and used by successful business unit managers but less familiar to IS professionals.

In rightsized, less structured, and flatter organizations, mentoring can become a prime tool for individual survival and professional development. However, unless mentoring relationships are initiated with care, nurtured with discretion, and managed for organizational as well as personal benefit, they can also deteriorate into stressful, conflict-laden situations that cause harm and embarrassment to mentor and mentoree alike. This chapter explains how to use mentoring as a developmental strategy and gives suggestions for structuring healthy mentor-mentoree relationships.

BENEFITS OF MENTORING

A mentoring relationship may be the vehicle an individual needs to gain valuable insight, experience, and exposure to further a personal career. Mentoring relationships may also provide an opportunity to help further the career of others or to learn more about the organization's business, products, services, customers, and competition. For the ambitious and goal-oriented, mentoring may be a strategy for personal and professional development worth investigating.

Although well accepted as a career development strategy by those in an enterprise's business unit, mentoring is rarely practiced by professionals within IS departments. Mentoring as a deliberate, intentional, and planned career development strategy is not that familiar to IS professionals. Despite attempts to align IS more closely with the business units, IS professionals are still relatively isolated in many organizations—even to the point of being physically separated from the other staff departments and line organizations. In addition, many IS professionals are introverts and may thus have some difficulty seeking out and initiating relationships with potential mentors in other units of the enterprise.

IS professionals can benefit from mentoring relationships, especially in the midst of organizational restructuring, delayering, and rightsizing. Maintaining a mentoring relationship with a colleague in another segment of the enterprise can become a source of strength and personal advantage. The mentor-mentoree connection can serve as an early warning system of changes to come. The connection can also result in contacts for the mentoree, perhaps enabling him or her to relocate more easily within (or outside) the company. The mentor can also be a sounding board for the mentoree, providing feedback on possible courses of action as well as acting as an empathetic listener.

Given the benefits of mentoring, certain key questions must be considered before it is adapted as a management development strategy:

- What are the attributes of mentor-mentoree relationships?
- Why is mentoring not more widespread?
- What are the guidelines for mentoring?
- How can mentoring relationships be established?

GENERAL NATURE OF MENTORING RELATIONSHIPS

Mentoring is a career development strategy. It is a process whereby a more experienced member of an organization becomes involved in a relationship with a less experienced colleague to communicate information, insight, knowledge, tips, techniques, and advice and counsel about the culture of the organization, its key players, their strategies and the strategies of the enterprise, and the politics of how work gets accomplished.

Mentoring relationships can be simple, focusing on immediate job-related and career concerns. They may also become more complex and deal with deeper, psychosocial issues. These may include advice and insight into attitudes, behaviors, and values that may be appropriate or inappropriate in a given context or set of circumstances.

For example, a mentor and mentoree may choose to establish, maintain, and limit their relationship to discussing and dealing with such straightforward job and career concerns as who is the best source to talk to about a particular issue, how to gain access to that person, what to cover during a conversation or meeting, how to structure the conversation, what to avoid saying or implying, and when and how to make commitments.

Expectation Sharing

A mentor and mentoree may, however, decide to shape the relationship so as to include discussion of broader issues, such as the time and travel demands of a job and career on the mentoree and his or her family, ethical considerations surrounding courses of action, and costs and benefits of career opportunities. Either way, a critical success factor when establishing a mentoring relationship is the process of establishing the expectations between the mentor and the mentoree. This represents a contract of sorts between the two parties. These contracts are most likely not put in writing, but they are nonetheless vital to the success of the relationship. If the expectations between mentor and mentoree are unclear at the outset of the relationship, it becomes difficult to clarify them later on. Even if the operational details get straightened out, there can still be a residue of ill will remaining between the parties.

Mentoring relationships are usually long term and may also transcend changes in organizational affiliation. A mentor and mentoree may begin a relationship while both are employed by the same enterprise. One or both may leave and the relationship may continue. For any mentoring relationship to succeed, both persons must perceive that their needs are being met. This is especially true for relationships that span years and organizations. For best results, these needs should be discussed openly and in detail during the expectation-sharing phase and revisited regularly. Both parties to a mentoring relationship would do well to live by the old (but still true) adage: assume nothing.

Mentoring relationships must always be based on a high degree of trust and respect. Mentors and mentorees may become involved in each other's lives and may become aware of confidential information. Indeed, the closeness that often develops between mentor and mentoree can become a major issue in cross-gender relationships. (Some organizations try to discourage the forming of mentor-mentoree relationships for this reason.)

Distinction From Manager-Subordinate Relationships

Usually, mentoring relationships are not manager-subordinate relationships, even though the best of such relationships involve coaching, counseling, and championing of the subordinate by the manager to others. This is not to say that effective mentoring relationships cannot evolve from manager-subordinate experiences; they can and do. But manager-subordinate dynamics encompass expectations and responsibilities that can get in the way of establishing mentor-mentoree relationships.

For example, an important part of the manager-subordinate relationship is the cycle and process of establishing objectives, conducting performance reviews, and appraising performance. A manager may participate in this cycle with many subordinates; a mentoring relationship with one of them may create conflict not only between the mentor and mentoree but among all the others reporting to the manager as well.

Managers have dual roles and responsibilities with subordinates: to evaluate them and to develop them. These dual roles eventually clash as managers attempt to mentor as well as manage.

A preferable arrangement is for managers to manage their subordinates and mentor the subordinates of other managers. In this way, the sometimes conflicting roles of evaluator and developer can be kept separate.

Furthermore, mentoring relationships may be cross-functional, involving participants in different line and staff departments. For example, a manager in the marketing department might serve as a mentor for an IS professional, or an experienced IS manager and a less-experienced person in the finance department might team up as mentor and mentoree.

Mutual Commitment Required

However mentoring relationships are constructed, mutual benefits are at the heart of those that are the most productive. Each person must perceive and believe that he or she has needs that can be met through the mentoring process. If the needs of only one participant are met, the relationship seldom achieves its potential and may be short-lived.

Mentoring is a mutual commitment demanding a major investment in time and energy. Mentor and mentoree alike share responsibility for managing the expectations that surround the mentoring relationship.

Successful mentoring relationships sometimes transcend the workplace. They may include the spouses or companions of the mentor and mentoree and be primarily social in nature, or they may involve a mix of business and social activities that includes only the participants themselves. There is no one best way. Mentoring can be informal, with only the mentor and mentoree involved, or it can be formal, with organizations providing a degree of structure to the mentoring relationships and activities. Mentoring can thus take on aspects of a project, except that there may be no predetermined end. Certain activities (i.e., courses or seminars) may conclude, but the personal relationships may continue.

PEER-TO-PEER MENTORING

In most mentoring relationships, one of the participants is senior to the other, in age as well as in experience. There is an important exception to this tendency, however, and it offers IS professionals an opportunity to broaden their business knowledge as well as build a network of colleagues throughout the enterprise. The exception to the rule is peer-to-peer mentoring.

Peer-to-peer mentoring involves building a support relationship with a peer in another department of the enterprise. This peer should not be a user/client, nor should either individual be a direct stakeholder in the activities of the other person (e.g., project team member or colleague). Relationships among project team members can be difficult enough without introducing a mentor-mentoree relationship into the mix.

The common ground necessary for effective peer-to-peer mentoring is that each person must possess some knowledge, skill, or insight that is not possessed (at least to the same degree) by the other but that the other needs in order to be successful. Furthermore, each person must be willing to share this knowledge, skill, or insight and encourage the other person to use the information or skill when and where appropriate. This requirement is more difficult than it sounds, especially during periods of rightsizing, when individuals may guard information they believe gives them competitive advantage over their colleagues.

In a well-crafted peer-to-peer mentoring relationship, each person becomes a stakeholder with the other in terms of common career ambitions, required knowledge and skills, and a desire to develop their careers even without formal learning resources being available. Each person becomes, in effect, an internal consultant to the other.

EXTERNAL MENTORS

A form of mentoring needed in downsized organizations is external monitoring, or the establishment of peer-based mentoring relationships primarily through professional associations. Some IS professionals, especially those at senior levels, are extremely successful at this. The majority of IS professionals are not. Many IS professionals are not joiners and thus fail to take advantage of opportunities to establish contacts outside their organizations and build human networks of peer-to-peer relationships.

Human networking becomes an increasingly important career management strategy as organizations rightsize and staff size shrinks. The external contacts and relationships established through professional associations are valuable sources of information, not only about job opportunities but about best practices in a wide variety of organizations. For example, the Society for Information Management (SIM), a leading professional association for IS executives, consultants, and academics, invites its members to participate in working groups to examine best practices in quality management within information systems. Some SIM chapters also offer CIO members the opportunity to participate in roundtable, focused discussions of topics of interest to CIOs.

These opportunities for external peer-to-peer human networking and mentoring do not just happen. Interested individuals have to seek out the contacts, determine whether the programs, information, and benefits will be helpful, and establish the relationship. Initiating and cultivating these contacts requires an investment of time and energy. Individuals must be willing to do more than attend occasional meetings, which alone will not yield the benefits that flow from in-depth participation. Those who get the most out of external peer-based human networking and mentoring are those who become involved in committee work, program development, and officership.

WHY MENTORING IS NOT MORE WIDESPREAD

There are several reasons why mentoring is not widely practiced among IS professionals, some of which have been touched on previously:

- Lack of familiarity with the mentoring concept and process.
- Lack of contact with potential mentors from business units and other staff departments.
- Physical separation of IS departments from other departments of the enterprise, making contacts with potential mentors more difficult.
- The introverted nature of many IS professionals, which may inhibit them from initiating contacts.
- The commitments of time and energy required for successful mentoring.
- The close personal nature of some mentoring relationships that may discourage some people.
- Lack of a perceived balance of benefits for mentors and mentorees alike. For example, mentors may perceive that there is more in the relationship for mentorees than for themselves and thus be reluctant to become involved.

- Lack of role models. If a person has not had a mentor during his or her career, that person is probably unaware of the benefits of such a relationship.

The issue of gender, racial, and ethnic differences is also a consideration to be faced by mentors and mentorees. Those on both ends of the relationship (i.e., potential mentors and mentorees alike) have their own feelings about becoming involved in developmental relationships with persons of the opposite sex, as well as those from different racial and ethnic backgrounds. There are, of course, many special groups in which members meet others like themselves, make contacts, and learn the ropes, but they cannot necessarily take the place of an in-depth, one-on-one mentoring relationship in which the mentor is committed to helping another person grow a career.

The issue of differences, while perhaps unsettling to some people, should not be a deterrent to successful mentoring. Differences exist; they are a fact of life, and denying their reality is not useful. It is better to discuss openly and honestly the feelings the potential mentor and mentoree have about the differences during the experience-sharing phase.

A discussion of differences and expectations can help get a mentoring relationship off on the right foot. It can also avoid conflict and embarrassment by allowing both individuals to share their feelings and opinions under conditions of relative confidentiality. In addition, it enables each person to gain valuable experience in dealing with feelings and emotions that are not usually expressed as openly.

MENTORING GUIDELINES

There is no one best way or specific model for successful mentoring. Mentoring relationships are unique to the persons involved, because of the personal chemistry between mentor and mentoree. There are, however, some common themes and broad parameters to consider. Organizations may develop guidelines to govern aspects of the mentoring process, including:

- How mentors and mentorees are selected and paired up.
- The roles and responsibilities of mentors and mentorees.
- The availability of formal educational experiences, including courses and seminars.
- Evaluation of the participants and the process.

In the majority of organizations, mentors and mentorees determine for themselves how to establish and manage their relationships and mutual expectations. Few organizations may have guidelines, but this may be a strength, not a weakness, for it allows and encourages mentors and mentorees to grow relationships that best meet each other's needs while at the same time serving the needs of the enterprise. The issue of whether to establish predetermined policies, rules, and requirements to govern mentoring relationships is a good example of a situation in which the principle "Less is more" applies.

Mentoring relationships can be primarily job and career related and focus on such hard issues as:

- Expanding the mentoree's job opportunities (outside the enterprise, when appropriate, but primarily within the organization).
- Understanding how to approach specific situations and problems.
- Learning about key people in the organization and how to handle them.
- Understanding the culture of the enterprise, including the psychological and social contracts that govern relationships.
- Undertaking tasks that increase personal visibility.
- Taking on stretch assignments that may require new learning and risk-taking but that can result in increased self-esteem and new contacts.

On the other hand, mentoring relationships may deal more with such soft issues as:

- Attitudes and behaviors.
- Value judgments surrounding particular issues and decisions.
- Ethical considerations.
- Personal and professional goals.
- The need to cultivate close personal relationships in increasingly impersonal workplaces.

It is difficult to separate all of these issues. As a result, a mentor may offer advice and counsel on ways to approach a specific problem or troubling situation and at the same time raise the issue of the values and ethics involved in the various approaches. Thus, the pros and cons of each approach can be analyzed, but in the broader context of a values-based discussion.

CONFLICT BETWEEN MENTOR AND MENTOREE

Conflict is inevitable in mentoring relationships; indeed, it is invaluable. The mentoring experience would be diminished if conflict did not arise, because conflict is a part of everyday organizational life. If mentoring is to be a useful experience, mentorees must profit from learning how to analyze and manage conflicts that arise between themselves and their mentors; these lessons can then be applied to the conflicts they need to analyze and manage between themselves and their colleagues, managers, and subordinates on the job.

How Much Time to Give

A major source of conflict between mentor and mentoree is the amount of time and energy that must be invested in the relationship by the mentor. This may be grossly underestimated by both participants. If either participant enters into the mentoring relationship without having examined in advance the demands in personal time and energy required and having determined that these demands are acceptable, the mentoring relationship may falter or be counterproductive, setting back the cause of effective mentoring within the enterprise by months.

The way to deal with this source of conflict is first to recognize its inevitability and second to realize that it must be managed, discussed, and agreed on before the relationship begins. If the decision of how much time to devote to the relationship is not mutually acceptable, either person must feel free to leave the relationship.

Personal Style and Values

There are two other sources of likely conflict: conflict over personal style and conflict over values. Personal style is easier to observe and easier to discuss and change than is a conflict over values. Personal style is in part a combination of learned traits or characteristics; it may even be based on the style of an admired friend, colleague, or public figure. Values, however, are deeply ingrained in a person's personality, character, and makeup. Values are difficult, if not impossible, to change.

Style- and values-based conflicts should not be avoided, however. They are symptomatic of the conflicts that arise within the enterprise, and a mentoring relationship may be the ideal vehicle for gaining firsthand insight and experience into managing them more effectively. They cannot be avoided on the job, nor should they be in mentoring relationships. The reality of conflict should likewise not be an excuse for discouraging or avoiding mentoring relationships. Rather, mentoring should be encouraged for precisely this reason: the more experience a person can gather on the practice field, the easier it will be to handle the real thing when it occurs during game time. That is what mentoring is about.

HOW TO ESTABLISH A MENTORING RELATIONSHIP

If the prospective mentor and mentoree are employed by an organization that has a formal mentoring program in place, the program is usually administered (or at least coordinated) by someone from the corporate human resources department, and there is probably a cadre of preselected and prescreened mentors ready and willing to become involved with less-experienced colleagues. Problems may still arise, however, because the choice of mentors may be limited to those already on HR's approved list and there may not be a good fit among them for everyone interested in a mentoring relationship.

Equally disturbing (for some) is the notion of a predetermined program for mentoring. This may include prescribed mentor-mentoree meetings, seminars, and conferences. Although such a corporate commitment is to be applauded, it may not enable or encourage the customization of mentor-mentoree relationships around mutual needs and benefits.

The reality is that most IS professionals who desire to develop and further their careers through a mentoring relationship will have to establish and grow this relationship on their own. The following action steps are designed to help them.

ACTION STEPS

Step 1. Individuals should be as clear as possible about their career goals and objectives, for the entire mentoring experience is based on these. If individuals are unclear about their career direction, the mentoring experience may help clarify options, but the individuals must at least be able to discuss where they are in their careers before approaching potential mentors.

Step 2. Individuals must be equally clear about what they need from a mentoring relationship. A person may, for example, simply be seeking a colleague in another department with whom to kick ideas around. Other individuals may want to locate a more senior person in a line department who can help them understand the enterprise's direction and strategy. The potential mentoree must know what he or she needs and why.

Step 3. Individuals should talk with friends and colleagues who are in mentoring relationships about their experiences in order to benefit from what they have learned. What aspects of these relationships work well and why? What works less well and why? By thinking about what others have learned, a person can begin to think about what he or she might do differently.

Step 4. A person may not know anyone who is, or has been, in a mentoring relationship, so it may be necessary to learn as much as possible about the organization's culture and the different jobs and responsibilities in the business to be able to locate people in other departments (or even other levels in the organization) with the experience the mentoree is seeking. The more a person knows before approaching a potential mentor, the better.

Step 5. The next step is to draw up a list of potential mentors and to clarify why each one would be an appropriate mentor, what can be learned from each prospective mentor, and what the reciprocal benefits will be. It helps also to learn whether there are extenuating circumstances surrounding any of the prospects that would influence the decision to ask them or their decision to accept an invitation.

Step 6. The first five steps are meant to help a person prepare to approach the prospective mentors. Some people will decline the offer, but that is no reason to be discouraged. When someone accepts, a meeting should be scheduled to review mutual needs, expectations, and benefits. The mentoree and prospective mentor must determine the parameters of the relationship. Will the relationship be formed to work only on hard-core career issues or on a combination of hard and soft issues?

Step 7. It is important to set an initial timetable and a review and evaluation procedure to establish some bases for continuing the relationship or discontinuing it.

Step 8. Assuming that both people have made a mutual commitment to begin the mentoring relationship (after taking into consideration all the issues discussed in this chapter), they must then continue to review, assess, and evaluate the relationship to determine whether they should continue to move forward on the original basis or reevaluate expectations and take appropriate action.

CONCLUSION

Mentoring is a developmental relationship that can be valuable to mentoree and mentor alike. A successful mentoring relationship can help mentorees survive enterprisewide restructurings and rightsizings. As a career development strategy, mentoring is more widely used outside of IS than it is by IS professionals. Although there are reasons for this situation, IS professionals can overcome them by understanding the nature of the mentoring process and its requirements for success.

Section V
Client-Based Computing

WITH THE PROLIFERATION of personal computing, many organizations have established help desks to provide technical assistance to the user community. Unfortunately, help desks have all too often suffered from a lack of attention by departmental management. In many cases, they have not kept pace with their customers' changing requirements, nor have they been positioned to encourage staff longevity. As a result, some help desks that were initially successful are no longer effective. Chapter V-1, "Improving the Help Desk," addresses the problems that face mature help desks and proposes a course of action to fine-tune and upgrade them, restoring their credibility within the organization and positioning them for success for years to come.

The process of fine-tuning the help desk begins with evaluating the current situation, setting obtainable goals, and developing a plan for the future. The final step in the process is ensuring that implementation procedures are followed according to the plan and that initial goals are met. Chapter V-1 also outlines the change management required to facilitate the help desk transition.

As business users assume more and more responsibility for processing their own information and as personal computers become ever more common in the workplace, IS managers at all levels are concerned with what role they will play in the information processing function in the future.

The trend toward decentralized computing on intelligent and powerful desktop workstations—and the subsequent decreased demand for data center, or mainframe, services—does not necessarily signify the demise of the IS department or its managers. Although the technology is changing, the technology management issues beyond which hardware is used will not change. These issues remain just as critical to the ultimate success of the organization. For this reason, experienced IS professionals can often successfully apply their skills and perspective to the microcomputer environment. Chapter V-2, "Applying Management Principles in Downsized Environments," suggests an approach IS managers can take to effectively manage and adapt to the expanded use of microcomputers and therefore remain valuable and contributing members of their organization.

Over the years the problem of computer viruses has become more widespread and has gained much public attention. The sensationalism that occasionally surrounds the appearance of another virus only serves to complicate the problem for the IS manager, who is usually expected to control such outbreaks.

Systems break down for many reasons: hardware fails, programs are subjected to odd circumstances, and users find unexpected ways of doing simple, straightforward tasks. One way a system can fail is by the introduction of a harmful, self-replicating program, better known as a computer virus. A virus is a type of software used for malicious purposes; types include Trojan horses and worms.

Computer viruses are a high-profile software threat, comparable to the biological entities of the same name. Chapter V-3, "Control of Computer Viruses," reviews some of the characteristics of viruses and the products and procedures for combatting them.

V-1

Improving the Help Desk

Christine B. Tayntor

WHEN FIRST INTRODUCED, the help desk's mission was simple: to help users operate their personal computers and obtain a basic proficiency with the software installed on them. The challenges were straightforward. Not only were the PCs standalone machines, but the software packages being used were usually limited to word processing and spreadsheets.

The world of end-user computing has changed dramatically, however, with a new level of complexity being added in three key areas: hardware, software, and customer requirements.

In many cases, standalone computers have been replaced by PCs linked into extensive local and wide area networks. This has increased both users' dependence on their machines and the possibility that one person's error could affect an entire community. It has also complicated the help desk's responsibilities. To be successful, the help desk staff has had to expand its area of expertise to include at least the fundamentals of network operating systems.

Word processing packages now include many of the tools that were previously found only in high-end desktop publishing products, and spreadsheets boast integrated spell checkers and query tools. In addition, many users have migrated from DOS to Windows, adding complexity as they run multiple products simultaneously. For the help desk staff, problem diagnosis has become substantially more difficult. Not only have they had to develop expertise in the new, more complex applications, but they now need to understand the relationships between the applications.

The help desk's customer base has also grown more sophisticated, and users have a far higher comfort level with personal computers. Many are highly computer literate and willing to experiment with packaged software. They want in-depth explanations of how to link a spreadsheet with a graphics package and tie them both into a word processing document, then send the results to a dozen people by electronic mail.

As customers' levels of expertise have grown, so too have their demands on the help desk staff. They expect nothing less than excellence and are frequently vocal if their expectations are not met. If the help desk is to be successful, it must adjust its services and skills to meet the new requirements.

FINE-TUNING THE HELP DESK

Three basic steps can facilitate an orderly transition to the help desk of the future:

- *Defining the ultimate help desk.* This is the vision of excellence for the future. It will become the benchmark against which performance can be measured.
- *Establishing the baseline.* This involves determining where the organization is now. Comparing current performance to the goals established in the first step can help identify the areas in which performance improvements are required.
- *Managing the evolution.* After the plan has been developed, basic management techniques are needed to ensure that the plan is implemented rather than becoming only a historical document.

DEFINING WORLD-CLASS SERVICE

Before a company initiates any organizational changes, it should have clearly established goals and a plan to achieve them. Without such a formal vision, change is unmanageable and may have unpredictable results. Three fundamental tasks are required to define the ultimate help desk: establishing a vision, identifying the services to be provided, and defining optimum service levels.

Establishing a Vision

One of the key elements in defining the future is to clearly outline the functions that the help desk can and cannot perform. Before this level of detail can be reached, however, the organization needs an overall framework. In short, the help desk needs a mission statement.

Identifying Services to Be Provided

Although the mission statement addresses services in general terms, management should define them very specifically, because what the team is expected to do directly affects both the staffing level and the skills that are required. Specific questions should be answered at this point.

Is the help desk responsible for resolving the majority of all problems, or is its primary function to route questions to the appropriate expert? The answer to this question determines how large the staff must be, because solving a problem takes substantially longer than simply routing it to another person. Similarly, the more problems the help desk is expected to resolve, the greater the depth of product knowledge and training required.

Should the help desk provide services other than problem resolution? Some companies have expanded the role of the help desk beyond problem resolution to include such functions as:

- Installing and upgrading software.
- Performing preventive maintenance on personal computers and servers.
- Providing product training to customers.

This expansion of services can have both positive and negative effects on the organization. On the negative side, if the help desk is to assume additional responsibilities, increased staff and more training are required.

From the staff's view, the added responsibilities can be either positive or negative, depending on the personalities involved and the corporate culture. The new functions can be perceived as job enrichment and a way to learn more about the hardware and software the team supports. They may also be viewed as diluting the primary mission of the help desk: resolving problems.

Defining Service Levels

After management has decided which services the team should provide, the next task is to determine performance levels. It is not sufficient to state that the help desk can respond quickly to customer inquiries, because quickly is a subjective term. Instead, the help desk should have specific, measurable performance targets. Examples include:

- Of all calls, 95% should be answered before the third ring.
- Of all problems, 93% should be resolved with no callback (i.e., customers receive their answer during their first call to the help desk).

Benchmarking. Because help desk performance is measured against the target performance levels, those service levels must be achievable. One way to establish acceptable performance measures is to benchmark other companies, determining the levels that they have set and that they meet. Some basic rules to follow when benchmarking include the following:

- The companies' environments should be similar. A help desk that supports dumb terminals attached to a mainframe running core transaction processing systems has different performance expectations from one that supports personal computers attached to LANs running personal productivity tools.
- The companies being benchmarked should be recognized as providing above-average or excellent service levels. Learning how a mediocre performer sets its goals does not facilitate developing a world-class help desk.

Although it is important for service levels to be achievable, it is even more critical that they meet customer expectations. Too often management develops targets in a vacuum without consulting the user. Although some companies are reluctant to ask for customer input to the goal-setting process, this is an essential step toward improving satisfaction. One way to obtain user requirements is with a customer survey. A sample survey section is included as Exhibit V-1-1.

Customer Survey—Help Desk Services

Help, please! The help desk needs your feedback to know what services it should provide. We urge you to complete the attached questionnaire and return it to us by _____. Please answer only for yourself, not for your entire department.

Hours of Operation—Please indicate the hours when you would like someone from the help desk to be available to assist you.

Weekdays: from _____ to _____

Weekends and holidays (check one):

_____ from _____ to _____

_____ on call (able to reach the office within one hour)

_____ in the office when arranged with _____ hours advance notice

Call Answering

1. When you call the help desk, your phone should be answered in:

_____ 2 rings

_____ 3–5 rings

_____ 5–7 rings

_____ 8–10 rings

_____ more than 10 rings

2. The call should be answered by:

_____ a person who can answer the question

_____ someone who can transfer you to a person with the answer

_____ a receptionist

_____ voice mail

3. If you leave a message with voice mail or a receptionist, you should receive a follow-up within:

_____ 5 minutes or less

_____ 15 minutes or less

_____ 30 minutes or less

_____ 1 hour or less

_____ 2 hours or less

_____ 4 hours or less

_____ the same working day

_____ the next working day

Problem Response

1. The first help desk person you talk to:

_____ should be able to help you immediately

_____ should be able to help you after a short (less than one minute) hold

_____ may call back with the answer

Exhibit V-1-1. Sample Help Desk Customer Survey

2. If it is necessary for someone to call you back, follow-up should be within:

_____ 5 minutes or less

_____ 15 minutes or less

_____ 30 minutes or less

_____ 1 hour or less

_____ 2 hours or less

_____ 4 hours or less

_____ the same working day

_____ the next working day

3. The time from when you first call the help desk until you get the correct answer should be:

_____ 5 minutes or less

_____ 15 minutes or less

_____ 30 minutes or less

_____ 1 hour or less

_____ 2 hours or less

_____ 4 hours or less

_____ the same working day

_____ the next working day

Exhibit V-1-1. (*continued*)

ESTABLISHING AND EVALUATING THE BASELINE

After the first step is complete, the organization knows what it considers to be a fully functional help desk and is typically anxious to proceed with implementation. An essential intermediate step exists, however, that must not be ignored. The organization must measure its current performance and compare that to the goals established by the vision. Without this step, the organization is proceeding blindly, making changes without being certain of their impact or knowing whether those changes are treating symptoms rather than resolving underlying problems.

Before an effective implementation plan can be developed, the organization must complete three key tasks:

- Establishing a baseline of current performance.
- Determining how large a gap exists between the present help desk and the ideal that was identified.
- Performing a gap analysis (i.e., determining the underlying causes of the discrepancies).

For those companies that have implemented formal metrics programs for their help desk, measuring current performance presents no challenge. Many other companies, however, have few if any statistics about the help desk and must compile them.

Although automated tools can simplify the collection of metrics and increase the accuracy of the data, statistics can also be gathered manually. At a minimum, each member of the help desk staff should record the number of calls answered each day, how many are forwarded to someone else for resolution, and how many require follow-up. Although it is more difficult to compute manually, it is also helpful to calculate the minimum, average, and maximum length of time before a call is fully resolved. These are important metrics that are used to measure future performance.

Customer satisfaction, which is a key element of current performance, can be obtained either by interviews (e.g., in person or by telephone) or through a survey. One approach is to expand the customer requirements survey shown in Exhibit V-1-1 to include two columns, one to record the current situation and the other to indicate the customer's needs.

For organizations that have not yet implemented metrics programs, the following recommendations are given:

- *Be honest with the staff.* Measurement is frequently perceived as an attempt by management to identify and punish poor performance. Management should explain that the statistics are used to measure improvements for the group as a whole, rather than for individuals. It is simply a measurement of the current situation. Future performance and widening the gap between that and current performance are key.
- *Do not rush.* A meaningful baseline cannot be established in a day or a week. To ensure that seasonal swings in activity do not skew the statistics, they should be gathered over a period of at least a calendar quarter.

After the goals and the baseline have been established, it is relatively simple to determine the gap between them. This third task, determining the causes for these discrepancies, requires substantially more time and effort. The proper focus, however, can minimize the length of time needed.

Because of the type of work the help desk performs, only three key variables in performance exist: the staff, the automated tools they use, and their customers. Because the help desk cannot mandate changes in its customer base, the fine-tuning program should focus on the help desk and its tools. By analyzing each of these, the manager can identify areas for improvement.

CHANGE MANAGEMENT

Although the transition from the current status to the ultimate vision of the help desk is more evolutionary than revolutionary, marked by a series of continuous improvements rather than a single dramatic change, the organization can take several steps to increase the likelihood of meeting its goals.

Upgrading the Staff

Although many organizations consider staff upgrades to be synonymous with technical training, three other aspects should be considered:

- Hiring the right people.
- Ensuring that the skill set of existing employees is the correct one.
- Retraining the staff.

Traditionally, managers hiring help desk staff have sought candidates with an existing knowledge of the hardware and software being supported. Although this approach has its merits, it does not address the primary function of the help desk: customer service.

Candidates with backgrounds in telemarketing who might not have been considered because of their lack of technical knowledge have proved to be excellent additions to the staff because they had expertise in dealing with customers, including difficult ones. Because telephone skills are vital for the help desk staff, some organizations have conducted their preliminary employment interviews by telephone. Not only does this prescreening save time for both the candidate and the hiring manager, it permits the manager to assess candidates in the same way the help desk customers will—by the sound of their voices. Although face-to-face interviews are still necessary, telephone screening can be a valuable first step in the hiring process.

Upgrading staff involves more than hiring the right people; it also includes assessing current staff members to be certain they should remain on the help desk staff. Many help desks are staffed with technicians, some of whom have neither the skill nor the desire to be in customer service positions. A careful evaluation of the staff members' performance as well as their long-range career goals helps identify members who should be transferred to another function.

Training is the key to upgrading the remaining staff. The gap analysis performed after the baseline has been established frequently demonstrates the need for specific training. Classes should be conducted to address immediate needs. In addition, a program should be developed to ensure that training is not just a one-time effort but becomes part of the culture. Such training may include formal classes on hardware and software products, an apprenticeship program for new hires, and ongoing coaching by both the help desk manager and the staff. As members of the staff gain expertise in specific products, they should be encouraged to share their knowledge with the rest of the team.

Team Spirit. The final challenge is to ensure that the newly trained staff remains with the organization. Because of the nature of the work, the help desk staff is subject to burnout. Ways to encourage staff longevity do exist. One of the most important of these is the development of a team esprit de corps, and that cannot occur until the help desk functions as a team.

The key to developing a team is to treat the group as one. Recognition should be based on the group's performance rather than on one individual's, although some measurements will necessarily be individual. For example, the following factors should be considered:

- *Policy*. The entire team receives recognition (e.g., an award, a bonus, or a dinner) when the number of calls handled per day increases by 10% as compared with the same period the previous year and when 95% of all customer satisfaction ratings are 8 or higher on a scale of 1 to 10.
- *Measurements*. The factors being measured are the number of calls per day (by individual and aggregated for the team) and customer satisfaction ratings (by individual and team).
- *Effects*. In a fully functioning team, if employee A is resolving fewer problems per day than the rest of the team, and employee B's satisfaction ratings are so low that they jeopardize the overall rating, the team itself resolves the problems. Someone works with A to determine why calls are not being closed. Someone else listens to employee B's calls and then provides coaching on techniques to improve customer satisfaction ratings. The result of these actions is that the team resolves internal problems, improves its performance, and reaps the rewards without management intervention.

Establishing Service Agreements

Customer satisfaction is the primary goal of the help desk; at times, however, it may seem an elusive goal. It is important that both the help desk staff and the customer departments have a realistic—and common—understanding of what level of service should be provided. Similarly, customer satisfaction surveys should be based on the help desk's performance against those predefined commitments rather than on an individual customer's requirements.

One way to develop shared expectations is to establish written service agreements. These outline the services that the help desk provides, the specific products to be supported, the help desk's hours of operation, guaranteed response time, and penalties for nonperformance. Agreements such as these provide clear targets and an objective way of measuring performance.

Monitoring Performance

After performance targets have been set, they must be monitored. Monthly or quarterly status reports, although necessary, are insufficient. Instead, the organization should strive for continuous monitoring so that problems can be addressed and resolved before they escalate. One technique that successful help desks have found valuable is holding daily problem meetings. The entire team meets briefly each morning to review the previous day's problems—both outstanding and resolved. Not only does this improve communication among team members, it encourages everyone to participate in problem solving and helps transfer knowledge.

Customer surveys are another technique for monitoring performance. Although these tend to be conducted on a monthly or quarterly basis, some organizations have found it helpful to contact customers soon after the call has been resolved, thereby ensuring that their memory of the events and the service they received is clear. Although it is desirable to obtain all customers' feedback, many organizations do not have adequate resources to perform a complete survey. For them, a random sampling of 10% of all calls is usually sufficient to determine whether any problem areas exist.

As metrics are established, it is key that they be communicated to the staff. Some organizations post call statistics on a central bulletin board; others carry them on a data base accessible by the entire staff. In either case, the important element is timely communication. Without it, the staff cannot react to and resolve problems.

Addressing the Root Causes of Calls

Although the help desk cannot change the composition of its customer base, it can help customers resolve some problems without having to call the help desk. This accomplishes two goals: faster problem resolution and freeing the help desk to address more complex problems.

The easiest way to assist customers is to determine the cause of their most common problems and then give them the information they need to solve those problems themselves. These self-help tools can include:

- A customized user guide, with such job aids as quick reference cards for commonly used software.
- Access to an internal bulletin board containing common problems and their resolution. To ensure that the data base is used, queries must be both easy to construct and flexible.
- Electronic mail alerts when a common problem occurs. The E-mail message includes a brief description of the problem as well as the resolution. This information should then be added to the bulletin board.

Promoting the Help Desk

The help desk of the future must market itself and its services if it is to remain an essential part of the organization. This self-promotion can take several forms, including:

- *Periodic newsletters.* These provide the opportunity to improve customers' product knowledge by including answers to commonly asked questions. They also serve as a regular reminder of the services the help desk provides.
- *Surveys.* Although most commonly used to gauge customer satisfaction with current services, surveys can also gather information about the desire for new services. The danger of overloading customers with too many surveys is constantly present, but when properly constructed, surveys can be a valuable communication tool.

- *Internal trade shows.* Some organizations conduct annual or semi-annual trade shows during which they display new hardware and software. Although vendors may be present to demonstrate the products, the help desk staff serves as the hosts. Open houses can serve as an ad hoc training tool, because customers frequently ask questions while they watch product demonstrations. Perhaps most important, they increase the visibility of the help desk staff, affording customers the opportunity to connect faces with the voices they have heard.

Like any other service organization, the help desk must ensure that its customers are aware of the benefits it can provide, and self-promotion is the surest route to increased visibility.

MAKING A BUSINESS CASE

Any help desk that has been in existence for two or more years is a candidate for fine-tuning. Although the fine-tuning varies with each company and may require from months to years to accomplish, the steps required to determine the scope of the upgrade vary little. The goal of this project should be to accomplish the first two steps of fine-tuning: establishing the vision of the future and determining the gap between current and desired performance.

The first step of the update involves determining the level of senior management commitment to improving the help desk. If no perceived need exists or if senior management is reluctant to provide either financial or staffing support, the project will fail and should not be undertaken.

Obtaining senior management commitment can frequently be accomplished by creating a business case for the upgrade. The following steps can be used to generate a compelling argument for improving the help desk.

Quantifying the Problem. The help desk manager should identify and quantify any problems that exist. A chart showing the number of calls that require more than a day to resolve, the degree of customer dissatisfaction with the current level of help desk support, and the staff turnover rate can focus senior management's attention on the problem and demonstrate that it is worth resolving.

Identifying Costs and Benefits. Because most managers make decisions on the basis of a cost/benefit analysis, the help desk manager should provide statistics about the costs (both hard and soft) of the current process. Hard costs include recruiting fees and training costs for new employees, which are the result of low employee morale and its related high turnover. Soft costs include low customer satisfaction, which can cause the entire IS department to have a tarnished reputation. An estimate of how much these costs can be reduced can help sell the program.

Networking with Other Companies. No business case would be complete without a comparison of the current process with other companies' handling of the same process. Although formal benchmarking is a lengthy process, informal networking, which can be done through structured telephone calls, can identify other companies' basic processes quickly. This information can be used to demonstrate the need for a change and the benefits that other companies have derived from one.

Many managers are visually oriented, responding more favorably to written reports and charts than to oral presentations. For this reason, a simple but clearly outlined business case may persuade them to approve a help desk upgrade program after a spoken plea for help was unsuccessful. In addition, by presenting their arguments in a written form, the help desk managers have demonstrated that the problem is a real one, important enough for them to expend the time defining it.

The next step requires managers to identify budgetary constraints. This provides a reality check for the project. If, for example, a one-time $50,000 limit exists, the project may focus on upgrading or purchasing an automated tool rather than hiring 10 new staff members.

After the budget constraints have been identified, a team must be formed. Because the purpose of the team is to establish a vision of the future, the team should include one or more customers as well as members of the help desk staff. Ideally, different levels of help desk staff should be included to provide different perspectives.

Next, a project schedule must be established. A formal plan with target dates and deliverables should be developed. In the case of fine-tuning, this project should be time-boxed into a period of 90 days or less. If the project extends beyond three months, it will lose momentum, and higher-priority projects may force it to be abandoned.

The final step is to actually begin the work. Fine-tuning the help desk requires a commitment of time, effort, and, in many cases, money. Because of this, some organizations cannot undertake the project. For those that do, the benefits are greater efficiency for the help desk and improved productivity for its customers.

V-2

Applying Management Principles in Downsized Environments

John P. Murray

IS THE MAINFRAME likely to disappear from the data center? No one today can say with any degree of certainty. What is likely is that in the future, much smaller, less expensive yet increasingly more powerful and efficient information processing hardware will become the norm. Many more IS fuctions are likely to reside in functional units outside a centralized IS department, and in fact, increased control of many IT processes by business unit users is already quite common.

The expansion of the use of microcomputer technology is an inevitable reality. More powerful, intelligent workstations offering greatly increased functional capabilities and productivity are becoming more common in user departments. Personal computers have already begun to change the manner in which the IS department is managed and the demands placed on those charged with that management responsibility. IS managers may be uncomfortable with this scenario, but because its occurrence is inevitable, they cannot ignore it. These changes need not signal the end of the computer operations function. On the contrary, astute IS managers develop an understanding of what is occurring and take the steps required to capitalize on the changes.

THE REQUIREMENT FOR MANAGEMENT CONTROL IN CLIENT/SERVER ENVIRONMENTS

IS managers deal with many issues daily that do not entirely depend on the technology involved. To a considerable extent, these issues apply in any environment—mainframe or microcomputer. Responsibilities for the procurement and management of IT hardware, processing control, security, the backup and protection of the organization's data, and the selection and management of personnel are still critical. The requirement to remain current with changes in technology also remains important in the world of desktop computing.

Protecting Data Assets

Perhaps most important, the requirement for the central storage and control of the organization's data is not going to vanish because of the movement to microcomputers or client/server technology; it may even assume greater importance in a mostly decentralized computing environment. Companies usually find that they must retain some mainframelike hardware to store and secure the organization's most valuable data assets. That hardware may remain in a centrally located data center or be dispersed throughout the organization.

Because client/server processing is going to play an important role, one issue IS managers should consider is what the server looks like: Is it a mainframe or a series of microcomputer servers? Where will the server or servers reside? Will they be in a central location or dispersed throughout the organization?

In many installations, the first step toward the client/server environment is through the existing mainframe. For installations that own or have long-term operation software leases, continuing to use the mainframe as a server for a period provides an increased return on that investment. In addition, the phased movement to client/server, through the continued use of the mainframe, reduces the risk inherent in changing the processing environment. The phased approach allows for planning and training that can be valuable through the transition.

What the final client/server installation looks like depends on the plan developed by the particular organization to deal with this new environment. The IS manager can provide valuable input to the planning process and should stress that attention be paid to the issues of control and support. As IS functions become increasingly dispersed, the requirement to control, secure, and protect the data increases.

There are already many examples of the difficulties encountered when individual departments become responsible for the security of their data assets. Failure to routinely back up the data on standalone PCs is a common example of the type of difficulty such circumstances can cause. When that situation occurs and data is lost, the damage is usually minor. Because typically only one or two people are affected, the result is often more an annoyance than a serious issue. However, with an expanding microcomputer environment that involves both local and wide area networks (LANs and WANs), the opportunities for serious disruption to the organization from the failure to back up data increase dramatically. Although business unit managers may be capable of protecting the data, they are often unaware of the requirement to back up the data or they lack the discipline data center professionals gain from years of experience performing regular backups. In addition, their focus remains on the business functioning of their department, and worrying about the data may be viewed not as a departmental problem but an IS problem.

Organizationwide provisions for the management and control of the data assets must be established wherever the data resides. Final decisions are likely to depend on the action of the IS manager. Managers who develop a sound plan to retain control, and construct a business case to do so, will be in a favorable position. Those who simply bide their time and let things take their course are probably going to lose control.

DIFFERENCES AND SIMILARITIES IN MAINFRAME AND MICROCOMPUTER MANAGEMENT

The basic management principles that apply to the management of the data center apply equally well to the management of a microcomputer environment. The primary difference is one of scale. Some management approaches are different in a smaller dispersed atmosphere, and microcomputer terminology is somewhat different. However, none of these should deter the experienced IS manager from taking proactive steps to adjust to the new environment. The growth in PC technology can offer many benefits to those in the data center who make an effort to understand the technology and how to use it. The skills that make managers successful are exactly the skills required as the industry embraces microcomputer technology.

As the technology evolves, parallels between the microcomputer environment and the current mainframe environment become evident. For example, the use of LANs and WANs is nothing more than the current mainframe teleprocessing environment. In addition, the concepts and processes found in the microcomputer world are similar to those associated with the mainframe world. The need to capture data, to process that data, and to make the resulting information available to those who need that information is precisely what is done in the data center today. Many of the same issues that arose in the early days of the development of the mainframe installations are reappearing as microcomputing expands.

The benefits of microcomputer use are less complexity, less cost, and the ability for nontechnical individuals to gain greater control of their data. Those benefits are offset by the greater difficulty in managing, coordinating, and controlling these new environments, and, possibly, getting new responsibilities. Gaining direct control over their environment means that users must accept ultimate responsibility for managing that environment.

Even in centralized environments, many organizations do not have a strong grasp of how much data they have, the accuracy of the data, or where it is stored. IS managers continually encounter problems with providing adequate disk storage capacity to hold existing islands of data. Yet disk storage is only a part of the problem from the perspective of the IS manager. The time and effort required to process various jobs because the data is not well structured and organized is a growing problem, and its implications are beginning to become more pronounced as organizations move to data base processing. This problem, unless addressed and managed, may grow worse as individual departments gain more control over their data. This is why strong active management of the emerging microcomputer processing world is so critical.

In many organizations, data that has become critical to the continued business functions of the organization resides on standalone microcomputers.

When that data is lost and it is impossible to re-create, there are organizationwide implications. The person using the microcomputer may not back up the file. The person controlling the data or managing the application may leave the organization. Before leaving they may erase the data, but far more likely the person replacing the employee may inadvertently destroy or mismanage the data. Replacing that data may or may not be possible, and even in the best scenario, replacing the data is likely to take a considerable amount of time, money, and effort.

Managing the Networked Environment

By understanding this problem, the IS manager can gain control over this data, just as in the current data center operation. Because the potential problems associated with islands of data are not apparent in many installations, raising the issue and building a case to move against the problem before it becomes serious is not going to be an easy task. However, aggressive action by the IS manager can bring both the manager and the organization considerable benefit. Managers can save their organizations time and effort by doing whatever they can to ensure that their companies are not forced to relearn the lessons of the past.

Other problems that have been dealt with in the mainframe world, and mastered by the IS management team, are likely to appear in the microcomputer world. Problems of the availability of LANs and WANs and of adequate response times across the networks are serious issues. In addition, there must be a method to anticipate the growth of the processing load. As the processing load grows, it is going to have to be managed.

Management of the processing work load growth requires developing a strong microcomputer network management function as a part of the IS department. The first step of such an approach is to develop a plan to move all standalone microcomputers to LANs.

Although the impression may be that the introduction and effective use of PC technology, once standalone units are networked together, is a very arcane area only mastered by a few highly skilled individuals, experience has shown otherwise. Success has to do with dedicated, quality people and effective and thorough planning. A background in computer operations can be a distinct help in managing the LAN environment.

The installation of WANs, by their nature, may represent a more difficult challenge. However, it seems unlikely that people who have had experience with the installation and management of remote online communications installations in the mainframe world would find much difficulty in the WAN area. That premise is, again, based on the availability of sound operations management skills.

Tapping into Current Operations Management Skills

An organization may believe that it is more cost-effective for the installation and maintenance of LAN hardware to be handled by the vendors, rather than by company employees. However, many vendors that offer PC hardware and services do not have personnel with the skill or experience necessary to handle the installation and continuing management of LAN technology. In too many cases, however, an organization that expects to successfully use the technology finds it has to develop the required skills within the organization or look outside for someone with those skills.

As the use of and the reliance on microcomputer technology in business expands, one lesson companies are learning is that they must make a provision to address the planning, installation, and continuing management of the components of the microcomputer hardware and associated operating software. One solution may be to assign the responsibility for the design, installation, and continuing support of the LAN environment to the data center staff. Maintenance of the microcomputer inventory may also move to the computer operations group.

It is the stated intent of many organizations to move to a downsized IS environment. That means that over the next several years there will be a dramatic reduction in mainframe processing. With a strong long-term education plan, an organization can define its LAN and WAN management requirements and move that function under computer operations. The result is to transfer existing staff skills to the new environment.

OPPORTUNITIES FOR THE INFORMATION SYSTEMS STAFF

Computer operations professionals should concentrate their efforts on the management of the hardware and the operating environments. In addition to the aspects mainframe and microcomputer management have in common, several new areas must be addressed.

First, beyond the continuing management of the various operations concerns, the PC environment presents the opportunity to gain control over the mechanical aspects of the process. Tasks such as the layout of the LANs and the selection and installation of the wiring for the LANs can be placed within the purview of the data center staff.

A second area the IS manager should seek to manage is the continuing maintenance of the microcomputer hardware; the problem should be understood and its potential explored. PC maintenance contracts may be costing the organization a lot of money. However, because the hardware is becoming more standardized and modularized, hardware failures are increasingly being solved by replacing complete components. In that case, people with a reasonable amount of mechanical aptitude and an interest probably could meet the bulk of the repair problems of the organization. The data center staff is in an ideal position to develop an in-house maintenance service.

The data center staff's experience with upgrading mainframe hardware can also apply well to the microcomputer environment. Because of the movement to modularity, a shift to hardware that can be upgraded to more powerful versions is taking place. In some cases retrofitting the old hardware is an option.

Communications is a third area the IS manager should try to become involved in or gain control of. The installation and use of LANs and WANs present several opportunities.

The structures of the PC and communications industries consist of many vendors providing a variety of goods and services; however, the quality of the products offered, the experience of the people involved in the industry, and the levels of service provided vary. Customers are often forced to deal with several vendors. When difficulties arise, the vendors are often more adept at placing blame than they are at correcting problems. The same problems existed in the management of the data center 8 to 10 years ago. IS managers have the experience to direct PC and communications vendors to deliver the levels of service that will be demanded in the future.

Bringing management skills to these evolving microcomputer and communications areas is a circumstance requiring attention in every organization. IS managers who recognize the opportunity and take the initiative to move ahead are going to enhance their careers, whatever computing platform their organizations ultimately decide to use.

V-3

Control of Computer Viruses

Roger B. White, Jr.

A COMPUTER VIRUS is an executable piece of code that is programmed to make copies of itself in other executable files. A simple virus is a standalone program that makes copies of itself when it is run. A sophisticated virus hides in other executable files. Either way, however, a virus must be executed to perform its function of self-replication. A virus can corrupt, destroy, or change the data in data files, but to do this and to infect other files, a virus must run as a program—it must be executed. This means a virus cannot spread or cause damage from a data file unless that data file is somehow transformed into an executable file.

Virus programs are not new. One of the first viruses took the form of a program called Animals, an artificial intelligence exercise. Animals is a simple computerized version of 20 questions. The computer wins when it guesses the player's answer correctly. When the computer loses, it asks the player for two things: the correct answer and a question that can differentiate the new answer from its best guess. It then stores these responses and is ready to play again. Eventually, a computer programmer added code to the front end that told Animals to copy itself automatically onto any new storage media it could find. The Animals virus was not harmful; it just replicated itself.

The point of this story is that viruses are just another programming tool. They can be thought of as an undocumented feature that automatically adds itself to other programs. A virus becomes a systems manager's concern when it carries malicious code in addition to its self-replicating nature.

Viruses can be designed for any computer system, and most models have had at least one or two written for them at some time in their history. This chapter, however, deals specifically with viruses for IBM PC-compatibles and the Macintosh.

PC-COMPATIBLE VIRUS CHARACTERISTICS

PC-compatible viruses can be categorized by the kinds of executables they infect; their varieties include standalones, executable infectors, boot sector infectors, systems infectors, and mutating viruses.

Standalones. Standalones are programs like the Animals virus mentioned previously. They simply replicate themselves and do not affect programs around them. Standalones are rare and are generally not a problem because they are so easily identified.

Executable Infectors. The executable infector virus is code that adds itself to other .EXE or .COM files. The simplest form of infection occurs in the following manner: most of the virus is appended to the tail end of the .EXE or .COM file, and a hook is added to the front of the program that instructs the computer to immediately go to the tail and run the code there.

When the infected program is executed, the virus code searches for other files to infect and does whatever else it has been programmed to do. When the virus code has finished, it sends control back to the beginning of the file and the application the virus is hiding in begins its normal execution.

Executable infectors have no size limit, so they can be the most versatile of viruses. They are also the kind that can spread the fastest through a local area network. If one of these viruses gets into a file server utility commonly used for logging on (e.g., CAPTURE on NetWare LANs), it will be in every workstation that uses CAPTURE thereafter.

Boot Sector Infectors. When a PC starts up, the first thing it does is load code from a specific area on a disk and execute it. This area is called the boot sector; on PC-compatibles it contains the startup code for MS-DOS. It can, however, contain a virus instead—the virus moves the MS-DOS startup to another place on the disk. This is called a boot sector virus. One of the first of these was the Pakistani Brain virus (so named because it was developed in Pakistan and has the word *Brain* as part of its text message).

Boot sector viruses are always small and more of a problem when systems are booted from diskette rather than hard disk. The viruses do not move through networks, because the virus spreads by copying itself onto the boot sectors of new disks, not by being part of a copyable, executable file.

Systems Infectors. System file infectors are a cross between executables and boot sector infectors. One of the first of these was the Friday the 13th virus. These viruses infect only specific system files, not every kind of executable. System files rarely change, so the virus can be fine-tuned for its environment.

Mutating Viruses. The newest wrinkle in PC-compatible viruses is the mutating virus. This is a virus that encrypts part of its code and fills the unencrypted part with a changing amount of meaningless statements. One of the first of these is called Dark Avenger. Mutators are hard to spot with the static pattern recognition techniques that are the mainstay of antivirus scanners, so antivirus developers are designing dynamic scanners to deal with this latest development.

MACINTOSH VIRUS CHARACTERISTICS

The Macintosh architecture and the Macintosh programming environment are quite different from those of the PC-compatibles. As a result, Macintosh viruses look different from their PC-compatible counterparts.

Resource Adders. Resources are a way of adding to a Macintosh program without recompiling it. They are also an easy way to add a virus. Resource adders are the equivalent of PC-executable infectors; they can be big and versatile and they can infect many kinds of files.

Desktop File Infectors. One file on the Macintosh changes continually: the desktop file that keeps track of where icons and windows are located on the screen. The program that updates the file is a prime target for Macintosh virus developers.

DETECTING WHERE VIRUSES ARE LIKELY TO OCCUR

All computers can be afflicted with viruses. The difference in the seriousness of the problem is one of magnitude: how often does a virus attack occur and how hard is it to eradicate once it is discovered? Virus problems get worse when:

- The computer model is common.
- The computers are operated by many people with different skill levels, so many users cannot detect the signs of virus infection or that their programs are not operating correctly.
- The computers are used with many kinds of software, so new programs on new disks are introduced to the computers regularly.
- Great flexibility exists in new application design. This makes programming easier, but it also makes it easier to slip a new virus in without notice.
- The computers are networked. The programs being transferred can be virus-infected, so networking is a way of spreading viruses quickly. In fact, one of the quickest ways to spread a virus is to get it into a commonly used network utility (e.g., one used during log-on).
- No antivirus tools or procedures are in place. Virus attacks are now just another IS hazard, and tools and procedures are available for dealing with virus attacks just as for dealing with hard disk failures and all other system failures. Available tools and procedures can stop virus damage when they are properly implemented, but they cannot help if they are not used.

The difference between viruses and traditional programs is simply that the distribution is uncontrolled. This means that viruses move through some channels and pool in some places more readily than others.

One method of infection occurs when a program on the home computer gets infected and the home user takes a copy of an infected program to work. A similar potential source of infection are sales representatives or temporary technicians who bring a disk full of entertaining and helpful utilities to the office. If they pick these programs up from various informal sources and do not check for viruses, it is highly possible that a virus can be present.

Another source of viruses is disgruntled employees. It can be an employee who is close enough to the technology to develop a virus or someone who merely acquires an infected disk from someone else and introduces it into the office environment.

COMMONSENSE PREVENTION TECHNIQUES

Viruses are widely recognized as a threat to computer systems, and the prevention measures are straightforward.

Computer viruses are not diseases, but it is helpful to think of them that way. There are at least two rules for keeping viruses from moving through systems.

Avoid Booting from Strange Disks. Boot sector viruses are active only during the boot process. By consistently booting from a disk that is known to be uninfected (e.g., the local hard disk), spreading boot sector infections can be avoided.

Scan Disks Before Loading. Many antivirus packages are available today. These can be used to scan a disk before it is loaded and before any virus has a chance to move from the disk into RAM and from RAM to other storage devices.

If the system is virus-free, any new disks or disks brought back to the office after being run on outside-office machines should be scanned. The scanning software alerts the user if a problem exists.

Scanning software should be used properly. If the user is sloppy in the scanning procedure, it is not uncommon for the virus scanning software to become virus-infected. When that happens, the virus moves quickly.

CONTROLLING VIRUS DAMAGE

Because a virus is a program, it can only do damage that programs can do. It can be a devious program, but it is only a program. Viruses that put up strange messages or reprogram the keyboard are alarming to watch, but are not going to cause serious damage to office data. Serious virus damage occurs when data on disks is affected. Virus damage at its worst can be as direct as a command to format a disk or as insidious as a command to add random data to random sectors on a disk. In either case, the effect of the virus attack is much the same as the effect of a failure of disk hardware: data on the disk is either no longer accessible or no longer reliable.

Restoring Data from Backups

The first line of defense against virus damage is diligent backup procedures, so that when the damage is detected the backups can be used for recovery. Keeping backups current and using stringent and thorough backup procedures are the important first steps in minimizing virus damage.

Viruses can infect only executable files. Their activity can corrupt data files, but they cannot be stored in data files. Executable files rarely change much from the time they are installed, so one convenient way to avoid reintroducing a virus from a backup tape is to never restore executables from a backup tape. Instead, all executables should be restored from their original disks. If it is more convenient to restore executables from the backup system, they should be scanned after the restoration to make sure they are clean.

What to Do When Under Attack

If a virus is spotted, the antivirus scanner should be used. Most antivirus packages disinfect (i.e., remove viruses from executable programs) as well as detect. If an antivirus package cannot disinfect a file, the infected file must be deleted and a fresh copy must be made.

If the virus is caught on a disk coming from the outside, it is probably not necessary to do more than alert the owner of the disk that it has been exposed and any system that the disk has recently been used with should be scanned. If the virus is discovered on an in-house disk, the rest of the in-house computers, disks, and networks should be scanned to determine how far the virus has spread. All copies of it should then be identified and disinfected.

If the virus has been in-house for a while before being discovered, it is likely that it has been saved in the backup-archive files as well. It may be necessary to expunge the virus stored on tape. The virus cannot damage the tape or files on the tape. The hazard is simply the prospect of reinfection if one of the virus-infected files is restored from the tape. A compromise is to document on older tapes what viruses they may contain and in which files those viruses are likely to be found (this would be a list of files that the scanner had to disinfect when the virus is discovered) and then never restore those files from tape.

Up-to-Date Antivirus Software

New viruses are being developed all the time. Antivirus developers can only respond to, not anticipate, new viruses; it takes months to years for a PC-based virus to spread widely and only days to weeks for antivirus developers to analyze the virus once they see a copy.

It is important to keep virus-scanning packages up to date. If a package is more than two years old, it is probably not going to catch current waves of infection. Most developers of virus-scanning products offer upgrades, and many of these upgrades are available on disk and as downloads from either the producer's bulletin board system (BBS) or a commercial service (e.g., CompuServe). Because bulletin board services are often plagued by viruses in disguise, however, downloading to a test machine first is a common precaution.

MYTHS AND REALITIES

Viruses have recieved more publicity than all other computer problems combined, but not all of the stories about them are true. There are some popular virus myths.

Viruses Can Do Everything and Be Everywhere. Viruses are programs. They can do only what programs can do. Viruses can in theory come in all sizes, but the bigger they are, the easier they are to spot. If a million-byte virus tries to hide in a 50,000-byte COMMAND.COM file, it will soon be apparent that the COMMAND.COM looks too big. If the virus program is not big, its actions are not going to be too complicated. There are limits on how subtle a small program can be.

The other limit that a big, complex virus program faces is debugging. It is no easier to design a flawless virus than it is to design any other kind of application flawlessly. For instance, the Internet virus attack of 1988 was caused by a virus with many bugs. One of those bugs protected many kinds of computers on the Internet from attack—the program was incompatible with certain types of UNIX. Another bug, however, made the virus virulent on those machines it was compatible with. That bug kept the virus from sensing whether another copy of the virus was already running on the computer (the program was supposed to run only one copy of itself per machine). Instead, the virus reinfected computers repeatedly—each piece stealing a little processing power and using a communications line to find a new computer to infect—until the virus had commandeered so many computer and communications resources that the network was clogged up with virus traffic.

A Virus on a Macintosh Can Spread to a PC. Viruses are executable programs. It is nearly impossible to design an executable file that runs on both Macintoshes and PC-compatibles. Application developers would love it if the task were easier, but because it is not easy for traditional application developers, it is not easy for virus developers either, and so far they have not succeeded. Should one be developed, it would be likely to look like such an oddball file in both the PC-compatible and Macintosh directories that it would be easily spotted and removed.

Most Mysterious System Malfunctions Are Virus-Related. Long before viruses were discovered, computer systems experienced failures for reasons that were not immediately obvious. They will continue to do so. The three most common causes of mysterious system failures are operator error, a hardware problem (e.g., a loose connection), and a software bug already identified by the developer. If testing for the first three has been exhausted without finding an answer, it is time to consider a virus problem.

VIRUSES AND NETWORKS

Local area networks (LANs) aggravate virus problems in some ways and alleviate them in others. The aggravation comes because the computers of a LAN are interconnected. Viruses can move quickly through a LAN. Reinfections are likely and they move just as quickly. Once a virus gets into a LAN environment, it takes much work and vigilance to eradicate it completely.

The alleviation comes because applications that are centralized on file server disks can be scanned and protected easily, and boot sector viruses cannot spread through a LAN connection. The tight connection makes it possible to alert users to the virus problem so remedial action can start quickly. The following specific actions can be taken to control viruses on LANs.

Using Security to Control Virus Propagation. Executable files that are made read only in some fashion cannot be infected. They can be made read only at the file level or at the directory level. This can protect many applications but not all of them; it does not work for those that modify the executable every time users change their configuration. When viruses are around, those files must be watched carefully. If all applications are stored near each other on the directory tree, it makes it easier for the network manager to scan through them quickly.

Disinfecting a Network. If a virus has been established on the network for some time, four places must be checked: file server disks, local disks on each workstation, diskettes that users have for moving programs on and off the network, and the backups.

Supervisor Equivalence. A user reports to the administrator that a machine is acting strangely. Not realizing that a virus infection is present, the administrator tries running the application on his or her workstation to confirm the problem. The administrator's machine is now infected, and it, too, acts erratically. The administrator now logs in as supervisor to see whether the problem can be cleared up by trying other copies of the application. The administrator's infected machine with supervisor equivalence (which overrides the read only protection system) infects CAPTURE. While the administrator continues to research the problem, every user that logs in subsequently is infected. When the administrator finally recognizes that a virus is the source of the problem, it will have spread much further.

Server-Based Virus Scanners. Products are available to scan file server disks in real time, which makes controlling a virus much easier. Some of these packages have attack logging. In one case, this attack logging solved the mystery of a weekly virus attack on a LAN. It turnout out the culprit was a user on another LAN attached by a remote bridge. That user mapped to a file server on the LAN in question, then ran an infected program. The virus used the drive mapping to jump from one LAN to the other. The attack logger recorded that the attack was coming from over the asynchronous bridge that connected the two LANs, and the mystery was solved.

Hierarchical Security. If a particular system maintains a hierarchy of security, virus searches should begin at the top. Hierarchies are great virus concentrators; the user who can run all the programs can catch all the viruses.

ERADICATING VIRUSES

The easiest way to eradicate a virus is to use an antivirus scanner to disinfect the executable that contains it. This works in most cases—as long as the scanner can recognize the virus. If the scanning package is old and the virus is new, the package may not recognize the virus. If the scanner cannot find the virus, the IS department, the reseller of the package, and the scanner's developer can be questioned to determine whether an update is available.

If a scanner cannot be found to recognize and disinfect the virus, the following method should be used (it is crude, but it works):

* Any surely infected and possibly infected executable files should be deleted.
* The files should be restored from their original disks.

All the diskettes that come in contact with the personal computer or workstation that the virus is found on must be checked. If a virus has successfully penetrated to shared files on a network drive, this means checking every workstation on the network and all the diskettes that are used with those

---

* *Unusual disk activity.* A virus attack is the act of writing something new to the disk. This unusual disk activity may be too subtle to detect until after it has been confirmed that a virus really is at work, but if a disk is working strangely and the anomaly cannot be attributed to failing hardware or unusual software, a virus could possibly be the cause.
* *Changes in the size or date stamp of executable files.* For instance, if COMMAND.COM has grown by a few hundred bytes, or its data stamp indicates it was written two days ago, not two years ago, it has been infected.
* *Consistent crashing of a PC workstation on a LAN.* Many viruses use the same system resources that LAN drivers do. The conflict will crash both and usually foil the virus attack. This may leave a bit of mystery—the virus will be causing problems, but it will not be spreading to files on the LAN. Unless the infected disk is checked, the virus will not be found.

Exhibit V-3-1. Symptoms of a Virus

workstations. Extra vigilance for a few weeks may be required; reinfections from forgotten diskettes are very common. Reinfection can be reduced by finding out where the virus came from and alerting the user of that system that a virus is present. Exhibit V-3-1 describes other symptoms to look for to control viruses.

CONCLUSION

Viruses have been around long enough to be a well-characterized part of the IS environment. New viruses will be introduced from time to time, but procedures and products are available for dealing with them. The threat they represent is as manageable as any other that computer users must deal with.

Section VI

Systems Development and Programming

DEVELOPING AND MAINTAINING systems continues to be one of the most important functions in IS organizations. The chapters in this section cover the full range of systems management—from analysis and design, to creating the user interface, to testing systems after they are implemented.

Chapter VI-1 covers "Object-Oriented Systems Analysis." The object-oriented approach to systems analysis has been slow to evolve. Although the methodology has been gaining popularity among analysts, modelers, and practitioners, a lack of commonly accepted techniques and procedures still prevails.

Beginning with a discussion of four fundamental types of object classes in information systems, this chapter describes a systems analysis approach that merges object-oriented, functional, and dynamic methodologies. A case study involving three phases of abstracting information is used to demonstrate the technique.

Data modeling usually plays a significant role during systems design. The development team must identify and organize the required data entitites, determine the relationships between them, and communicate effectively with the users of the intended system to ensure that the system will meet their needs. Data models—graphical representations of a system's data elements—are used to facilitate these efforts. Chapter VI-2, "Data Modeling in Systems Design," discusses the components of the data model and then focuses on five important and commonly used data modeling notations from which to choose.

The user interface is the way the user sees the system. A flexible user interface permits the greatest possible convenience to the user. The user interface relates to the total hardware and software system. Although a flexible user interface helps users complete subordinate tasks more efficiently, the system designer must ensure that this efficiency also helps to accomplish overall corporate goals. "Building Flexible User Interfaces" is the subject of Chapter VI-3, which explains how interface design can conform to user goals.

A rigorous test process and a definable, repeatable test environment will lower development costs and improve applications quality. The elements of such a testing process and environment are discussed in Chapter VI-4, "Automating Applications Testing." IBM Corp.'s test tools, WITT and SATT, are discussed to illustrate how automated tools can promote rigor and reusability in applications code.

VI-1

Object-Oriented Systems Analysis

Shouhong Wang

USING THE OBJECT-ORIENTED approach, analysts can model a system by identifying a set of objects along with their attributes and the operations (i.e., internal operations and messages) that manipulate the object data. Objects are grouped into classes with common properties. Classes are organized into hierarchies in which the subclasses inherit the properties, including the data definitions and operations.

Identifying object classes is subjective, because it depends on the problem domain. In addition, the operations on each object class are often less intuitively identified; a great deal of functional refinement is often necessary. Functional (i.e., structured) and object-oriented hybrid methodologies offer a possible solution to these problems. However, a uniform paradigm that merges functional, dynamic, and object-oriented methodologies as an exploratory analysis approach is still lacking.

This chapter discusses how to use an integrated, object-oriented systems analysis approach specifically for information systems analysis. It investigates fundamental types of object classes in management information systems, develops an output-input backward-tracing analysis approach that embraces the generic structured aspects in an unstructured systems analysis process, and outlines three systems analysis phases involved in the process of abstracting information requirements.

FUNDAMENTAL OBJECT CLASSES

Four fundamental object classes exist in information systems: physiomorphic objects, events, output objects, and input objects.

Physiomorphic Objects. This term refers to a physical entity—for example, a person (e.g., a customer or a salesperson), a property item (e.g., a machine or a building), or an organizational unit (e.g., a company or a department). A systems analyst usually has no difficulty identifying physiomorphic object classes for IS development purposes. The attributes of each object class, however, may or may not be identified completely at first glance.

The operations on the object classes are even harder to uncover. For example, an analyst of a marketing information system can easily identify CUSTOMER as an object class. A list of attributes can be presented, but these attributes may be incomplete or redundant. It is also difficult to ascertain which operations would be involved without considering other object classes. To elaborate on physiomorphic object classes, iterations of refinement are usually needed through identification of other types of object classes.

Events. In systems analysis, time-dependent aspects must be included because events are associated with state transitions of the system and explicitly express the system's dynamic aspects. Therefore, a fundamental object-type event is needed. Some events could be routine operations or transactions (e.g., pay invoice, order product, or schedule work). Others could be decision-making activities (e.g., approve credit or promote personnel).

Events are noticeable in the management environment. A systems analyst should identify events on the basis of day-to-day business operations and decision-making activities. An event is associated with a nonphysiomorphic object, which is called an event object. For example, the pay-invoice event is represented by the INVOICE-PAYMENT object. Searching events will reveal those event object classes.

An event typically involves a trigger. In other words, an event is caused by or causes other events. A trigger could take one of the following forms:

- Timing (e.g., once every five days or 5 PM every day).
- The state of an attribute of an object reaches a critical point (e.g., the inventory level reaches a reorder point).
- The value of a variable involved in an operation of an object falls within a certain range (e.g., the after-tax income is greater than a certain amount).
- Exchange of information with entities outside of the system (e.g., a telephone call or a receipt of an invoice).

Descriptions of events in turn provide the systems analyst with hints to help identify object classes. For example, in an office system, the physiomorphic object class of SECRETARY is obvious, but other nonphysiomorphic object classes (e.g., MEETING-SCHEDULE) and their operations are probably less apparent unless the systems analyst searches all the events involving the SECRETARY.

Output Objects. An output object is a report (e.g., a sales summary, invoice, or credit certificate). It is considered a fundamental type of object class on the basis of several facts. First, output objects have attributes describing output properties (e.g., format and frequency). They must be independently included in the object class descriptions. These attributes are called nontraceable attributes, because they have little relationship with other object classes.

Second, a significant number of IS operations involve data base query and printing functions. These operations should be associated with specific output reports to make object modules more cohesive. In other words, the physiomorphic and event object classes contain a few generic printing operations and are more concise. The output object class contains most of the output operations, making the system easy to modify when responding to changes in information requirements. For this reason, an output object class can maintain attributes (called traceable attributes) whose values come from other object classes. Finally, identifying output object classes and their operations and tracing backward to system input will help the analyst identify object classes and expose relevant operations.

Input Objects. Input objects are representations of the information entities that enter the system. Examples include customer orders or government statistics for marketing forecasts. Input objects are a fundamental object class because they have specific attributes (e.g., format and frequency) that must be included in the descriptions of the object classes. As previously mentioned, tracing backward from an output object is a feasible way of identifying and checking physiomorphic and event object classes and their operations. Whenever an input object class is reached, the trace is ended.

BACKWARD-TRACING AND ITERATIVE PROCEDURE

The object-oriented analysis approach proposed in this chapter uses a trial search, backward tracing, elicitation, and progressive and iterative refinement. The iterations involve three phases:

1. Identifying output, physiomorphic, event, and input object classes, along with their attributes and operations, on a trial basis.
2. Tracing backward from output to event and physiomorphic object classes, as far as input.
3. Refining the inheritance structures.

Although the analysis process is iterative, theoretically, all three phases could be executed in parallel fashion. The following sections describe the phases in more detail.

Identifying Object Classes on a Trial Basis. In this phase the systems analyst identifies object classes and their attributes and operations. Each identified object class contains attribute names and operation names. Because the entire process is iterative, after phases 2 and 3, the analyst repeats this phase and identifies new classes on the basis of the results of the tracing and refining phases. If incompleteness or additional object classes or inconsistencies are found after phases 2 and 3, the analysis process converges and the iteration stops; otherwise, a further exploration is required.

Backward Tracing. After identifying outward object classes and their attributes, the analyst uncovers all relevant classes and their properties by tracing backward. This is achieved in three ways: by locating the event that triggers the object class currently investigated, by locating the messages and the receiver object classes to acquire the data items of the attributes, and by defining the internal manipulations on the data items of attributes.

For example, in a payroll system, the output object class of PAYCHECK and its attributes (e.g., EMPLOYEE-NAME, GROSS-PAY, INCOME-TAX, and NET-PAYMENT) have been identified. After creating a record for the PAYCHECK object class, the analyst then considers which event triggers the class and where the data items of these traceable attributes come from. This returns the process to phase 1. The analyst finds the PAYDAY event that triggers the PAYCHECK object class. The PAYDAY object could trigger other output objects and is in turn triggered by the SYSTEM-CLOCK object—for example, once every two weeks.

The analyst also considers where the data EMPLOYEE-NAME came from. The analyst identifies the EMPLOYEE object class according to the elicitation. If the system includes some personnel functions, the data of the EMPLOYEE object class eventually comes from the input object class HIRE-EMPLOYEE. In addition, the analyst may then uncover the internal operation INCOME-TAX-CALCULATION that generates income tax data. In this example, an analyst may not stop a trace until the system boundary (e.g., the SYSTEM-CLOCK or REGISTRATION object class) or a terminal operation (e.g., INCOME-TAX-CALCULATION) has been reached.

Refining Inheritance Structures. One of the characteristics of object-oriented systems is inheritance, which enhances software reusability. Creating effective inheritance structures in systems analysis is crucial for future implementations. In this phase, the analyst refines the classes by building and elaborating on the inheritance structures. Identifying inheritance structures is a complicated process, particularly when object libraries are involved. For the sake of simplification, discussion here is restricted to the cases without an object library.

In the refinement phase, the analyst searches all identified object classes, attributes, and operations. If several attributes or operations have the same name, the analyst should create a superclass for the classes sharing the common attributes and operations. For example, the analyst might identify the EMPLOYEE and EMPLOYER object classes, which have the same attributes (e.g., name or address). After checking these attribute names, the analyst will find that the two classes of EMPLOYEE and EMPLOYER could inherit attributes from a superclass. The analyst may then generate a superclass named LEGAL-ENTITY.

OBJECT-ORIENTED ANALYSIS APPROACH

To demonstrate the suggested object-oriented analysis approach, a simple but typical example of an information system is examined. The example is a payroll system adapted from J. A. Senn's *Information Systems in Management* (Belmont CA: Wadsworth, 1990). For the sake of demonstrating the

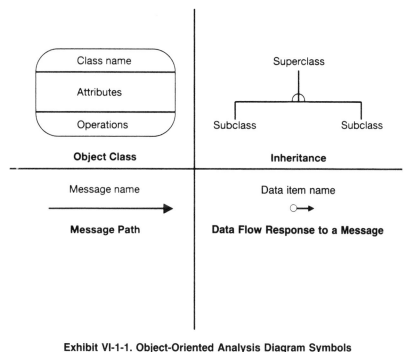

Exhibit VI-1-1. Object-Oriented Analysis Diagram Symbols

inheritance construction, a minor modification is made. The system is supposed to determine pay, produce a paycheck, and store relevant payroll information for each employee. There are two types of employee: full-time and part-time. The system determines pay from time cards for part-time employees and flat pay rates for full-time employees.

In the object-oriented analysis method, four symbols—object class, inheritance, message path, and data flow response to a message—are used for diagrams (see Exhibit VI-1-1). These symbols are used in the following exhibits to represent the information system.

In the payroll system analysis, the suggested object-oriented analysis procedure comprises the following three steps: identifying output object classes, tracing backward from output object classes to other classes, and refining inheritance structures.

Step 1: Identifying Output Object Classes. According to the system descriptions, three output object classes, Paycheck, CashAccount, and PayHistory, along with their data items (i.e., attributes) are identified (see Exhibit VI-1-2). No other information about their operations is known at this point.

Step 2: Tracing Backward from Output Object Classes to Other Classes. This step involves finding the events that trigger the output. An

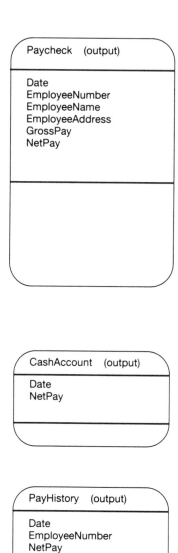

Exhibit VI-1-2. Payroll Example Output Object Classes

event called Payday triggers the three output objects of the system. Messages that will be sent by the Payday event to the output objects must be defined. Generic output functions (e.g., PrintRecord) are then specified. Data flows indicating the communication between the classes (e.g., Date) can also be identified. Because the analysis process is iterative, some data flows may not be identified immediately and will be completed later on.

With further backward tracing, an event called SystemClock can be defined—this event triggers the Payday event. The object-oriented approach has advantages in representing timing factors, compared with traditional structured analysis. In this example, the SystemClock object could be a real system clock or a set of transaction commands. Exhibit VI-1-3 shows what the object-oriented structure looks like at this point in the analysis procedure.

To trace backward to physiomorphic classes, the modeler can check attributes of the defined object classes to find the messages and receiver object classes and then obtain the data items of these attributes. In Exhibit VI-1-3, no source of the data items in the Paycheck object (e.g., EmployeeNumber, EmployeeName, and EmployeeAddress) has been defined. Accordingly, a physiomorphic object class of Employee is uncovered. Exhibit VI-1-4 depicts the expansion of the diagram.

Tracing backward from the output object class to the input object class requires checking attributes to find internal operations. Exhibit VI-1-4 diagrams the search for operations that generate the values GrossPay and Net-Pay for a Paycheck object. To calculate gross pay for an employee, time cards for part-time employees or flat pay rates for full-time employees are required. The input object class TimeCard is then uncovered. In addition, it is found that an Employee object could be either FullTimeEmployee or Part-TimeEmployee. For the sake of clarity, the intermediate analysis result of the Employee class is shown in Exhibit VI-1-5. To calculate net pay, tax tables are needed, which prompts a search for the input object class TaxTable. The completed diagram of operations needed for the attributes of the Paycheck class, as well as all of the messages and data flows required by the operations, is shown in Exhibit VI-1-5.

Step 3: Refining Inheritance Structures. The final step of the object-oriented analysis approach is to create effective inheritance structures for software reuse purposes. In the example, FullTimeEmployee and Part-TimeEmployee are two subsidiary classes of Employee. The inheritance relationship between them is shown in Exhibit VI-1-6.

Several iterations of the three steps involved in the approach are usually performed to complete the analysis of a system. In the simple example described here, however, all information requirements have been described completely after one iteration. The final object-oriented analysis diagram is shown in Exhibit VI-1-6.

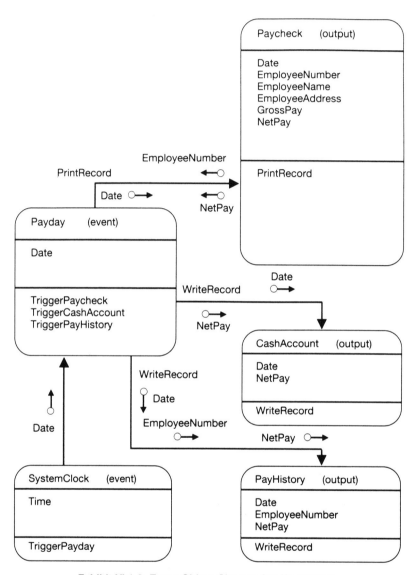

Exhibit VI-1-3. Event Object Classes Are Uncovered

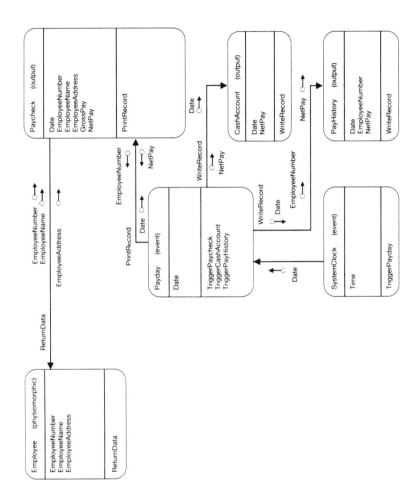

Exhibit VI-1-4. Physiomorphic Object Classes Are Uncovered

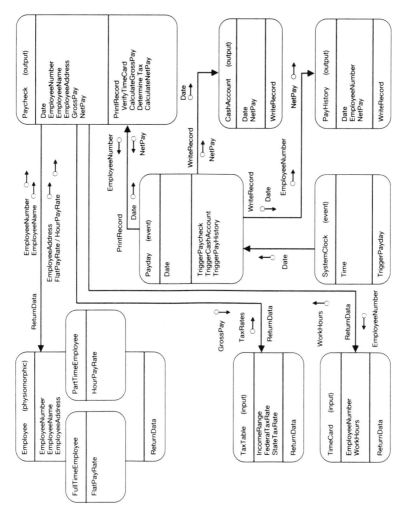

Exhibit VI-1-5. Input Object Classes Are Uncovered

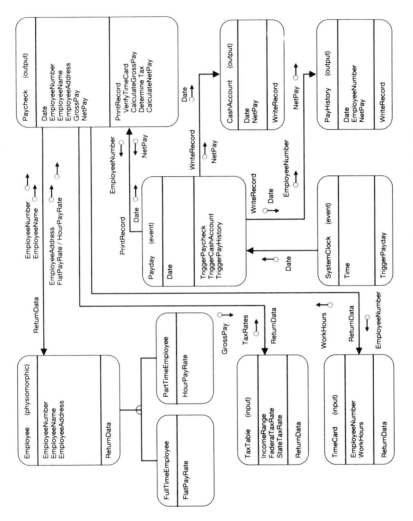

Exhibit VI-1-6. Final Refined Object-Oriented Analysis Diagram

CONCLUSION

Object-oriented systems analysis methodologies have become more popular in information systems; however, there is still a lack of commonly accepted approaches. This chapter has described an object-oriented analysis approach that could be relatively effective and efficient for management information system analyses because of its three characteristics.

First, the approach integrates the descriptions of the three aspects of an information system—namely, object, function, and dynamics—into a single object-oriented analysis diagram. As discussed, the approach describes not only tangible objects in a usual way but also dynamic (i.e., timing) properties of a system by defining event object classes. It also describes the functional properties of a system by specifying data flows between the object modules.

Second, the suggested approach includes structured algorithms in systems analysis, called iterative and backward-tracing processes. They substantially reduce the requirements for artistic skills in systems analysis.

Finally, the analysis products (i.e., diagrams) of the approach are easy to convert into object-oriented programs. The diagrams generated by this approach offer the features of both systems analysis and systems design, compared with the traditional structured systems analysis approach.

VI-2
Data Modeling in Systems Design

Stephen McHenry

MOST DATA MODELING highlights the data that an organization needs to do business. The modeler uses data modeling to view the data elements used by each group within an organization. Usually, an IS organization performs this kind of modeling before developing a set of applications for each of the groups represented. Consequently, a data model depicts information about an enterprise as a whole.

Data modeling serves several purposes. First, it can be used as a vehicle for identifying and describing a system's data elements. A model also helps the designer determine the relationships among data elements.

During system design, a complete data model—or more precisely, the knowledge that comes from developing one—improves designers' decisions. With models, designers make fewer false starts and backtrack less frequently during a project's design phase. Data models also facilitate the intelligent discussion of phasing for functions that cannot be implemented all at once.

A data model can also help data base design. However, not all entities in a data model have corresponding tables in the data base. Indeed, for organizational data models, the data base may not contain all of the data elements in the model. Although it is likely that the data base will be structured differently from the model (usually for performance reasons), the model still indicates what data must be represented in the data base.

BASIC COMPONENTS OF A DATA MODEL

At its most basic level, a data model represents the data elements in an organization or system and the relationships among them. It is also a statement of business rules that govern an organization or system. Each basic data model contains entities, relationships between entities, and attributes of entities. Additional notations are often added to qualify the types of relationships or attributes.

Entities. Entities are things that are meaningful to an organization. They may be tangible (e.g., employees, dependents, departments, and vehicles), or they may be less tangible (e.g., events, routes, or locations). An entity is anything about which some data must be stored.

Relationships. Relationships depict how entities relate to one another. For example, an employee (i.e., an entity) works for (i.e., has a relationship with) a department (i.e., another entity). Relationships are depicted in a data model by lines between entities, sometimes with boxes or other symbols that specify the relationship.

Attributes. Attributes are the information that must be kept about each entity: the fields that describe an entity. Examples of attributes for an employee are name, address, age, and Social Security number. For a vehicle, they might be make, model, color, and gross weight.

Cardinality. A fourth component that is frequently depicted is cardinality. Cardinality is the allowable quantitative relationship between two entities. More specifically, cardinality answers the question: For each entity A, is it proper to have zero, one, or many of entity B? Examples of cardinality include:

- One-to-one (1:1). For each entity A, there must be one and only one entity B.
- One-to-zero or one (1:0, 1). For each entity A, there may be at most one entity B.
- One-to-zero or many (1:0, M). For each entity A, there may be zero or more of entity B.
- One-to-one or many (1:1, M). For each entity A, there must be at least one entity B.

Cardinality depends on the direction in which it is expressed. For example, each DEPARTMENT may have one or more employees, but an EMPLOYEE is assigned to one and only one DEPARTMENT. Therefore, the cardinality from DEPARTMENT to EMPLOYEE is one-to-one or many and the cardinality from EMPLOYEE to DEPARTMENT is one-to-one.

Constraints. A final component usually found in data models is constraints. Although each data modeling notation supports different types of constraints, most specify the various conditions that dictate the presence or absence of related entities. Constraints ensure referential integrity and various other integrity checks imposed by an application.

DIFFERENT TYPES OF DATA MODELS

Five notations are commonly used for data models:

- Chen.
- Merise.

- Nijssen's Information Analysis Methodology (NIAM).
- ICAM Definition Methodology (IDEF1X).
- IBM Corp.'s Repository Manager.

Chen was the first notation widely used. Shortly thereafter, the Merise notation was introduced as a minor variant. Their expressive power is approximately the same. NIAM extends the expressive power of modeling languages and adds the ability to represent some complex constraints between relationships. IDEF1X also extends basic notations. Repository Manager has approximately the same expressive power as IDEF1X.

Currently, Chen and Merise notations are rarely used. NIAM has developed what could be described as a cult following—those who use it are completely devoted to it. Because in most cases IDEF1X has similar expressive power and is less cumbersome to use, much modeling done today involves IDEF1X. Repository Manager's notation is a little different. Repository Manager does not provide substantially more expressive power than IDEF1X. A discussion of each of these notations follows.

Chen

This notation shows basic entities as boxes (see Exhibit VI-2-1) and the relationships between entities as diamonds. The boxes contain the name of the entity, and the diamonds identify the relationships.

Cardinality is also depicted in this model. The symbols "1,1", "1,M", "0,M", and "0,1" next to the second entity in a relationship denote the cardinality of that relationship. For example, the DEPARTMENT entity contains one or more employees; this is shown by the "1,M" next to EMPLOYEE.

Exhibit VI-2-1 also illustrates several business rules. For example, an employee must be responsible for one and only one project; however, a project may have one or more than one employee assigned to it. An employee can be married to at most one spouse and a spouse must be associated with only one employee. There is, however, a weakness in Chen's expressive power. Relationships, as stated, are not necessarily reciprocal and often make sense only in one direction. For example, an EMPLOYEE is responsible for a PROJECT; however, it is not true that a PROJECT is responsible for an EMPLOYEE. A project is the responsibility of an EMPLOYEE. With Chen notations, each relationship has only one direction for expression. Usually this is not a problem because the inverse relationship is relatively easy to derive.

Merise

The Merise notation is functionally equivalent to the Chen notation (see Exhibit VI-2-2). It also shows entities as boxes (with rounded corners) and relationships as circles. The direction of its relationships is expressed explicitly with arrows. This eliminates any confusion about how a relationship is to be read.

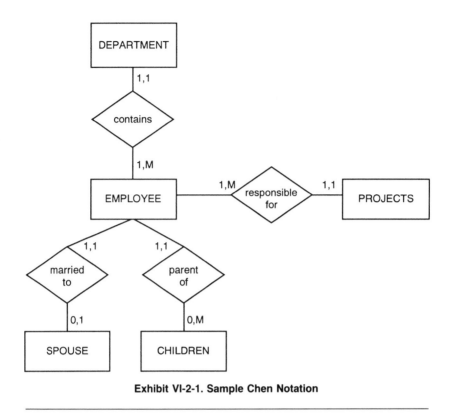

Exhibit VI-2-1. Sample Chen Notation

NIAM

NIAM modeling was pioneered during the early 1970s. Like the other techniques, it represents entities and relationships and supports cardinality. It differs, however, in its ability to name a relationship in both directions. Exhibit VI-2-3 depicts a basic NIAM relationship between two entities. Entities are depicted by solid circles; relationships (called roles) are shown by boxes between them. The relationship is always given for both directions. The example in Exhibit VI-2-3 reads DEPARTMENT contains EMPLOYEE and EMPLOYEE is assigned to DEPARTMENT

NIAM modeling allows a similar graphical depiction of the relationship between an entity and each of its attributes. Exhibit VI-2-4 shows the relationship between the EMPLOYEE entity and one of its attributes, NAME. (Attributes are represented by dashed circles.) Entities are often referred to as nonlexical object types and attributes are often called lexical object types.

Also supported is the distinction between optional and mandatory relationships. DEPARTMENT contains EMPLOYEE signifies that a department may contain employees; but a department is not required to have any employees. The inverse relationship, EMPLOYEE is assigned to DEPARTMENT, is not

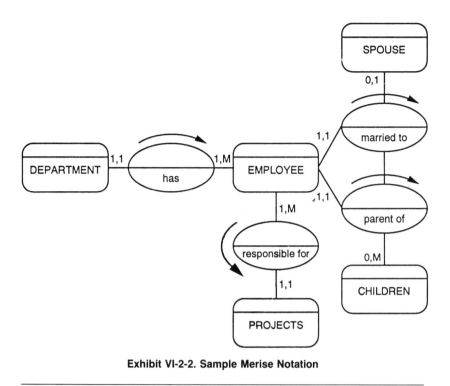

Exhibit VI-2-2. Sample Merise Notation

optional. If an employee exists, that person must be assigned to a department.

In NIAM modeling, mandatory relationships are known as total role constraints and are depicted with a V near the entity (see Exhibit VI-2-5) for which the relationship is required. Every EMPLOYEE must be assigned to a DEPARTMENT, because a V is on the line next to EMPLOYEE. It is not necessary for a department to contain employees because there is no V on the line next to DEPARTMENT.

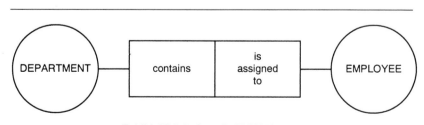

Exhibit VI-2-3. Sample NIAM Notation

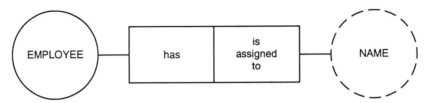

Exhibit VI-2-4. Relationship Between an Entity and Its Attribute Under NIAM

The four types of cardinalities are shown in Exhibit VI-2-6. The cardinality of each relationship is depicted by a dark solid line above the appropriate role.

NIAM also supports supertype and subtype entities. This notation is used when an entity (or supertype) contains subentities (or subtypes), each of which has additional attributes. The supertype entity contains all attributes and relationships common to all subtypes. Additional attributes and relationships that apply only to a specific subtype are shown with that subtype. In the example in Exhibit VI-2-7, the entity VEHICLE can be broken down into CAR, MOTORCYCLE, and TRUCK.

A simple NIAM model for the relationships between DEPARTMENT and EMPLOYEE, including attributes for each, is shown in Exhibit VI-2-8. Even an uncomplicated model can be quite large.

IDEF1X

IDEF1X notation has most of the expressive power of NIAM but is a little less cumbersome to use. Like the other methods, it depicts entities as boxes and relationships as lines between them. Like NIAM, it allows the attributes of entities to be listed, but it does not support the relationships between an entity and its attributes. IDEF1X allows further classification of entities as dependent and independent and provides for the categorization of the relationships into identifying and nonidentifying. Attributes are specified by expanding the entity box and adding the attributes inside the box. Primary key attributes are added above the line; the remaining attributes are added below.

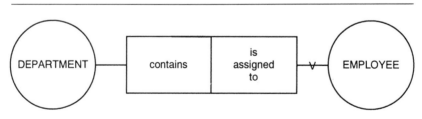

Exhibit VI-2-5. A Mandatory Relationship with NIAM

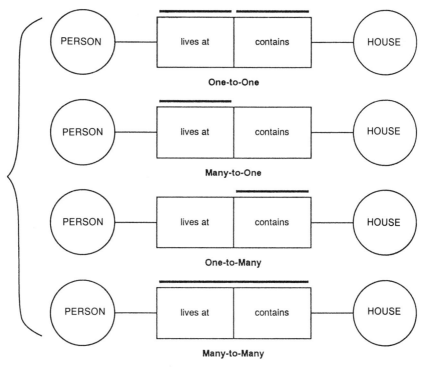

Exhibit VI-2-6. Cardinality of Relationships Using NIAM

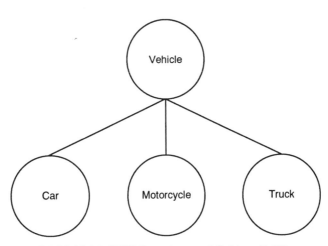

Exhibit VI-2-7. NIAM Supertype and Subtype Entities

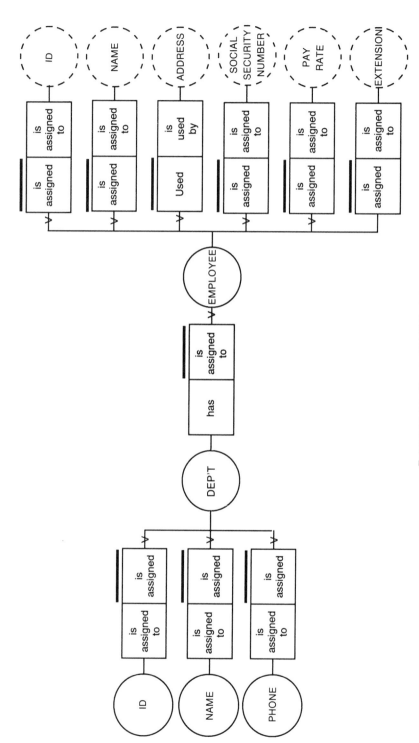

Exhibit VI-2-8. Simple NIAM Model

IDEF1X also allows alternate key and foreign key attributes to be identified. The IDEF1X version of Exhibit VI-2-8 is shown in Exhibit VI-2-9.

With IDEF1X, two types of boxes are used for entities, depending on whether they are the independent (square corners) or the dependent (rounded corners) entities in a relationship. Exhibit VI-2-10 shows both an independent and a dependent entity. In every relationship, one entity is independent and one is dependent; however, because an entity can participate in more than one relationship, it is possible (indeed likely) that it is the dependent entity in one relationship and the independent entity in another. In Exhibit VI-2-11, AIRLINE owns PLANE. AIRLINE is the independent entity and PLANE is the dependent entity. PLANE is assigned to FLIGHT is another relationship. Here, PLANE is the independent entity and FLIGHT is the dependent entity.

Relationships between entities can also be characterized as nonidentifying or identifying. In nonidentifying relationships, entities can be identified without reference to each other. For example, in Exhibit VI-2-12, departments and employees have IDs, but each can be identified without reference to the other. In contrast, courses in a university cannot be identified uniquely with simply a course number. The department number is also necessary (e.g., ECON 103, ART 103). In this case, the relationship between DEPARTMENT and COURSE is called identifying, because the department ID and course ID are both necessary to uniquely identify a course. In an identifying relationship, the key of the independent entity is part of the key of the dependent entity. In a nonidentifying relationship, the foreign key is just another non-key attribute. Identifying relationships are depicted by solid lines and nonidentifying relationships by dashed lines.

IDEF1X also shows the cardinality of a relationship (see Exhibit VI-2-13). Normal relationships, in which one instance of entity A can be related to zero, one, or many instances of entity B, do not have a special symbol. Other relationships do use special symbols, however, Relationships in which one instance of entity A must be related to one or many instances of entity B are represented with a P. Relationships in which one instance of entity A can be related only to zero or one instance of entity B are represented with a Z; and when one entity is related to an exact number of another entity, the exact number is shown next to the relationship.

Additional notation depicts certain attributes as alternate or foreign keys. Alternate keys (shown next to the field as AK) are fields that can also be used as the primary key, which uniquely identifies a row to a table. An employee's Social Security number could also be used to uniquely identify an employee. Foreign keys (shown next to the field as FK) are fields that are present in an entity because of its relationship with another entity. For example, an EMPLOYEE entity contains the ID of the employee's department. Because this field is the primary key of the DEPARTMENT entity, it is shown as a foreign key in the EMPLOYEE entity (see Exhibit VI-2-9).

The notation shown in Exhibit VI-2-13 expresses the forward direction of the relationship (i.e., a CAGE has 0, 1, or more ANIMAL_TYPEs), but it says nothing about the reverse direction. Must an animal type be in a cage? Phrased differently, is this a mandatory relationship for ANIMAL_TYPE? In

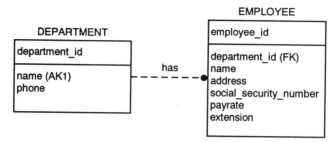

Exhibit VI-2-9. Simple IDEF1X Model

Exhibit VI-2-14, the answer is indicated by the presence (or lack of) a diamond on the first entity. The CAGE may contain 0, 1, or many ANI-MAL_TYPEs. In the first example, however, an animal type must be in a cage (in other words, the cage_id field in the ANIMAL_TYPE entity may not be null). In the second example, the diamond on the CAGE side of the relationship indicates that an ANIMAL_TYPE may exist without being assigned to a cage (the cage_id field may be null).

IDEF1X also supports categorizations for entities (see Exhibit VI-2-15). A categorization, also known as supertype or subtype, allows an entity to be decomposed into multiple, mutually exclusive entities, depending on its type (e.g., a vehicle may be decomposed into a car, motorcycle, or truck).

Repository Manager

Like all of the other data modeling notations, the IBM Repository Manager supports entities, relationships, attributes, and its own brand of cardinality and constraints. In Repository Manager, entities are represented as boxes with the name in the upper left corner. An attribute is separated from its entity name by one or more spaces. The primary key (i.e., the attribute that identifies unique instances of the entity) is listed first, followed by the

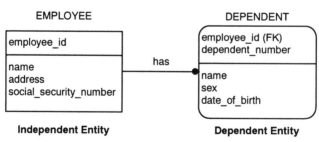

Independent Entity   Dependent Entity

Exhibit VI-2-10. Independent and Dependent Entity with IDEF1X

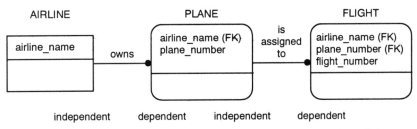

Exhibit VI-2-11. An Entity That Is Both Dependent and Independent Using IDEF1X

remaining attributes. As with IDEF1X, attributes are optional and may be omitted.

A relationship is depicted by writing a verb phrase on or adjacent to the line connecting entities, as it is with IDEF1X, and the phrase works in the same way as its IDEF1X equivalent. Optionally, the inverse relationship may be explicitly stated and shown in parenthesis, usually below the primary verb phrase. A simple Repository Manager model is shown in Exhibit VI-2-16.

One difference between Repository Manager and the other notation methods centers around complex relationships and constraints on them. Repository Manager supports *n*-ary relationships. In most other modeling notations, no more than two entities may participate in a relationship. When more than two entities logically exist in a relationship, a new entity is cre-

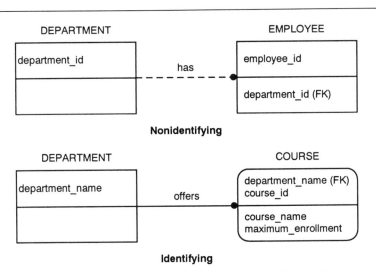

Exhibit VI-2-12. IDEF1X Notation for Nonidentifying and Identifying Relationships

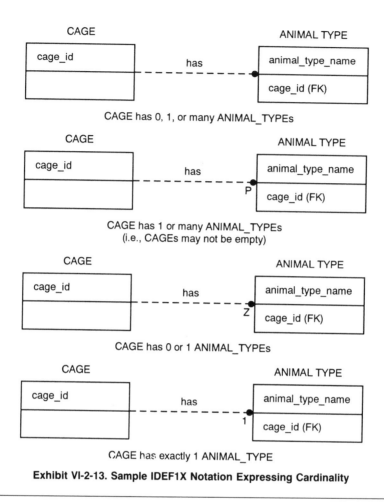

Exhibit VI-2-13. Sample IDEF1X Notation Expressing Cardinality

ated that has a binary relationship with each of the original entities. Repository Manager has this capability, but it also supports a relationship-to-relationship capability. Exhibit VI-2-17 shows both approaches for the same trinary relationship.

Repository Manager lacks a categorization entity. Although the relationship between the various entities can be captured in Repository Manager with an "is a" relationship, this notation does not adequately contain all of the semantics needed to represent the classification. For example, the Repository Manager entity on the right side of Exhibit VI-2-18 does not specify whether its subtype entities must be mutually exclusive.

Repository Manager refers to the cardinality of a relationship as instance control. It differs slightly from IDEF1X in that it actually corresponds to the maximum cardinality at the designated end of the relationship. Exhibit

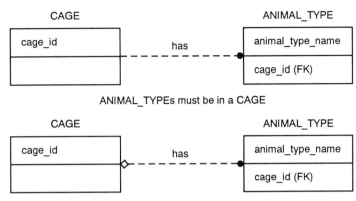

ANIMAL_TYPEs must be in a CAGE

ANIMAL_TYPEs are not required to be in a CAGE
(some animals may be allowed to run free)

Exhibit VI-2-14. Sample Mandatory and Nonmandatory Relationship with IDEF1X

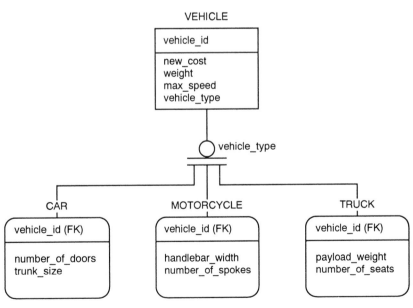

Exhibit VI-2-15. Categorization with IDEF1X

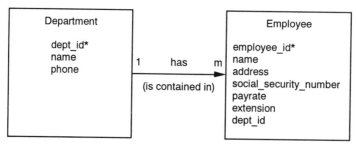

Exhibit VI-2-16. Simple Repository Manager Model

VI-2-19 illustrates how Repository Manager expresses the cardinality of relationships.

Repository Manager also allows mandatory, controlling, and ordered set constraints to be placed on a relationship. Each of these constraints is depicted by its first letter. A mandatory constraint determines the minimum cardinality permissible for a relationship. In essence, the mandatory property is used to maintain referential integrity when rows are inserted into the tables.

The controlling property enforces referential integrity when rows are deleted. It states that if the constraining relationship is removed, the constrained object must also be removed. Consequently, if all of the organizations (see Exhibit VI-2-20) to which a person belongs are removed, the person must also be removed. In most situations, mandatory and controlling properties are used together.

Repository Manager supports one additional constraint that is not found elsewhere: ordered set. This constraint indicates that rows will be retrieved in the order that they were created. If it is not specified, rows are retrieved in the order of the primary key. The order in which rows are retrieved from an entity can be considered an application issue, in which case the presence of this information is inappropriate in a data model.

Repository Manager supports dependent entities. However, rather than depict them graphically as IDEF1X would, Repository Manager calls for a D placed at the end of the relationship that is the dependent entity. This eliminates the problem in which an entity may be the dependent entity in one relationship and the independent entity in another relationship. Exhibit VI-2-21 illustrates how Repository Manager supports dependent entities.

CONCLUSION

The decision of which data modeling notation to use is largely subjective. It depends on such factors as familiarity, corporate mandates, and the availability of automated tools. Each of the five notations detailed in this chapter

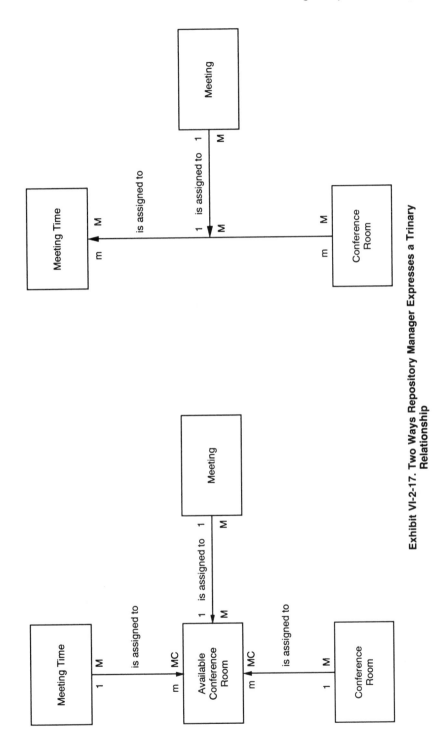

Exhibit VI-2-17. Two Ways Repository Manager Expresses a Trinary Relationship

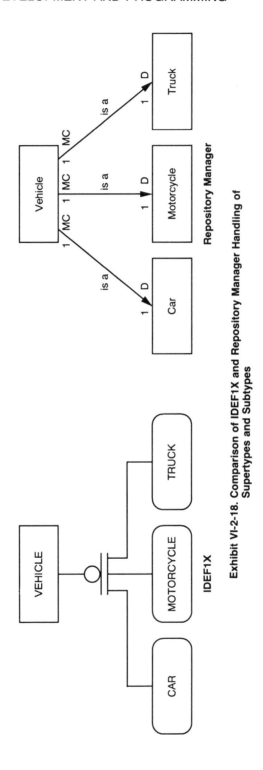

Exhibit VI-2-18. Comparison of IDEF1X and Repository Manager Handling of Supertypes and Subtypes

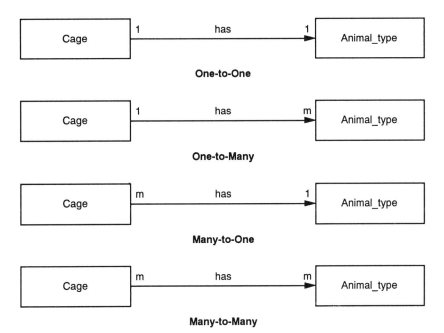

Exhibit VI-2-19. How Repository Manager Expresses the Cardinality of Relationships

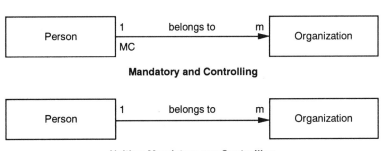

Exhibit VI-2-20. Sample Repository Manager Notations

Exhibit VI-2-21. How Repository Manager Supports Dependent Entities

has its strengths. Whatever notation modelers choose, however, they should also use an automated tool to keep track of data changes and to generate pictorial versions of the model until it is complete.

VI-3

Building Flexible User Interfaces

Paul Nisenbaum

A USER INTERFACE is a mechanism that allows people to interact with machines. For example, a bicycle seat enables a person to sit on a bicycle. A keyboard enables a person to send instructions to a computer. A flexible user interface is a mechanism that lets people customize a user interface to their needs. A rider can adjust a bicycle seat. A user can define what certain keys on a keyboard will do.

THE NEED FOR A FLEXIBLE USER INTERFACE

Most computer hardware and software, either purchased or developed in-house, provides some degree of flexible user interface that allows users to control their computing system. For example, users can adjust the contrast on a display monitor, assign synonyms to commands, create macros, and split the screen for multiple windows.

Over the years, these and other components of a flexible interface have become expected standard features. Most people probably do not even think about whether the interface is flexible, but if they did not have the ability to customize function keys or set the time to military or AM/PM format, they would no doubt notice its absence.

PC users demand the ability to easily control hardware and software. Even minicomputer and mainframe vendors now offer personal computer-like interfaces. The trend toward client/server systems that let PC users access mainframe information also signifies that people want to control their computers on their own terms. Without a doubt, people want the ability to tailor their own computing systems.

GOALS OF FLEXIBLE USER INTERFACES

Even though a system may have a flexible, efficient, and intuitive user interface, it may be counterproductive unless it enables users to complete goals, not just subordinate tasks. For example, an inventory control clerk has the ability to customize the online data entry application and workplace environment in the following ways:

- The online form can be rearranged to make typing data easier.
- Both fonts and colors can be changed.
- Abbreviations can be used, so that by typing a few characters and pressing a function key, a whole phrase (e.g., a product description) is displayed.
- The keyboard can be adjusted to prevent carpal tunnel syndrome.
- The monitor and chair can be adjusted for optimal position.

If the goal is to quickly and accurately itemize the inventory, however, a portable bar code system could be a better solution. Working with users to define the goal initially would have been much more useful in this case.

Monitoring a Workload. Defining the goal first does not guarantee an efficient way to reach the goal. Take the example of the data center goal of monitoring a workload such as the payroll system. The monitoring software can display four workload states: not scheduled to run, running on schedule, running behind schedule, and unable to complete on schedule.

To provide maximum user flexibility, hardware and software could be provided that would allow each staff member on each shift to highlight these states with a choice of 1,000 colors. Although this might be beneficial for a single user, each time another person approached the console, the new user would have to determine which color represented a particular state. This user in turn might spend time reconfiguring the colors to his or her liking. The situation may then be repeated when yet another person approached the console. Time would be lost figuring out the color scheme and customizing the highlighting. A more efficient solution would be to limit either the color choices or the customization privileges, or to limit a combination of the two with default settings. Although the user interface with 1,000 color choices may be easy to use and efficient, it wouldn't necessarily help with the overall goal of monitoring the workload.

Navigating from One Panel to Another. Another example of a flexible interface involves the subordinate task of navigating from one panel to another. Variations of this example can be seen in microcomputer, minicomputer, and mainframe systems. The user can choose several ways to select the name of the destination panel. For example:

- Select panel destination choices from a sequence of menus.
- Select a labeled push button.
- Type the destination panel name on the command line.
- Type the destination panel abbreviation name on the command line.
- Type a user-created synonym for the destination panel name on the command line.
- Select the destination panel from a help panel.
- Select an icon (system provided or user created) representing the destination panel.
- Select the destination panel from an index.

Balancing Flexibility and Productivity. In both user interface examples described—assigning colors to objects and navigating between panels—there needs to be a correct balance between too little and too much flexibility. Are the many color selections and the navigation techniques helpful in satisfying the varied desires and needs of users? Do they help users reach stated goals and improve productivity, or do they simply carry a flexible interface to a superfluous extreme? If the user has to spend too much time deciding which way to do something or learning a multitude of techniques, productivity may suffer.

CREATING USABLE AND PRODUCTIVE SYSTEMS

Three steps are key to developing systems with beneficial flexible user interfaces:

- Identifying the users and their characteristics.
- Identifying user tasks.
- Involving users continuously.

Users and Their Characteristics

The first step in design is to determine who will be using the completed system. If information about the users is collected in an organized fashion, fewer items will fall through the cracks and similarities and differences among users will become apparent. The system can then be designed to accommodate the various user characteristics.

Helpful information includes current and previous job titles or levels, formal and informal education, and experience with various computer systems. Less tangible, but equally important, may be the user's motivation for learning and using new systems.

Collecting User Information. Whether to poll all users or only a representative sample depends on the number of potential users. If 10 people will be using the system, then it probably makes sense to question all of them. For 2,000 users, a sample would be sufficient. The sample should include users with various job classifications and skill levels who will actually use the system.

For example, if the payroll manager and IS manager agree on building a new payroll application, they will no doubt have definite ideas about the design. However, once the application is up and running, they may have only peripheral involvement with it. Within the payroll department the application administrator and others may be interested in customization and various bells and whistles. However, the primary users of the application, the data entry staff, might not have the skill, time or desire to explore computer applications. Therefore, it would be essential that the everyday data entry users, as well as the more experienced and the less frequent users, be included in the collection sample.

Exhibit VI-3-1 gives a sample form for collecting information on user characteristics; it can assist the designer and can be tailored or used as is.

Part 1: User Characteristics	
For project	
Date(s)	
Department	
Observer	
Name	
Job title	
Job level	(entry-level, senior)
Department	
Education	
Degrees	
Additional courses, seminars	
Experience	
Previous job titles	
Current job	(years)
Subject area	(years)
Microcomputer	(years)
Minicomputer	(years)
Mainframe	(years)
Use computer on current job	(daily, quarterly)
Motivation	(reluctant, eager)
Part 2: Current Hardware	
Mainframe or minicomputer terminal type	(monochrome, four color)
Personal computer	(display: monochrome—amber or green, VGA, SVGA; sound; RAM; hard drive; LAN or host emulator cards)
Data entry	(Keyboard, mouse, touch screen, voice)
Printer	(local, remote, paper type, speed duplex, multiform)

Exhibit VI-3-1. Sample Form for Collecting User Information

Modem	(Internal, external, baud rate, LAN connected)
Miscellaneous	(Swivel monitor stand, printer stand, adjustable chair or desk, lighting)

Part 3: Current Software Applications		
Application, Brand, and Version	**Frequency Used** (Hourly/Quarterly)	**Expertise** (Novice/Expert)
CAD/CAM		
CASE tools		
Customer support		
Data base		
Desktop publishing		
E-mail		
Financial planning		
Graphic presentation		
Help desk		
Human resources		
Inventory		
Operating system		
Payroll		
Printer management		
Problem management		
Programming (languages)		
Service-level management		
Spreadsheet		
Statistics		
System administrator (name system)		
Tape management		
Utilities		
Word processing		

Exhibit VI-3-1. (*continued*)

For increased efficiency, it may make sense to combine the step of gathering user characteristics with the next step: identifying current goals and user tasks.

Identifying User Tasks

The importance of identifying user tasks cannot be underestimated in the development of systems and user interfaces. Therefore, special attention needs to be given to collecting this information. User tasks can be as broad as getting the payroll out and as narrow as deleting a looping transaction with one keystroke. It is crucial to identify goals and their subordinate tasks.

Examples of Goals and Subordinate Tasks. The system designer needs to determine the level of detail that needs to be gathered. For example, if the goal is to restore an accidentally deleted file, the tasks are to phone the data center and ask to have the file restored, locate the tape on which the file resides, and request a tape mount.

If the goal is to print the monthly problem management report, the tasks are: collect the daily and weekly reports from remote machines by uploading to the mainframe, run the job to create the monthly report, set up the printer with preprinted forms, and submit the print job. Exhibit VI-3-2 breaks down another goal—getting payroll out each week—with keystroke by keystroke detail.

Understanding Human Nature. Bear in mind that, as with other endeavors involving people, things are not always what they appear to be. People may not be as forthcoming, direct, or honest as might be expected. There may be conscious and unconscious reasons for their particular responses. Personal agendas and corporate politics transcend even the most seemingly cut-and-dried situation.

When approached with questions, some people may feel they are being judged and must give a correct answer. They do not want to appear ignorant to the observer or their peers or supervisors. Their answers may not be an accurate reflection of their job. Other people may not speak candidly for fear of retribution, no matter how much assurance to the contrary they are given. They may have been reprimanded in the past or they know of others who have had a similar negative experience. Still others may emphasize only a small part of their job because that is the area in which they feel most competent. It may be beneficial to make several visits over several days or weeks to gain a more balanced view of some users.

Many approaches for gathering information about user goals and tasks can be used concurrently to cover a wide variety of users and their settings. These recommended approaches can be adapted or expanded to the particular needs of the designers:

- Be open to surprises. Really observing a user without preconceived notions can lead to startling revelations for both the designer and the user.

Goal: Get the payroll out weekly
1. Gather time cards from employees on Monday morning. If Monday is a holiday, collect them on the previous Friday.
2. Log on to the system by typing the user ID, then pressing Enter. Type the password, then press Enter.
3. Enter time card data into the online system
   a. Select the time sheet data entry application
   b. Type the week ending date and press the tab key. Type the employee's number, then press Enter.
   c. Type the hours worked and tab to the appropriate column for overtime, holidays, sick time, and vacation time, then press Enter.
   d. Repeat for all time cards.
   e. Exit application by typing QUIT, then pressing Enter.
4. Select the payroll tabulation and printing choice by typing the appropriate number or mnemonic on the highlighted entry field, then press Enter.
5. Log off system by typing LOGOFF, then pressing Enter.
6. Take the output from the printer to the mailroom for distribution.

Exhibit VI-3-2. Sample Goal and Subordinate Tasks

- Meet with a single user at a time.
- Meet with a group of coworkers who share common responsibilities.
- Observe the user or users on several occasions. There may be personal issues at stake. In addition, the system may be slow on a particular day, a rush project might have been given to the user, or the user might be doing the work of absent workers.
- Ask the user's supervisor and director what they think the necessary goals and tasks for a particular job are.
- Meet with coworkers of an employee to see what they think the tasks and goals of other jobs are.
- Meet with vendors.
- Meet with customers (in-house and actual).
- Ask users why they do tasks in a certain way. Then listen. Ask users if they are satisfied with the current way of performing tasks. If not, ask why or how it could be different.
- Ask if the task is essential to complete the specific goal.

Continuous User Involvement

Including users in an iterative design process can help ensure that the final product allows users to meet their overall goals and provides appropriate facilities for users to customize the user interface. The iterative process includes demonstrations of work in progress to users at various developmental stages. Paper and online prototypes can be used initially, with the actual product demonstrated as it evolves. Sessions can be held both for individuals and for groups, with hands-on sessions scheduled when appropriate. The designer needs to constantly monitor user input and adjust the product accordingly.

First Iteration. When the designer initially sorts through the collected user characteristics, goals and tasks, and other information, the overall goals will probably appear fairly obvious. A high-level design based on these goals must be presented to users. Without a confirmation of this system view, the entire project may face an uphill battle. The designer needs to demonstrate that the system is a tool to make the users' jobs more productive.

The Cycle Continues. As the design evolves, care should be taken to incorporate common areas of concern noted during the examination of the user input. When the users view the next level of design, they should express confidence in their new tool. Designers who listen to and incorporate feedback from users into the next design iteration not only make the users feel part of the process but give them a stake in the eventual adoption and use of the system.

This cyclical process needs to progress quickly so the users do not lose interest. Using rapid prototyping techniques can optimize effort and feedback. Actual scenarios give life to the design and users can participate by asking their specific questions, such as, "What if I selected this field?" or "What happens on the last Friday of the quarter if it is a three-day holiday?" Eventually, live data should be used in the user review sessions to help test the system and generate enthusiasm. Once again, feedback about the use of the system needs to be carefully evaluated and, if appropriate, incorporated into the next iteration.

CONCLUSION

At some point, the system will meet the completion criteria. However, user involvement can still continue after the product is released for general use. After all, it is their tool. As in most systems, improvements can be added to the next version.

Although the participation of users in the systems development process can clearly lead to better systems, their involvement needs to be carefully managed. It bears repeating that the designer should always remember that people sometimes bring personal agendas into the workplace that may have a negative influence on a seemingly impartial opinion. When involving users in design, designers should work to maintain a positive environment.

One rule to remember is that users may expect their input to be visible in the product. If they do not see their requests in the design, they may reject further participation, become hostile to the project, and discourage others. If they are paying customers, they may even begin buying from other vendors.

Users may become defensive when the tasks they have been doing a certain way turn out to be inefficient or unnecessary. They may contradict or seek to invalidate the statements of others because of office politics. All this is part of the process, and designers must learn how to manage it.

VI-4

Automating Applications Testing

Philip L. Arthur

TO MANY, THE COST of applications testing seems too high. This impression is dispelled when they closely examine the applications testing process. Typically, testing includes such activities as creating test scenarios, identifying and creating input data, establishing test data bases, running test cases, evaluating test results, and debugging and resolving code deficiencies. At least one of these activities is repeated until the application is considered ready for production. Testing a sophisticated application requires planning, designing, validating, and examining for completeness; in many cases, separate groups test the entire application. These activities are often repeated for enhancements or code fixes with little or no reuse of test data.

Many times, application programmers control application code quality. Programmers receive requirements, write the code, create a few test cases, run some unit test cases, probably use a debugging tool to run test cases and identify defects, and put the code into production when they believe the code is ready. This process depends on subjective judgment, and it is repeated and reinvented for every enhancement or code fix; nothing is reused.

Programmers often test the same code they wrote, and this code may not meet the application requirements. To test the code that should have been written requires developing test cases from the requirements. Yet testing is seldom defined during the requirements phase. In addition, application function testing may not uncover defects that occur in a high-volume production environment.

The solution to these problems is a test environment in which testing is performed as a rigorous process and in which reuse is promoted. This chapter examines the activities involved in a rigorous test process. Testing tools have automated some of these activities and play a key role in promoting a rigorous test process and testing reuse. Two testing tools from IBM Corp., Workstation Interactive Test Tool (WITT) and Software Analysis Test Tool (SATT), are discussed to illustrate the role of tools in an automated testing environment.

APPLICATIONS DEVELOPMENT AND TESTING

The traditional software development process has one quality checkpoint—after the product has been built, the application code is tested. A more effective development process has quality checkpoints at each development phase. The software development life cycle then becomes a series of work products and releases, permitting continuous assessment of product quality and allowing changes to be introduced during the development process. The following sections examine the testing components of an effective development process.

Rigorous Requirements Definition. Rigorous requirements definition requires a rigorous mathematical definition and focuses on error prevention instead of code error removal. At each level of design, mathematical proofs of correctness are used to ensure the accuracy of the evolving design and the continued integrity of the product requirements. This design method introduces module and procedure primitives (e.g., sequences, branches, and loops) to handle the packaging of software designs into products and provides a clear and concise set of programming specifications for the application programmer to write high-quality code. Rigorous requirements definition, which includes data domain, data type, and allowed-values information, allows application testers to build a rigorous set of test cases and validate the test results.

Thorough Inspections. Studies indicate that inspections can uncover about 60% of total product defects and that the errors are found through applications testing. These inspections should be performed by a team whose members are from different areas in the project and include a moderator, developer, and inspectors. The diverse backgrounds of the inspection staff ensure continuity across work phases and work products, reflects multiple interests, and helps create varied scenarios of usage. For example, the requirements work product review should be inspected by a team of end users, analysts, and designers.

The cost of error removal increases the longer the error remains in the product. Therefore, requirements and design reviews are critical to developing quality software. Design inspections validate the interpretation of the requirements. Likewise, detailed design reviews verify the interpretation of high-level designs.

Unfortunately, inspections depend on qualified people having the time to perform thorough inspections, and the inspection process can become a bureaucratic checkpoint yielding limited results. Combining formal inspections and a rigorous testing methodology fosters the creation of software with fewer errors and with errors that are easier to find and fix. However, rigorous testing depends on thorough, high-quality requirements.

The thoroughness of test cases depends on the thoroughness of the requirements definition, which includes data domain values and application process descriptions. Most online applications test tools drive test cases from an end-user perspective through transaction screens. In addition, test coverage metrics are needed to evaluate the quality of both manual and automated testing.

Root Cause Analysis. A data base on software defects contains inspection and testing-identified errors. This data base is used for improving the development process by monitoring and controlling the development progress. Root cause analysis is performed on the entries in the data base to prevent further defects. The cause of the defect must be documented in the data base for future analysis. It is possible to forecast the number of production defects at each development phase from historical data; statistical analysis can be used for analyzing error density and distribution.

TEST LEVELS

Applications testing approaches are typically divided into black box and white box testing. Black box techniques test an application from a user perspective and focus on the user input and resulting output. The programmer or tester builds test cases and determines expected results from a combination of requirements, design, and user documentation. White box techniques test program logic rather than external specifications. Applications programmers often perform white box testing on the code they wrote. White box testing techniques focus on running enough test cases to ensure test coverage of the code.

Application developers usually perform structural or white box testing to verify that the code conforms to the design. This testing is usually performed in one or more steps, which are commonly defined as unit testing, string testing, and integration testing. These steps vary by development groups and differ primarily by the degree or scope of application integration. For example, unit testing may be performed on a single subroutine, paragraph, or module, and string testing may be performed on the entire transaction, which may consist of one or more modules.

Those who are not software developers perform functional or black box testing to verify that the function satisfies product requirements. This form of testing is also usually performed in one or more steps, which are commonly known as systems testing, acceptance testing, stress testing, and user-verification testing. The steps vary by development groups and are distinguished primarily by testing objectives. For example, systems testing tests the entire application for code quality: whereas, stress testing tests the entire application for performance bottlenecks and stress-induced failures.

BLACK BOX TESTING TECHNIQUES

Common black box testing techniques include space partitioning, boundary analysis, cause and effect graphing, and error guessing. These data-driven techniques derive test data from the specifications and help the tester to define a subset of all possible input and output elements that have a high probability of detecting errors.

Space Partitioning. This technique partitions input so that input items in each partition are treated the same. As a result, the space partitioning technique is sometimes referred to as equivalence testing. The tester selects at least one data element from each partition, which is either a valid or invalid item. The goal of space partitioning is to define partitions so that each piece of data in the partition produces equivalent testing results. This allows testers to minimize the number of test cases but to invoke many distinct input conditions.

The space partitioning technique requires identifying the partitions and defining the test cases. Often, one partition is a data domain, which may be described by a range of values (e.g., minimum and maximum), a set of values (e.g., a table look-up), or a number of input values. Conversely, another partition can be data that is invalid and outside the data domain. Therefore, most data elements need two or more test cases. For example, the number of working hours in a regular work week can be described by the following range of values:

$$0 \le x < = 40$$

where:

$$x = \text{the number of hours in a workweek.}$$

The valid data domain is 0 to 40 inclusive, and the invalid data domains are the values less than zero and those greater than 40. Therefore, three or more test cases, one for each partition (e.g., -1, 30, 50) are desirable, especially for testing entires or updates to a data base or file.

Boundary Value Analysis. This technique is a special case of space partitioning. The tester selects one or more data elements that identify the boundary of a partition or data domain. If the partition represents a range of values, the minimum and maximum values are tested. If the partition represents a set of values as in a table look-up, the first and last table entries are tested. In the example using the number of hours in the regular work week, the testing data values -1, 0, 40, and 41 are four desirable test cases. It may be desirable to test the maximum and minimum values permitted by the transaction's screen input field, which may not be consistent with the data base definition. Experience indicates that boundary value analysis and space partitioning techniques apply equally well to output data by testing maximum output values and values higher than the maximum output ones, as well as minimum output values, and no output. Experience has also shown that boundary value analysis has a higher payoff than other techniques.

Cause and Effect Analysis. This technique transforms a natural language specification into a formal language specification and identifies the causes and effects using a Boolean graph or a decision matrix. It is a more sophisticated level of testing that considers the effects of one or more combinations of input values. This type of testing is highly productive and identifies incomplete and ambiguous points in the specification.

Error Guessing. This type of testing makes use of intuition and experience. It is often productive when technology or the application environment changes. Error guessing should not be used in place of the other types of black box testing but should be used to enhance their effectiveness.

Testing from the User Perspective. IBM's WITT tests applications from the end-user perspective. This automated test driver tool provides keystroke and mouse movement capture and playback. In other words, the tool plays back keystrokes instead of the application tester. WITT can also capture and compare screens and supports noncompare areas. When performing black box testing, the tester creates test scenarios from the specifications, and these test scenarios are executed by using WITT.

WHITE BOX TESTING

White box techniques are used for testing program logic. These techniques include:

- *Statement coverage.* An attempt is made to test every statement in a program at least once; this is considered the weakest of testing techniques.
- *Decision coverage.* Enough test cases are developed so that each decision statement has at least one true and false outcome.
- *Condition coverage.* Each condition for a decision is met so that all possible outcomes are made at least once.
- *Decision/condition coverage.* Each condition in a decision is tested for all possible outcomes at least once, and each decision is tested for all possible outcomes at least once.
- *Multiple condition coverage.* All possible combinations of conditional outcomes for each decision are invoked at least once.
- *Flowpath combination coverage.* All possible combinations of flowpaths are invoked for each outcome for each condition.

IBM's SATT provides four types of coverage metrics at four different levels—paragraph (i.e., subroutine), module, component, and application. A component is an arbitrary division of an application (e.g., a batch component, online component, and an external interface component). The tool's four coverage metrics are the following:

- *Statement coverage.* This metric is the percentage of statements executed within a paragraph, module, component, or application, and the number of times a statement was executed. This metric corresponds to the statement coverage technique.
- *Logical paths executed.* This metric measures the percentage of local paths executed within a paragraph, module, component, or application, and the number of times a statement was executed. This corresponds to the decision coverage, condition coverage, and decision/condition coverage techniques.

- *Internal procedures.* This metric is the percentage of internal procedures (i.e., paragraphs) executed within a module, component, or
  application.
- *External procedures.* This metric is the percentage of modules executed
  within a component or application.

White box testing alone cannot identify application code that does not
meet specifications or is missing functional paths. In addition, it usually
does not cover data-sensitive errors.

Using SATT: An Example. SATT is used to create a structure diagram of
modules and their paragraphs. Exhibit VI-4-1 is a sample of such a diagram.
As shown in the diagram, application component CMP1 has three modules:
M3, TESTDATA, and KAIKI. Only 43.7% of the lines of code in component CMP1 were tested; 18% of the lines of code in the module KAIKI were
tested, and KAIKI comprises 50% of the entire component CMP1. A plus
sign is used in the diagram to indicate that the modules contain one or more
paragraphs.

SATT computes the coverage metrics from execution histories (i.e., trace
data) generated during testing of the programs. Coverage analysis reports
can be produced and ad hoc queries can be performed on coverage data,
which resides in the OS/2 Data Base Manager.

SATT helps the programmer understand programs and processes, so that
the programmer is better able to modify existing applications. Exhibit

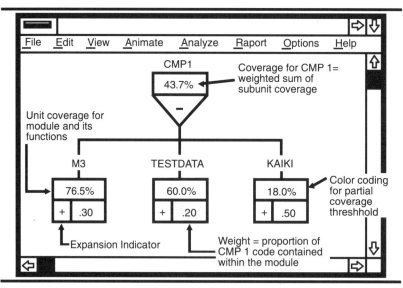

SATT180

Exhibit VI-4-1. Sample SATT Structure Diagram

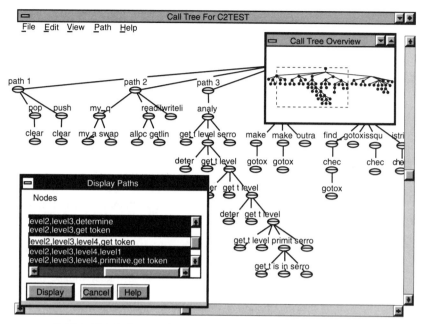

Exhibit VI-4-2. Sample SATT Display of Call Tree and Call Paths

VI-4-2 shows a SATT display of call tree and call paths for a sample piece of application code. SATT can generate the structure diagram, call tree, and call paths by reading and processing the compiler listings. It is also capable of animating the application flow sequence, which is a static replay of the execution history, by highlighting the application flow through each module and paragraph node in the structure diagram and the call tree. The tool displays the source code and animates the application flow through the source code by highlighting each line of code as it was executed during the test. SATT helps programmers identify and delete any unnecessary test cases and identify and create additional test cases to improve test coverage.

COMBINING BLACK BOX AND WHITE BOX TESTING

Black box testing techniques are sometimes capable of detecting and testing functions that are in an application but not in the specifications. White box testing techniques can be used to discover these additional functions; such a discovery necessitates changes in the program or documentation. On the other hand, white box coverage analysis cannot be used to find functions missing in the code but stated in the requirements specification. Nevertheless, white box coverage analysis can ensure the validity of the test case, and black box testing provides an efficient method for generating test cases.

Therefore, an effective testing method is to perform black box testing and white box coverage analysis. The rest of this chapter illustrates how such a method can be carried out with the two automated testing tools.

Testing During Development

A definable test environment features a data base populated with test data. This test data is known by the programmers, and the programmers have defined the expected test results for this data from the application transactions. A repeatable test environment features data bases repopulated with the same definable test data to establish a regression test environment. A definable and repeatable test environment is critical to realizing the maximum potential of an automated test environment.

Exhibit VI-4-3 illustrates how a repeatable and definable test environment is enabled through updating files and tables for applications testing before running test cases. Once the test files have been initialized, a base script can be built and enhanced for further automation. Initialization can be performed by a WITT test case.

This test case is a test script that consists of keystrokes, mouse movements, WITT commands, editor (i.e., 2/REXX) statements, and test case comments. Scripts can be created with an editor or through recording a test session using WITT. Once a base script has been created, it can be parameterized with 2/REXX statements. Testers can thereby use space partitioning, boundary value analysis, cause and effect analysis, and error guessing techniques. The data generated by these techniques can reside in a file and can be read by 2/REXX statements. In this setup, the tool can perform unattended multiple test scenarios, capture the results for validation, and archive the results for future comparison and regression testing.

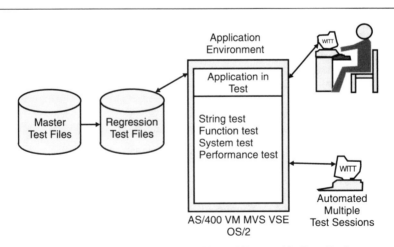

Exhibit VI-4-3. Components of a Definable and Repeatable Test Environment

A parameterized test script can be further enhanced to test an application's function keys, provide error handling of unexpected events, and initialize the application data bases. WITT commands and 2/REXX logic statements enable the interrogation of screen data, complex data, and further processing through external routines.

Ideally, a tester independent of the development team should review the testing results. Once test results have been verified, the screens should be archived for future use. Often, changes to the application can still use all or most of the test scenarios, which may need only minimal changes. In addition, all or most of the archived screens serve as a baseline for comparing results produced by changed code.

The tool compares the screens and highlights mismatches. Testers review the mismatches between the archive screens and the current ones. WITT keeps application documentation current by printing the screens to a file that can be embedded in the application documentation.

During new code development, programmers often correct code, which must be subsequently fully regression tested. All test scenarios are rerun to ensure that previously tested scenarios still operate properly. More elaborate and comprehensive testware can be created that corresponds to the complexity of the application. Parameterized WITT scripts serve as complete testware for functional verification of the code. The input file and WITT script represent the test plan documentation. This test testware should be reviewed and approved during the application design review, which occurs before writing the application code.

SATT Coverage Analysis Metrics. SATT's white box testing function complements WITT's black box testing functions by identifying any untested code or function. Subsequently, one would augment the test scenarios set to provide the test coverage where necessary. Using the execution history trace information, SATT animates the source code execution and thus allows the replay of test case execution. Programmers can replay failing test cases to determine the cause of the failure.

Network Stress Test. To ensure quality code for production environment, stress testing the application is needed to identify storage violations, inconsistent results, and performance bottlenecks. WITT test scenarios can be used with IBM's Teleprocessing Network Simulator (TPNS) test drivers for testing across development test phases and groups. TPNS can simulate a large network with hundreds or thousands of concurrent users to stress test the application.

Maintenance Test Scenario

Maintenance programmers can use SATT to understand program logic before they make any changes to it and to ensure test coverage of changes. SATT is used to display a program's structure diagram, call tree, and call paths. Once programmers understand application logic and have made the necessary changes, the new code must undergo regression testing.

Regression Testing. If necessary, the WITT test driver is edited to incorporate additional test scenarios and any changes to the transaction input screens and input data. The test driver is run on the changed code and is used to compare the current screens file to the archive screens file. Results are validated, differences in the screens are certified, and the current screens file is archived and will serve as the new baseline. Applications documentation is updated because the tool prints the newly archived screens to a file that can be embedded in the documentation.

CONCLUSION

The traditional application development life cycle focuses on writing code, unit testing with quickly devised test cases, and unit testing with a debugging tool. Testing activities and data are repeatedly re-created as the application is fixed, enhanced, and maintained and little or no test cases and data are reused. This practice does not promote high-quality application code or lower testing costs.

Testing theory put into practice, data domains, and automated test drivers can improve productivity and quality as well as lower costs. A rigorous test process, test case reuse, and a definable, repeatable test environment can be used to implement what is needed to improve quality and lower costs. This chapter has examined the elements of a rigorous test process and a definable and repeatable test environment and has shown the role automated test drivers play in it.

Section VII

Data Communications and Networks

MANAGING A DATA COMMUNICATIONS network is a real challenge. When the network also carries voice, video, and other signals, the challenge becomes even greater. As more and more IS managers assume responsibility for communications for their enterprises, the issues of network planning, network performance, and network reliability take on an importance equal to that of systems development and data management. The chapters in this section address all three of these issues.

A corporate network is in some ways a more extensive version of popular departmental networks; however, a corporate network adds value that cannot be achieved by its small-scale departmental counterparts. Chapter VII-1, "Framework for Network Planning," describes the planning, design, and deployment of a strategic corporate network that supports distributed applications.

It is commonly believed that technicians with extensive mathematical backgrounds and using sophisticated prediction models are needed to handle network performance specification measurement and to solve tuning problems. It's true that common carrier backbones and high-performance process control networks do merit significant attention, but this management is often handled by nonspecialists. Chapter VII-2 demystifies "Network Performance" for the IS manager by offering simple, effective methods for describing and improving network performance. A step-by-step approach is given for eliminating common problems while continually improving precision.

"Reliability and Availability of LANs" is the subject of Chapter VII-3. Local area networks are fast becoming critical elements in most data communications networks. In many companies they are already critical to the continued operations of the enterprise. IS managers with responsibility for LANs should know the distinction between network availability and reliability. This chapter briefly explains the LAN operating principles that affect availability and reliability, then describes topologies and hardware that can be used to ensure that reliability and availability are at their maximum in any network.

VII-1

Framework for Network Planning

Howard Niden

ALTHOUGH VAST STORES OF INFORMATION in a large organization can provide a competitive advantage, much of this information is inaccessible to those who need it most—in many cases because employees do not even know it exists. The corporate network can provide access to this valuable resource.

Most successful corporate network utility implementations are built on a robust network infrastructure that is able to meet current needs and efficiently adapt as requirements change. Such a project must be accomplished in a constantly changing environment that currently has no clearly superior vendor or technology solution.

This chapter discusses the planning, design, and implementation of a strategic corporate network capable of supporting a new class of distributed applications that puts corporate data into the hands of those who can make the best use of it. The discussion is limited to issues related to the deployment of the network itself, not the justification for or development of distributed applications. Specifically, the chapter addresses four topics:

- *The network paradigm.* The model describes and structures thinking about the network and its relationships with those requiring network services.
- *The corporate network as a monopoly.* This issue is among the most volatile, and a case is made for such an implementation.
- *The selection of and migration to an ever-evolving target network environment.* The relationships of current products to those expected to be provided by a future incarnation of the corporate network must be carefully mapped to ensure smooth transitions to the target network environment.
- *Network management.* As existing networks become integrated into a corporate network utility, the challenges associated with delivering an acceptable level of service to network users must be properly structured and managed.

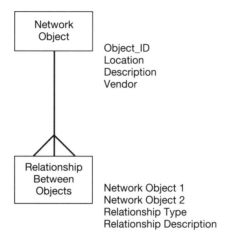

Note: In this greatly simplified model, the NETWORK OBJECT entity describes each relevant component of the network; the RELATIONSHIP BETWEEN OBJECTS entity describes a well-defined, finite set of relationships between entities.

Exhibit VII-1-1. Simplified Entity-Relationship Model Describing an Arbitrarily Complex Network

THE NETWORK PARADIGM

The network paradigm provides the structure against which to plan the corporate network implementation. The paradigm must be simple yet robust enough to describe any network that the corporation may deploy. It should also facilitate the development of a network that can evolve naturally and efficiently as improved technology becomes available. Finally, the paradigm should incorporate concepts that are well understood and generally accepted by those involved in the technical implementation of the network.

The paradigm provides the descriptive and schematic semantics that depict the network in terms of its components and their relationships to one another. The network can be viewed as a collection of objects, each of which is either a party to communication (i.e., a receiver or sender) or a mechanism over which communication occurs (i.e., a link). In one example, a terminal, a modem, the common carrier leased circuit, a second modem, and a CPU all qualify as network objects. Furthermore, at any given time, network objects may be either providers or requesters of network services.

Network Objects

Network objects can be either hardware (e.g., computers, terminals, wires, and leased communications links) or software (e.g., user applications or data communication programs and their components). These objects can be organized into hierarchies to reflect the relationships that exist among

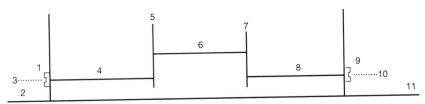

Receptacle 3 housed in faceplate 1 located in room 2.
Receptacle 3 attached to twisted pair 4 cross-connected to cross connect 5.
Twisted pair 6 connected to cross connect 7 connected to twisted pair 8.
Twisted pair 8 connected to receptacle 10 housed in
faceplate 9 located in room 11 (computer room).

Exhibit VII-1-2. End-to-End Connection as Constructed by Its Various Components

---

themselves. Exhibit VII-1-1 contains a simplified data model that describes the data structures necessary to capture relevant information about any network. This model allows for the description of arbitrarily complex networks to an appropriate level of detail for a particular implementation.

For example, on the basis of this model, a twisted-pair connection between a computer room and a desktop can be described simply as the physical connection—that is, a set with one member. If the situation demands, it could be described as a set of objects with more than one member and appropriate relationships. That set may include the connectors on either end, which are related both to the wire to which they are attached and to the faceplates into which they are embedded. In addition, the wire may be described as several objects, which include pieces of wire and punchdown blocks at which the wires are cross-connected (see Exhibit VII-1-2).

With this model, it is possible to extend the scope of the network description by simply including any additional object in the network and its relationship to a network stub. Because of the new object's position as a leaf on a network tree, the new object becomes the new stub.

For example, if the network is defined to terminate at the RS-232 connector on a faceplate at a user's desk, that is the stub. The network can be extended to include a cable and a terminal by defining these new components and then describing the relationship between the RS-232 receptacle in the faceplate and the new components (i.e., the cable and the terminal).

The relationships between objects on the network—whether between a pair of objects that are communicating or an object and a link—can be well defined and standard. This method permits designs and implementations that are modular, with components that can be upgraded easily and independently when technology becomes available.

The international systems community has adopted an architecture to structure and standardize the engineering of this type of computer communications system. The description is commonly referred to as the Open Systems Interconnection (OSI) reference model. The OSI model is generally accepted as the structure with which manufacturers describe network interaction, even if they do not yet support the OSI protocol stack. The reference model therefore provides an appropriate structure against which manufacturers' products can be systematically compared in terms of functions provided and the ease with which they can migrate to future implementations to take advantage of improved technology.

This way of thinking—that is, extending and formalizing the view of the network as a set of related objects by defining the network objects in terms of their interfaces rather than of any internal processing that they might perform—has far greater significance than technical design, operation, and extensibility issues. For example, the network paradigm, if properly implemented, can profoundly affect the way both users and vendors perceive the network and, as a consequence, the way they interact with it. A well-structured environment—one that conforms to OSI standards, is extensible, and provides economical support for current and future needs—is likely to be accepted even if it places some constraints on both users and vendors. Because vendors understand and appreciate the structure imposed by this network paradigm, it can be a powerful tool during the purchase cycle and beyond, providing a common basis for discussions and, eventually, agreements.

Finally, the paradigm offers an implementation-independent definition of a network. This definition in turn provides the framework for the consistent planning, deployment, and operation of a complex, ever-changing system.

Any sizable network is described in multiple, sometimes complex dimensions. A corporate network presents special challenges because of the diversity of its user population. This paradigm provides the robust conceptual structure necessary to manage the many technical and organizational challenges faced by corporate network implementation and operations teams.

THE CORPORATE NETWORK AS A MONOPOLY

A multitude of networks are in place at most large corporations. Usually, each network was installed because its implementer felt that the network products selected were somehow better than other alternatives. As true as this may be, a corporate network utility must be chosen and implemented on the basis of what is best for the organization overall.

The corporate network should therefore be operated as a public utility—that is, as a monopoly. As in the case of a public utility, the cost per unit of service for the entire entity (in this case the corporation) is lowest when there is a single network provider. Costs include those associated with the installation of the physical network and expenditures for managing and upgrading the network over time.

In this sense, the corporate network should be viewed in the same way as any other utility provided to the corporate user community. There are few who question a 120-volt/60-cycle standard for the provision of electrical service, or the ubiquitous 10-digit telephone number in the US, for example.

Nonstandard services can be provided—but they carry a cost. In the case of 240-volt electrical service, this cost is quite obvious; in the case of a common carrier's provisions for sub–10-digit dialing, it may not be quite so apparent, but it exists nonetheless. The additional expense includes the costs associated with interconnection to the network, as well as ongoing costs associated with making the nonstandard subnetwork operate within the context of the corporate network. If it is necessary to accommodate a nonstandard network when installing a standard corporate data network, the extra costs should be made explicit—and those requiring the service should pay the costs.

Forming an Oversight Committee. Inevitably, some network users may argue that they can service their own needs at a lower cost than the corporate network utility. This situation is one of the reasons that the corporate network should have an oversight body made up of network users and IS personnel. The body's charter should be to ensure that the utility, given its monopoly situation, provides service in a fair manner.

Chartering a corporate network oversight committee is a means to build support for the network as a utility among users. The committee is a vehicle for reaching a common understanding and setting user expectations regarding the level of service that users can expect. It is also effective in guiding users to think in terms of what is beneficial for the overall organization rather than what serves the parochial interests of individuals or small groups. Not implementing an oversight body is one of the biggest and most common mistakes that IS departments and managers make in providing strategic services to users. The development of a user oversight committee should not be an afterthought. The committee should be assembled at the beginning of the process and should continue to contribute throughout the network's life.

SELECTION AND MIGRATION

The selection of and migration to a common networking environment for a corporate network of any real size is a serious undertaking. A structured approach to requirements gathering, design, construction, and implementation of the network is essential to a successful effort. The structured approach ensures that network components (many of which are expensive in their own right) meet both today's and tomorrow's requirements. When subsystems within the network are upgraded or replaced, the infrastructure must be in place to support these endeavors without requiring undue effort.

For example, upgrades to the network operating system or the operating system of the thousands of nodes that reside on the network should not require visits to each machine. Similarly, upgrades to applications software made available to network users can and should be provided by the network, not through a manual installation process that retrieves the upgrade from tape or diskette.

Even more important, a careful, detail-oriented structured approach that accounts for both current and future requirements—often referred to as an architected approach—is necessary to the deployment of a basic network infrastructure that can economically endure the changes wrought by an ever-changing technology base. The ability to transcend the particulars of a given implementation, while at the same time maintaining a comprehensive, long-term view of the system's needs, is the mark of a successful implementation of a strategic corporate network.

The foundation of the architecture for the corporate network is defined in the network paradigm. The details of the architecture must be articulated during the high-level planning for the networking system. Then the details of the tactical and operational plans can be addressed.

The selection and migration effort is an ongoing process that, after the first iteration, becomes one of refinement. If the network has been properly defined on its first iteration, the process becomes one of anticipating and reacting to user requirements and technological change. The process adopts an evolutionary, rather than revolutionary, character. This approach tends to produce economical results and fulfills user needs. At all levels—strategic, tactical, and operational—the networking process must be user driven. If the network does not meet the needs of its constituency, the implementation is a failure.

NETWORK MANAGEMENT

Network management is the operational means by which the network comes into existence, is operated, and adapts to changes in the environment. Network management is often subdivided into the categories discussed in the following sections.

Configuration Management. These activities are associated with managing a data base that describes network objects and the topology of the network. In complex corporate networks, configuration management is essential to every other management activity. There are likely to be thousands, even tens of thousands, of components in a sizable corporate network. Without an understanding of the components and their relationships to one another, a network of this size can be difficult to maintain.

Ideally, the network management system should sense the network configuration and maintain a data base that accurately represents both the current and historical configuration. This data base is useful as an input to asset management, performance tuning, capacity planning, or to the process of tracking down subtle network problems. In practice, an automatic mechanism capable of dealing with complex networks is only partially implemented. Therefore, substantial manual effort is still required to maintain a useful set of information about the network.

Network Operations. Operations activities are subdivided into four categories: fault detection and isolation, security operations, performance operations, and statistics collection. All are real-time (or near real-time) activities associated with the immediate operation of the network and are complementary to other network management processes. A corporation's ability to deliver an acceptable level of service to network users is directly tied to success in these four activities, because they fully define the process of establishing and operating the network and accommodating network changes.

Fault Detection and Isolation. Unless network management personnel know there is a fault and what it is, they cannot fix it and the network won't be available. An ability to detect and isolate (i.e., identify) a fault in a timely manner is therefore essential to the delivery of the network service.

Security Operations. Security is the responsibility of all users of the network; however, a fully defined network management function includes processes to ensure that security practices are easy to follow and to check for events and patterns that indicate the possibility of a breach in security. Most of these mechanisms are implemented at the node (i.e., operating system) level and include routines to ensure that passwords are changed frequently and cannot be easily guessed as well as alarms that are triggered by unusual patterns of activity. To be effective, these mechanisms must be able to be managed centrally through an automated system.

Performance Operations. This activity, along with statistics collection, is related to the ability to match resource demand to capacity. It is only important in situations where capacity can be effectively adjusted in the short term. Segmenting an Ethernet to isolate a new server and its band-width-hungry clients is an excellent example of a performance operation activity.

Statistics Collection. This activity feeds the network planning process, which should be designed to focus on the longer-term capacity requirements of the network user community. Typical statistics collected include:

- Network loading factors as measured by percentage of network capacities used against various times frames.
- Types of traffic.
- Sources and destinations.

Each of these statistics provides important input into the long-term capacity planning process.

Network Planning. This effort includes all activities associated with the structure of the network. It includes capacity management, security management, and the development of the architecture and the implementation steps necessary to build the network. The result of the network planning process is implemented and maintained operationally by those involved in network operations.

Incident Tracking. These activities are closely related to network operations activities. In fact, incident tracking is sometimes included as one of the network monitoring activities. Incident tracking is listed separately because of its importance to the success of the implementation of a network utility. Incident tracking achieves two important objectives.

First, it provides a well-structured process by which users' operational-level network problems are addressed. Large networks generate a variety of situations that require attention. Incident tracking ensures that incidents are addressed according to priorities and procedures that can be understood by all parties involved.

Second, the data base generated during the incident tracking process provides an excellent objective source of information about the reliability of the network and the performance of the network management function. The incident tracking process provides the mechanism and data by which the service provided can be measured against expectations (set when defining the level of service that the network would provide). The incident tracking process is therefore an important part of managing these expectations and is in turn essential to the delivery of a product that will satisfy the customer.

CONCLUSION

A corporate data network utility is complex in its own right, and it is made even more complex by the many external systems (e.g., hardware and software) with which it must interact. This technical complexity at the operational level has a benefit: by replacing complexity at the user level, it makes the network more accessible and valuable to network users.

The process of planning and implementing a corporate network is too involved to be left to anything but a well-defined process. This process includes requirements definition, design at both the architectural and operational levels, construction, implementation, and management of the network. The similarity to a large software development process is not accidental; in both cases complex systems are being developed. There are several logical first steps in the process of successfully implementing a corporate network.

The Corporate Network Oversight Committee. The arguments for forming such a committee were made earlier in this chapter. It is essential that target users participate from the onset. This approach may not always appear to be the most expeditious; nonetheless, it is advisable to obtain user participation earlier than later.

The Detailed Strategic Networking Statement. The information presented here can help define the initial iteration of the strategic networking statement. The details for the corporation must be formally worked through and documented if the strategic view is to guide future tactical and operational efforts.

User Requirements for the Proposed Network. The product of this effort should be a well-structured statement of the services that a corporate network should provide if it is to serve the entire organization.

The Request for Information Document. This document can be used to query vendors regarding products that might fulfill the corporation's requirements. The document should be structured to support the selection of system components rather than a complete vendor solution, because it is unlikely that any one vendor will be able to provide a total solution. This strategy may encourage vendors who understand that they cannot provide a complete solution to participate in the process and may reduce wasted efforts by the corporation, as components from various vendors are mixed and matched to design the best possible solution.

VII-2
Network Performance
Howard C. Berkowitz

IN PRACTICE, the solution of network performance problems begins the same way as the solution to any business problem: the customer's expectations and objectives must be defined. Technical analysis then follows, which involves a comparison of the user's performance requirements with the internal network and host components that influence the performance factors that are visible to the user.

The IS manager's next task is to define the simplest practical methods for measuring performance. This can be accomplished by the following steps:

- Setting service-level goals (both at internal and external system interfaces) with the appropriate customer.
- With favorable response time as a goal, identifying the components whose cumulative delays—from user input or user output—make up the response time.
- Formalizing the service-level agreement. If the system is new, performance goals must be set as part of component design, and the components must be built. A continuing monitoring program must also be planned.
- Looking for, and correcting, simple problems first. The system must be kept on track with short-term tuning and long-term capacity planning and enhancement.

SETTING GOALS

A useful approach to performance specification, applicable both externally (e.g., to service-level agreements) or internally (e.g., to component design goals), relies on the architecture of ANSI X3.102. That architecture assumes that all data communications performance can be specified in terms of the performance of a measured communications facility that connects a service user with a service provider. (Network users may be either human users or computers. A packet switch uses a high-speed trunk to connect it with another switch, much as a human terminal user connects a dumb terminal and a timesharing host.)

Only three performance factors are experienced by a user:

- The probability that the network is available to do work.
- The probability that it will do the work incorrectly.
- The time it will take to do that work.

Parameters dealing with the first factor include percent availability and mean time between failure (MTBF).

Performance Time. The most general approach to measuring the last performance factor (i.e., time) is to examine the statistical duration of network activity to perform some meaningful service for the user. Because there are both human and automated users, it is helpful to think of users as end users or intermediate systems. End users either originate traffic and expect a response (terminal users) or they receive traffic and generate a response (hosts). Intermediate systems receive data and pass it along, possibly with no concern for the response. End users perceive the time component as response time, while intermediate systems perceive it as transit delay.

For intermediate systems in particular, it is better to report cumulative delay statistics than to report individual transaction measurements. The time component should be represented as a threshold (e.g., 95% of transactions complete in less than six seconds) rather than an average response time. Threshold specifications of this type can be used with simple statistical decision models.

Poor performance involves quantifiable costs, expressed as losses to the user and as penalties to the service provider. In each of these cases, a risk-to-reward tradeoff exists. For example, if a service provider guarantees a given service level, inaccuracies in the provider's measurement tools can lead to an inability to defend against a user's accusation of poor performance. At some point, risk avoidance using better (but more expensive) measurement becomes more costly than paying occasional penalties on marginal measurements. Variability of performance time can be even more important than its absolute value. Users are more likely to complain of a steadily increasing, or wildly fluctuating, response time than they are of a response time that is slower but remains constant.

IDENTIFYING RESPONSE TIME COMPONENTS

The ANSI X3.102 measurement model divides complex communications systems into sets of one-way paths through a measured network. Using this model, paths connect a source user and a destination user. These users may be any arbitrary users of a system: they may be two people, they may be a terminal and a host, or they may be two local area networks (LANs) connected through a media access control (MAC) bridge. X3.102 does not define response time measurement, but response times can be calculated accurately by combining the one-way performance on each path from originating user input to originating user output. Using this model, the host becomes a measured network between communications input and communications output; processing time becomes network delay.

The communications process, in X3.102 terms, has three phases: access, user information transfer, and disengagement. Access and disengagement are null in connectionless protocols. Each phase begins with a protocol-dependent interface event that maps into an abstract reference event, which starts a performance trial. Performance trials have an outcome, which reflects either successful performance of the phase, misperformance of the phase, or nonperformance of the phase.

Success means that the desired purpose of the phase occurred in a specific period. Misperformance means that an undesirable outcome resulted from the starting event (e.g., a wrong number when dialing a telephone). Nonperformance means that no response resulted from the starting event (e.g., no dial tone in response to lifting a telephone from its hook).

Successful performance is measured in units of time, from the starting event to the event that denotes success. The probabilities of the occurrence of different error types are the parameters for misperformance and nonperformance. These error types include delivery to incorrect destination, delivery of data containing errors, or duplication or loss of data.

End users of interactive applications are concerned with response time, not one-way delays. X3.102 is applicable to response time measurement, by defining response time as a series of one-way delays from input to output. The actual one-way delays used are specific to the architecture and application, and selecting these delays is the process of defining network components.

Interface Responsibility and User Fractions

User actions can bias response time measurements. A measurement strategy must consider interface responsibility. Interface responsibility is the binary state that indicates whether or not a measured unit of information has reached the system under measurement. If a network interface is ready to accept or deliver data, the network transfers responsibility to the user. For example, if a measured network delivers data—a line of print—to a terminal, the network is not responsible if delivery to its ultimate destination—the printer—is delayed because the printer must be refilled with paper.

If the user starting a service trial is not ready to complete the process, or the receiving user is not ready to receive, the transferring network between source and sink cannot be blamed for additional user-associated delay. Because this type of delay is part of the performance measurement, X3.102 has a set of user fractions that quantify various performance times. User fractions are dimensionless numbers that define the ratio of user-associated delay to the total time needed to complete a phase of communications. For example, the user fraction of access time in the telephone network is the additional time needed by the caller to dial, in comparison to the shortest dialing time that is possible.

Network Delay

The round-trip set of delays that compose response time occurs over several paths. Formulas exist for calculating the minimum time a message (and its protocol overhead) takes to cross a line that operates at a given maximum bit rate. Rules of thumb exist for estimating delay in network switching elements (e.g., 100 msec in front-end processors or concentrating computers that use conventional technology, and smaller, but vendor-dependent, times for new switching elements, like frame relay and fast packet switches).

Inside the network, it is rarely useful to track individual transaction delays. Response time is more easily estimated by using statistics for characteristic information units on specific paths. In addition, there may be different numbers of service trials in each one-way path. These numbers may differ because a user-perceived message can be split into smaller pieces, or can be joined with other transactions' messages into a larger block, by an intelligent communications network.

For example, a user input might consist of a screen of data containing 4,096 bytes. When this message flows through an X.25 network with a maximum data packet size of 1,024 bytes, the original message is segmented into four 1,024-byte packets. Each 1,024-byte packet experiences a statistically independent delay in transmission, which must be added to calculate the transmission time of the original message. The latter transmission time must also include the time needed for segmentation and reassembly.

Host Delay Component

An important component of response time is host (or server) delay, which is the time required to process an incoming transaction (incoming to the host) and return it to the network. Host delay can be calculated from the processing times of multiple messages, and may or may not include time in a communications processing routine (e.g., a front-end processor).

Host delay can be treated as a measured network in the X3.102 sense. In finding the start and end of the host delay phase, the start and end of host responsibility for the transaction must be identified. Host processing begins when the last byte of information in a given inbound transaction arrives at the host. It is not useful to start timing host delay when the first byte of an incoming message arrives at the host, because the delivery delay between start byte and ending byte is often paced by the network, not the host.

Allocating Delays

Response time objectives set a budget, measured in units of time, which must be allocated among the various components that can cause delay. Each component, including transmission lines, must be examined and a maximum delay allowed for each component must be allocated. This allocation process may show that the desired response time cannot be provided by the set of components selected. For example, a subsecond response time for a complex transaction is not possible when using satellite communications, because of the speed-of-light delay implicit in sending signals to and from the satellite. When a goal cannot be realized, either the goal must be renegotiated or the network design must change.

A series of node components (e.g., switches) and transmission media make up end-to-end connections, even in a single direction. Delay is not described as something that occurs at a node; it is rather something that is described as occurring through a node. For planning (not tuning), other measures complement nodal delay. Some measure of capacity (e.g., throughput) is useful in gross planning. When dealing with components operating above the link control level, measures (e.g., messages or protocol data units per unit time) are more useful than traditional bits or bytes per second.

Packet switching equipment, for example, often spends much more time processing packet headers than processing the body of the packet. Packet count limits the capacity of packet switches more than the absolute number of bytes received by the switch. Packet switch vendors sometimes inflate their capacity claims by citing a packet per second throughput based on packets of maximum length; such a throughput may not be realizable with short packets (e.g., those used in credit authorization).

DRAFTING THE SERVICE-LEVEL AGREEMENT

The next step in solving a performance problem is to draft the service-level agreement. This is accomplished by first describing the application and then establishing parameters and measures of their variability. Next, the terms and conditions of measurement (e.g., times during which the service-level agreement applies and rules for assessing the effects of downtime) need to be defined. Finally, values for the service-level parameters must be specified.

Characterizing Workload

Service-level agreements need to have workload definitions under which they are valid. Service providers have an unfair advantage when allowed to prove they meet the service-level agreement under conditions of little or no load; service users are unfair to providers if they expect performance to remain acceptable given an infinitely increasing workload. The following represents a basic list of questions to answer when defining communications workload:

- How many users will be served? If various users have various use patterns, all parameters should be specified.
- Who or what is responsible for the service accessed through the measured communications network? Are there different hosts to service different user requests?
- At what times is service available? Are there designated periods of unavailability? Is the network provider responsible for repair downtime?
- How many transactions do users initiate per unit of time?
- What is the rate at which users start transactions? A distinction should be drawn between simple query-and-response transactions and those involving multiple interactions.
- What is the size distribution of responses?
- What is the length distribution of user transactions?

Often there are factors, not obvious and frequently system-dependent, that affect the provision of a given service level. For example, IBM TSO has a time parameter called system logical wait time. When a user is inactive for more than this time value, the user process may be swapped from RAM to disk, so the next user transaction is delayed not only by network and host processing, but by time needed to load the user environment from the disk. System logical wait time trains users to increase their transaction interarrival rates, sometimes by pressing the enter key. Service-level agreements in this environment must include a transaction interarrival time that can be validated with measurements; failure to maintain an adequately high rate will guarantee slower response time because of disk overhead.

Measurements of the host portion of response time vary significantly depending on whether the response measurement starts at the first, or the last, byte exiting the host. In measuring availability, service-level agreements should specify that downtime extends from a problem report to its correction. Alternatively, time periods without maintenance coverage should be subtracted from the total.

COMMON PROBLEMS AND SOLUTIONS

Although it is possible to come up with many components of performance, in practice it is important to identify the most common contributors to poor performance and correct them before taking performance measurements.

Simple observation reveals many problems, but others will be detected only with formal monitoring. Measurement can be simple or complex. It may be done in hardware or in software. In many user environments, simulation or modeling tools may complement or even replace instrumentation. One approach may be to avoid direct measurement of end-user response time, except as a check on calculated end-user delay. In networks of practical complexity, the insertion of response time measurement capability in end systems often adds needless cost and complexity and a burden of returning measured data to an analysis point. Several common contributors to delay are easy to identify, if not to measure precisely.

Eliminating Errors. Data error rates are a major determinant of communications performance. If, in a protocol that corrects errors by retransmission, incurring 30% to 50% errors means the line is effectively doing nothing but retransmitting errors, no useful work is being accomplished. If monitoring of the error log or other facilities available in such an environment proves that the error rate is inordinately high, no further performance measurement should be made until the source of errors is found and fixed; not to do so would bias measurements.

Isolating Host Delay. Another area that is simple to examine is the distinction between host and network problems. There are different views of performance: that of the end user, that of the systems developer on the host, and that of the network developer. From the perspective of the end user, any problems are due to the computer. There is a natural tendency for the host people to blame the network people for problems, and vice versa.

A simple method of finding the cause of delay exists. This approach involves measuring the application host delay from the perspective of a simulated user in the host, or alternatively at a local connection to the host (e.g., an SNA channel-attached controller). This measurement is compared to the delay measured from a network-attached terminal.

If the delay for the internal or local connection is roughly equal to that for the network connection, the problem is not in the network; user response time is limited by host delay. If there is a major difference, it must be determined whether the larger component delay is in the host or in the network. Only if the network delay portion is a significant fraction of the total delay can the network be suspected as the primary fault.

Evaluating Traffic Loading. Any network's performance will degrade when handling excessive traffic. Simple observations can be helpful in finding problems caused by excessive loading. If minimizing response time is the goal, and interactive users complain of poor response time, checks should be made to see if any noninteractive users are loading the network. Typical sources of noninteractive loads are large print jobs and file transfers. Backups often can present unusual loads, as can software maintenance involving sizable software downloading.

Loading from noninteractive sources often can be managed by assigning this traffic a lower priority than interactive traffic, if the network supports multiple priorities. Forcing large transfers to intersperse with interactive traffic and deferring the transfers to interactive traffic can often maintain throughput without degrading response time.

TUNING THE NETWORK: APPLICATION EXAMPLES

Specific tuning recommendations are protocol and implementation specific. This section offers some rules of thumb for the more frequently encountered environments. The network user must distinguish between short-term tuning and longer-term capacity planning.

X.25 Standard

Factors that can be controlled by a public packet switched network user are: virtual calls per trunk, access line speed, and packet size versus window size. Host delay, of course, influences response time but is not a network responsibility. If the application under study uses terminals connected by a packet asembler/disassembler (PAD)—a protocol converter—the PAD can introduce significant delays. Response time can be intolerably slow if the terminal expects local echoing of entered characters, and the remote host does this echoing. When echoing is needed, it should be done by the PAD. In polled protocol applications, the PAD should emulate the polling master station; polling overhead should not be sent across a packet network.

PADs can have parameters that control how quickly packets, or parts of packets, are assembled and transmitted. A tradeoff can exist between maximizing throughput by waiting for full packets to form, and minimizing delay by sending packet-encapsulated user data quickly. Transmission errors are a problem on the access line—not throughout the network. Error statistics on the line often are available, and until errors on the access link are minimized, other network measurements are not useful.

The number of virtual calls on a single link often is a major factor. Although the decision is always implementation specific, performance may be better on two 9,600-bps lines, each with half the virtual circuits, than with one 19.2K b/s line. This observation applies to two lines each using the single-link procedure for link control, not two lines using the multilink procedure.

Maximum data packet length and window size are strong determinants of performance. In general, a longer packet length leads to better performance. Small window sizes are best for interactive applications; long window sizes work better for file transfer.

When X.25 service is being provided through public data networks, network performance information available to the end user is limited. This is not a practical limitation when performance requirements are specified at the network interface. It is the provider's responsibility to tune the network internals to meet contracted requirements.

SNA 3270

Because polled 3270 terminals often coexist with printers, noninteractive devices must not monopolize the line. Fifty percent use is a desirable maximum if noninteractive devices are not present. Use can be much higher if noninteractive devices have a lower priority (i.e., are serviced less often), and the size of their transmissions—when they have permission to transmit—is limited.

Problems common to multiple devices need to be identified. Excessive delay affecting all devices on a line suggests a line problem (e.g., excessive errors or traffic). If the excessive delay is restricted to one cluster, there may be too many devices in that cluster. Solutions here include adding a new controller for some of the devices, increasing the speed of the line servicing the controller, or, where the physical situation permits, moving terminals to less busy positions.

When excessive delay is restricted to specific terminals, possibly on different clusters, unusual use patterns should be suspect. Those users may be entering transactions with unusual host processing needs or with unusually large volumes of data. The latter problem may be traced to an intelligent emulator doing uploads and downloads. 3270 emulation on intelligent workstations is common. Such emulation may be used for file transfers, and file transfers defeat the algorithms used to properly configure 3270 systems. Many of these algorithms assume typical, bursty rates of human input, not the continuous input of a file transfer. Emulators doing file transfer can be recognized in traffic statistics because they will have a higher transaction interarrival rate than true interactive terminals.

Systems network architecture (SNA) interconnects intelligent switching nodes with transmission groups, which can be built from one or more lines.

They allow multiple priorities. Multiline transmission groups impose much higher overhead than a single-line transmission group, so they should be used only when increased availability is necessary, or if no single line of sufficient bandwidth is available.

Response Time with Ethernet LANs

Several simple rules of thumb may be used to tune response time on LANs. The first rule is to decide whether the network performance is actually a significant part of response time. The second rule is to measure whether the LAN is overloaded.

To determine whether network performance is causing the slow response time, a transaction can be run on two identical workstations and the response time measured. A statistically significant number of performance trials of the same transaction is run with one workstation connected to the LAN and one connected directly to the server. Approximate network delay is calculated by subtracting the mean response time at the directly connected workstation from the response time at the network-connected workstation.

To measure whether a LAN is overloaded, a protocol analyzer is used. If busy hour use is 50% or greater, the network will soon need to be split into subnetworks. If use is 70% or greater, it must be split immediately. The network should not be split on the basis of measurements of maintenance activity (e.g., backups) during times in which end users do not access the network.

Diskless workstations present a special challenge. Although keeping data files on a file server is generally wise, and a reasonable number of system files can be kept there, significant improvements in workstation performance often result from equipping the workstation with a small local disk. On this disk are kept read-only operating systems and scratch or swap files that do not need periodic backups.

CONCLUSION

Although performance optimization is an integral part of the day-to-day maintenance of any network, the problems that arise are not insurmountable. The IS manager trying to solve these problems and increase efficiency at the same time does not need a specialized degree in queuing theory. By following a routine set of steps, like those detailed in this chapter, and by allocating a specific amount of time for unavoidable delays, the IS manager can systematically locate the root of any performance problem.

VII-3

Reliability and Availability of LANs

Nathan J. Muller

IN MANY BUSINESSES, organizations now depend on the reliability and availability of their computer networks for the continuity and efficiency of daily operations. Reliability refers to a local area network's capacity to operate despite failures in communications links and equipment. Availability is a measure of performance; it refers to the network's capacity to meet the communications needs of its users. High availability indicates that services are provided immediately; low availability indicates either that users have to wait for network access or that network response is poor.

This chapter discusses some of the technologies that contribute to LAN reliability and availability; by applying these, IS managers can ensure that their networks serve to enhance productivity in their organizations, not detract from it. Discussions refer to LANs according to their topology. Simple versions of the basic LAN topologies are shown in Exhibit VII-3-1.

RELIABILITY

Star topologies score high in LAN reliability. The loss of a link prevents communication between the hub and the node attached to that link, but all other nodes operate as before. The hub is the weak link; the reliability of the network is dependent on the reliability of the central hub, and if the hub malfunctions, all nodes will go down. If a peripheral node fails, only that node is affected.

A ring network topology, in its pure form, offers poor reliability in case of either node or link failures. Rather than each node being connected to a central hub, in ring networks link segments connect adjacent nodes to each other. Each node passes the data it receives to the adjacent node. The loss of one link not only cuts off one node but can bring down the entire network. Improving the reliability of the ring requires the addition of redundant links between nodes and bypass circuitry in the nodes. Reliability is improved, but at great expense.

Although link failures also cause problems on bus networks, node failure will not bring down an entire network. A redundant link for each segment

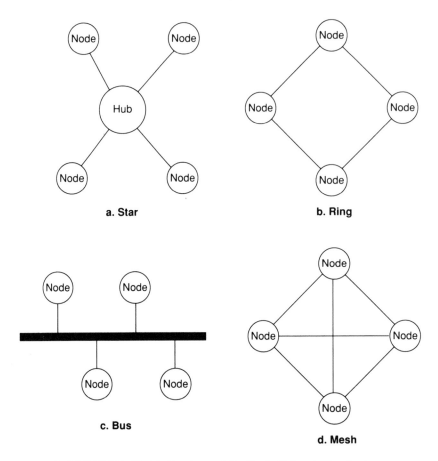

Exhibit VII-3-1. Simple Versions of the Basic Network Topologies

increases the reliability of the network, but as with ring topologies, it raises the cost.

Mesh topologies are used on the internetworks, the networks that connect geographically separated LANs. Mesh networks are the most reliable because there is always more than one route between nodes. But route diversity entails adding more physical links and the equipment (e.g., routers) to support them, again raising the cost of the network.

AVAILABILITY

Availability is a measure of performance dealing with the LAN's capacity to support all users who access it. A network that is highly available provides services immediately to users, whereas a network that suffers from low availability forces users to wait for access or degrades overall network performance when too many users are allowed onto the network at the same time.

Availability on a bus network depends on load, the access control protocol used, and the length of the bus. Under light load, availability is virtually assured for any user who wishes to access the network. As the load increases, however, so does the probability of information collisions. When a collision occurs, the transmitting nodes back off and repeat the attempt to transmit after a short interval. The chance of collisions also increases with bus length.

A mesh topology's multiple paths make it the most reliable of networks. In addition, because it provides the highest degree of interconnectivity between users, this type of network is always available to users who require access.

The capacity of a network based on a star topology is limited to the capacity of the central hub. Under heavy load conditions, users can be denied access. Hubs equipped with multiple processors can improve access in high-demand networks.

Although the ring topology does not provide the same degree of availability as a mesh topology, it is an improvement over the star topology. Its ring availability is lower than a mesh network's because each node on the ring must wait to receive the token (i.e., permission to send) before transmitting data. As the number of nodes on the ring increases, the time interval allotted to each station for transmission must, by necessity, decrease.

ACCESS METHODS

All LANs employ shared media, but the way sharing is done is determined by the access method, which plays a key role in determining the reliability and availability of the network.

Bus Networks

Ethernet, the major bus topology, is contention-based, which means that nodes compete with each other for access to the network. Each terminal listens to the network to determine whether it is idle. Upon sensing that no traffic is currently on the line, the terminal is free to transmit. The trouble with this access method is that several terminals may try to transmit simultaneously, causing data collision. The more terminals that are connected to the network, the higher the probability that such collisions will occur.

To avoid loss of data, the transceivers listen as they send, comparing what is sent with what is heard. If these are not the same, a collision has occurred. The transceiver notifies the attached node with a collision signal and sends error messages onto the Ethernet so that all nodes know of the collision.

Packets travel at nearly the speed of light over coaxial cable, so collisions may appear to be unlikely. In fact, during the very brief interval that it takes for a packet to traverse the network, terminals at the far end cannot know that the network is in use. This collision window imposes a practical limit on the length of a bus network that does not use repeaters. In its 802.3 standard for Ethernets, the IEEE recognizes 2,500 meters as the maximum bus length, regardless of data rate or cable type.

Ethernet is relatively simple to implement, so it typically costs less than other types of network. Because each node functions independently, the failure of one does not disrupt the operation of the others, and nodes may be added or removed without disrupting the network. Ethernet is media independent, functioning well over twisted-pair wire, coaxial cable, and optical fiber. The choice of media depends on desired rate, range, and immunity to interference from external sources of electrical noise.

Ring Networks

Token ring networks use a more efficient topology. The token-passing access method ensures all terminals an equal share of network time. Logically the network forms a ring; however, a particular wiring scheme may be physically configured as a star. The token consists of several bytes of data (also referred to as a packet) that circulate around the ring, giving each terminal in sequence a chance to put information on the network.

To transmit, the station holds the token, replacing it with a packet, and then reinserts the token on the ring. Only the addressee retains the message, and only the station that put the message on the ring can remove it. Because each terminal regenerates data packets and the token, token ring networks do not have the size and distance limitations of Ethernets.

A further advantage of token ring networks is that traffic can be assigned different priorities. Only if a station has traffic equal to or higher in priority than the priority indicator embedded in the token is it allowed to transmit a packet.

The token ring is not without liabilities. Special procedures must be followed to add terminals to the network without breaking the ring and to ensure that the new station is recognized by the others and is granted a proportionate share of network time. Because failed repeater circuits in a node can break the ring, bringing down the whole network, each station must be equipped with bypass circuitry.

A logical ring can be wired as a star, and bypass circuitry, if used with this configuration, will make it easier to correct failures of network equipment than if the bypass circuits are in the nodes. Each node is wired to a centrally located panel, which contains the bypass circuits. If a nodal or link failure occurs, the bypass circuit is activated, preventing the ring from being broken. Centralizing the bypass circuits in this way also facilitates moves and changes as well as fault isolation, because it is much easier to identify connections at a central point than to perform traces between offices and floors.

Token ring networks are vulnerable to anomalies that can tie up the network until the network manager figures out the problem. If a terminal fails before it has a chance to pass the token, the whole network goes down until a new token can be inserted. The token may even be corrupted by noise, to the point of becoming unrecognizable to the stations. The network can also be disrupted by the occasional appearance of two tokens, or by the presence of continuously circulating data packets. The latter situation can occur when data is sent and the originating terminal fails before it can remove the packet from the ring.

To ensure network availability, one terminal is usually designated as the control station to continually monitor network operations and do such necessary housecleaning chores as reinserting lost tokens, taking extra tokens off the network, or disposing of "lost" packets. To guard against the failure of the control station, every station is equipped with control circuitry, so that the first station detecting the failure of the control station assumes responsibility for network supervision. Such protective measures complicate the network and add to its cost.

Star Networks

The star topology consists of a central hub to which all devices on the network are connected. This topology is familiar in the office environment, in which each telephone is ultimately tied into the PBX. Another example of a star network entails several terminals sharing a single host. The star and the ring network share a key disadvantage in that the failure of a single critical node can result in the failure of the entire network, unless provisions are made for hardware redundancy or bypass. In the star topology the critical point, of course, is the central node.

An example of a LAN product that uses the star topology is AT&T's Datakit. In this case, all the network interface units and the interconnecting media are contained within a single cabinet to which the individual stations are connected through twisted-pair wiring. The system looks very much like a PBX, but it implements data communication. AT&T also offers StarLAN, which operates at 1M b/s, and StarLAN 10, which operates at 10M b/s.

Unlike the bus and ring networks, in which intelligence is distributed throughout the network, the star network concentrates all of the intelligence required to run the network at a central hub. The hub for StarLAN, for example, is a minicomputer. The failure of one terminal on the star network does not affect the operation of the others unless, of course, the faulty terminal happens to be the hub. Because network intelligence is centralized at the hub, safeguards must be taken to protect it from catastrophic failure. Such measures may include an uninterruptible power supply, an alternative computer on hot standby, or use of a fault-tolerant computer with redundant subsystems built into it.

Other steps may be taken to minimize the effects of a hub outage. For example, file servers in front of the hub may permit limited communication among the terminals connected to it. With such an arrangement, users would not be able to communicate with terminals not connected to the server, but they could at least continue to access files stored in the assigned disk area of the server.

EQUIPMENT RESTORAL CAPABILITIES

Data Switches

Data switches—also known as port-selection or port-contention devices—permit a number of terminals to share a relatively limited number of computer ports on one or more hosts or the hosts' associated peripherals. Data switches have evolved from relatively simple port-selection and port-contention devices to sophisticated communications controllers capable of managing access to local and wide area networks and of initiating restoral procedures.

Unlike matrix switches, which are designed for permanent connections under the control of the network manager, data switches are designed to establish connections dynamically under the control of individual users as their needs require. Such sophistication offers an economical migration path to LANs. For LAN users, the data switch makes an efficient LAN server or gateway to packet and T1 networks.

Terminals may be connected to the data switch in several ways. The most reliable connection is a direct connection by RS-232C cabling, at distances to 50 feet. For longer distances of one to two miles, between buildings for example, terminals may be connected to the data switch by line drivers or local multiplexers. Some vendors have integrated these devices into their data switches as optional plug-in cards. Terminal-to-switch connections may also use the twisted-pair wiring, whereas remote connections may be achieved over dialup phone lines.

Today's data switches have enough built-in redundancy to virtually eliminate the data switch as a possible single point of network failure. Not only is control logic concentrated on a single processor card, but optional redundant logic allows some data switches to automatically activate an optional secondary processor card if the first one fails. Configuration instructions are automatically copied into the standby card upon cutover, eliminating the need for manual reentry.

Some manufacturers offer redundant power supplies, which plug into the switch and activate automatically on failure of the primary power supply. The faulty power supply module may even be safely replaced with another plug-in unit with the data switch in operation to prevent unnecessary downtime.

The redundant or split backplane protects the switch from damage that may occur from the failure of components connected to the bus. In the event of a failure on the bus, the switch automatically cuts over to the spare backplane to maintain uninterrupted operation.

Some data switches perform continuous background diagnostic procedures so that faulty channels can be disabled automatically. If a requested port is out of service, a message notifies the user that the port has been busied out. When the appropriate channel board is replaced, the data switch automatically reenables it. The network manager still retains the option of using a terminal keyboard to disable any port from any terminal for any reason.

If the primary route is busy or out of service, the dynamic rerouting capability of some data switches allows users to reach any node on the network without performing manual reroutes. The process is entirely transparent to the user.

Data switches with built-in data rate conversion capability free the network manager from having to match terminals with computer ports; each computer port may be set at its highest rate. The buffer in the data switch performs rate conversion for any device that operates at a rate different from its assigned port. This means that users do not have to be concerned about speed at all, and network managers do not have to waste time changing the transmission speeds of computer ports to accommodate lower-speed devices. A computer port set at 19.2K b/s may send data to a much slower printer.

For reliable data rate conversion (i.e., with no loss of data) the connecting devices must be capable of flow control. When XON/XOFF is used for flow control, for example, the switch buffer is prevented from overflowing during data rate conversion. When the buffer is in danger of overflowing, an XOFF signal is sent to the computer, telling it to suspend transmission. When the buffer clears, an XON signal is sent to the computer, telling it to resume transmission. These settings are also used for reformatting character structures, enabling devices of different manufacturers to communicate with each other through the data switch.

These features, along with the various levels of redundancy, are especially important for data switches because they are usually configured in the center of star-type networks. The data switch is potentially the only single point of failure that could bring down the entire network. The modularity of today's data switches provide an economical method of network protection.

LAN Servers

Distributing LAN resources protects users against the loss of information and the unnecessary downtime possible if a network's resources are all centralized. Servers are used to decentralize LAN functions, including security and data protection, network management, and resource accounting.

Using servers to distribute resources minimizes the disruption to productivity that would result if all the resources were centralized and a failure were to occur. Moreover, the use of specialized devices as servers permits the integration of diagnostic and maintenance capabilities not found in general-purpose microcomputers. Among these capabilities are error detection and correction, soft controller error detection and correction, and automatic shutdown in case of catastrophic error. Some servers include such management functions as remote console capabilities. Protecting data at the server has become a critical concern. Some servers store multiple gigabytes of data; loss of this much data or even damage to it can have disastrous consequences.

Configuration Options. There are several ways to configure a server to minimize data loss, depending on the level of fault tolerance desired and the available budget. The drives on servers can be unmirrored, mirrored, or duplexed. The latest configuration is the redundant array of inexpensive disks (RAID).

An unmirrored server configuration entails the use of one disk drive and one disk channel, which includes the controller, a power supply, and interface cabling. This is the basic configuration of most servers. The advantage is chiefly one of cost; the user pays only for one disk and disk channel. The disadvantage of this configuration is that a failure in either the drive or anywhere on the disk channel could cause temporary or permanent loss of the stored data.

The mirrored server configuration entails the use of two hard disks of similar size. There is also a single disk channel over which the two disks can be mirrored. In this configuration, all data written to one disk is then automatically copied onto the other disk. If one of the disks fails, the other takes over, thus protecting the data and assuring all users of access to the data. The server's operating system issues an alarm notifying the network manager that one of the mirrored disks is in need of replacement.

The disadvantage of this configuration is that both disks use the same channel and controller. If either the channel or the controller fails, both disks become inoperative. And because the single disk channel and controller are shared, the writes to the disks must be performed sequentially; that is, after the write has been made to one disk, a write is made to the other disk. This can degrade overall server performance under heavy loads.

Disk Duplexing. In disk duplexing, multiple disk drives are installed with separate disk channels for each set of drives. If a malfunction occurs anywhere along a disk channel, normal operation continues on the remaining channel and drives. Because each disk drive uses a separate disk channel, write operations are performed simultaneously, a performance advantage over servers using disk mirroring.

Disk duplexing also offers a performance advantage in read operations. Read requests are given to both drives. The drive that is closest to the information will respond and answer the request. The request given to the other drive is cancelled. In addition, the duplexed disks share multiple read requests for concurrent access.

The disadvantage of disk duplexing is the extra cost for multiple hard disk drives (also required for disk mirroring) as well as the extra cost for the additional disk channels and controller hardware. However, the added cost for these components must be weighed against the replacement cost of lost information, plus costs that accrue from the interruption of critical operations and lost business opportunities. In view of these, the investment of a few hundred or even a few thousand dollars to safeguard valuable data is negligible.

RAID. An emerging method of data protection uses redundant arrays of inexpensive disks (RAID), which consist of many small disks instead of a single large one. Distributing data across several smaller disks offers protection from a crash that could cause the loss of all data if it is stored on a single shared disk. Multiple disks also ease disk I/O bottlenecks, thereby improving information throughput.

For a variety of technical reasons, current RAID solutions are not widely viewed by potential users as an option. RAID manufacturers have not yet perfected the means to put enough storage capacity (in the gigabyte range) onto the smaller 5¼- and 3½-inch drives. Intelligent controllers that steer and direct the placement and retrieval of data to and from the drives must be refined. RAID devices must also come down in price to compete with conventional disk storage. However, RAID may yet evolve to become the solution for massive storage chores implied by the advanced fiber-optic network architectures that will be introduced by IBM and other computer manufacturers during the late 1990s.

Bridges

The bridge is a protocol-independent interconnection device that operates at the data link layer. To be more specific, bridges interconnect at the media access control (MAC) sublayer and route using the logical link control sublayer. In working below the communications protocols, the bridge can interconnect LANs that use diverse communications protocols. As long as the bridge operates at the MAC layer, it does not need to perform protocol conversion. It monitors all traffic on the subnets that it links. In reading every packet, it looks only for the MAC-layer source and destination address to determine where the packet is going. This means that a bridge can interconnect DECnet, TCP/IP, or XNS networks without concern for higher-level protocols. Unless the LAN protocols are the same, however, bridging alone cannot ensure that applications from one network will interoperate with applications on another network.

As the user population of the LAN grows, performance may suffer. This is because many more users must contend for the same amount of bandwidth. This can be quite frustrating to the user who merely wants to send a message or print a document. Bridges are useful for partitioning sprawling LANs into discrete subnetworks that are easier to control and manage. Through the use of bridges, similar devices, protocols, and transmission media can be grouped together into communities of interest. This partitioning can yield many advantages, such as eliminating congestion and improving the response time of the entire network. Bridges can also make adding, moving, and changing devices on the network much easier, because only the effect on the subnetwork need be considered. Finally, partitioning makes problems easier to diagnose and isolate while enhancing overall security.

There are two types of bridges: dumb and smart. Dumb bridges must be told which addresses are local and which are remote, so they will know how to filter the packets. Smart or learning bridges have the intelligence necessary to figure out the address locations by themselves. Such bridges have distinct learning modes for intraLAN traffic and interLAN traffic. IntraLAN traffic requires that the bridge identify each device on the LAN. Some bridges accomplish this within several seconds, even for LANs with several hundred terminals. The locations at remote devices are automatically determined by a process referred to as flooding. A bridge broadcasts to all locations the first packet it receives that has an unknown destination address. When it receives a reply from the remote device, it updates its routing table.

Learning bridges are also used on networks that have many bridges and have several possible paths that traffic can follow between nodes. In this networking environment, it is possible for some packets to be duplicated, or endlessly looped between bridges. A smart bridge incorporates the spanning tree algorithm or some other proprietary routing algorithm to detect loops and shut down the redundant alternative path. If an active link fails, the smart bridge can detect the failure and activate an idle link automatically.

A bridge that is an integral part of a T1 multiplexer is under the control of the integrated network management system, so the available bandwidth can be allocated either for LAN-to-LAN communications or for voice or data communications—whenever such needs arise. The integral bridge allows the multiplexer's existing management system to monitor and collect error and use statistics. Furthermore, the bridge's filtering capabilities allow the network manager to restrict the types of packets that go out over the bridge, thus alleviating traffic bottlenecks.

Routers

The traditional router is a device that is similar to a bridge in that both provide filtering and bridging between subnetworks. Whereas bridges operate at the physical and data link layers, routers join LANs at a higher level: the network layer. Routers take data formatted for LAN protocols and convert it for wide-area packet network protocols, then perform the process in reverse at the remote location.

Whereas bridges are transparent to network protocols and are used for point-to-point connections between LANs, routers may be used to build complex internetworks. Routers also offer the highest degree of redundancy and fault tolerance, conducting congestion control in conjunction with end nodes to ensure that packets traversing large internets do not experience critical errors that can cause host sessions to time out.

Routing is intended to make the most efficient use of the network by sending data over the most available and direct route between nodes. Routers devise their own routing tables, which can adapt quickly to changes in network traffic, thereby balancing the load. Routers can also detect changes in the network to avoid congested or inoperative links. However, not all routers available today can use more than one path concurrently; some even cause loop problems.

Nevertheless, routers allow the partitioning of networks for tighter access control by eliminating the broadcast requirement of faster, cheaper, but less reliable bridges. Bridges are less reliable than routers because they deliver packets of data on a best-effort basis, which may result in lost data unless the host computer protocol provides error protection. In contrast, a router has the potential for flow control and more comprehensive error protection.

Recognizing the value of routers for network reliability, vendors of intelligent wiring hubs are now offering router modules that fit into their hub chassis. Moreover, the router-on-a-card strategy promotes a tighter coupling of the device's network management with the hub vendor's network management system, usually the simple network management protocol (SNMP). With SNMP, devices from other manufacturers can be managed from the hub. Because the router shares the hub's power supply, it does not introduce another potential point of network failure.

Another advantage of choosing a router module rather than a standalone version is that it eliminates the need to change the physical configuration of an existing LAN. With a standalone router at a central location, the user would have to run another riser cable from the router and add another port. This may cost much more than adding a module to an existing box.

Hubs now have such advanced management capabilities as protocol and traffic analyses, distributed network management, comprehensive port control, and relational data bases that archive historical information on network performance, store an inventory of interconnected devices, and keep service vendor contact information. These new hubs considerably enhance network reliability. Ultimately, the hub vendors will interface their equipment to enterprise management systems such as IBM's NetView and AT&T's Accumaster Integrator.

Some high-end hub vendors have introduced RISC architectures to help users avoid the transmission bottlenecks that may accrue as a result of embedding more and more internet functions into the hub. The move to RISC provides higher throughput for routing, bridging, and connectivity to high-speed LAN backbones (e.g., FDDI). With such hubs, it is even possible to use a high-speed backbone to connect several FDDI rings. All of this capacity is made available at the port.

Intelligent Wiring Hubs

As LANs become increasingly large and complex, they introduce important ramifications for disaster recovery. The bus and ring architectures have serious shortcomings in that a fault anywhere in the cabling can bring down the entire network; this weakness is compounded by the inability to identify the location of failure from a central administration point. This weakness led to the development of the intelligent wiring hub.

Such a device physically rewires bus and ring networks into star topology networks while logically maintaining their Ethernet or token ring characteristics. Cabling faults can affect only the link's node; more important, the intelligent hub provides a centralized point for network administration and control.

Cost savings accrue in several ways. Because unshielded twisted-pair wiring is used, there is no need to install new cabling. Redundant links are unneccesary, and bypass circuitry at every drop location is no longer needed to ensure network reliability.

A fully redundant backbone can be installed to interconnect LANs. Backbone redundancy can be achieved at two levels: cable and hub. A secondary physical cable links together all of the hubs to protect the network in case one of the cables experiences a break. To protect the network against hub failure, a standby hub must be cabled into the network.

The flexibility of the hub architecture lends itself to variable degrees of fault tolerance, depending on the mission criticality of the applications. For example, workstations running noncritical applications may share the same link to the same LAN module at the hub. Although this arrangement is economical, a failure in the LAN module would put all of the workstations on that link out of commission. A slightly higher degree of fault tolerance can be achieved by distributing the workstations among two LAN modules and links. That way, the failure of one module would affect only half the number of workstations. A one-to-one correspondence of workstations to modules offers an even greater level of fault tolerance, because the failure of one module affects only the workstation connected to it. Of course, this is also a more expensive solution.

Sometimes a mission-critical application demands the highest level of fault tolerance. This can be achieved by connecting the workstation to two LAN modules at the hub with separate links. A transceiver is used to split the links at the workstation; the ultimate in fault tolerance would be achieved by connecting one of those links to a different hub.

An intelligent wiring hub's subsystems are appropriate points for built-in redundancy. The hub's management system can enhance the fault tolerance of the control logic, backplane, and power supply by monitoring their operation and reporting any anomalies. With the power supply, for example, this monitoring may include hotspot detection and fan diagnostics to identify trouble before it disrupts hub operation. If the main power supply fails, the redundant unit switches over automatically or under management control without disrupting the network.

IMPACT ON SERVICE SELECTION

Interconnecting LANs over a wide area network requires the installation of devices that connect the LAN to a carrier's network. The selection of appropriate hardware can reduce the need for these services; for example, if the hardware is capable of error correction, the carrier's network need not perform this vital function.

X.25 packet networks, often used for LAN interconnection, have substantial error correction capabilities so that any node on the network can request a retransmission of errored data from the node that sent it. At the time X.25 networks were set up, errors had to be detected and corrected within the network because users' equipment did not usually have enough intelligence and spare processing power to devote to this task.

With much of the public network now converted to inherently reliable digital switching and transmission, there is less need for error protection. Today's intelligent end devices are more adept at handling error control and diverse protocols. Consequently, the communications protocol used over the network may be scaled down to its bare essentials, permitting an optimal balance of efficiency and throughput. This is the idea behind frame relay and the reason frame relay services are rapidly becoming the preferred means for interconnecting LANs.

CONCLUSION

As the strategic value of LANs increases, the concept of error detection, correction, fault detection, fault isolation, and reconfiguration become more important. Special precautions must be taken to protect information from loss or destruction through such means as disk mirroring and duplexing and, in the future, RAID. At the same time, the network must be equipped with appropriate intelligent devices that will ensure the highest degree of network reliability and availability.

Section VIII
Data Management

THERE IS A GROWING dichotomy between those IS departments that do an outstanding job of managing data and those that do not. IS departments using advanced techniques are making meaningful contributions to the information richness of their enterprises, while others cling to outdated methodologies and fall further and further behind.

Although the desire to structure data to meet global needs appears to be paramount, other pressures can force the IS manager to create a version of the data architecture that is quite different from the enterprise data model. These pressures stem from an organization's need to have summary, historical, and derivative representations of the data in the information data base. Chapter VIII-1 focuses on the implications of "Implementing the Information Data Base" as the data architecture.

Chapter VIII-2 offers an update on "Data Classification Concepts." The traditional terms and concepts used to discuss data modeling products and the design techniques that create them are proving to be inadequate in describing the growing variety of data modeling implementations and uses. This lack of terminology is especially noticeable in working with and describing entities. Terminology and concepts that are adapted from classification science provide much-needed assistance in producing a data model. This chapter describes how classification science applies directly to and can be used to explain many of the concepts, products, and techniques of data modeling.

VIII-1

Implementing the Information Data Base

Rom Narayan

MANY ORGANIZATIONS are struggling with the fact that operational production systems meet the day-to-day information processing needs of the business but do not meet decision support or executive information needs. This problem is exacerbated by the downsizing of operational systems to obtain cost and productivity advantages and the use of vendor-developed packages. In the first case, the data is increasingly dispersed on several platforms in a variety of data base management systems (DBMSs). In the second case, the organization does not have control over data structures in vendor-developed packages.

To make the information suitable for use by both senior management and decision support personnel, some organizations are undertaking an information data base or data warehouse project in which the data from production systems is extracted and stored in a data base that is founded on an enterprisewide data model. With this strategy, existing production systems continue to operate with their application-oriented data structures while creating a data base that represents a global architecture. In addition, it becomes possible to satisfy the information needs of different users and to provide for expansion to meet the needs of new users. Over a period of time, the information data base becomes the hub around which corporate information processing takes place, and the result is the propagation of data corresponding to the data architecture.

JUSTIFICATION

Many organizations can benefit from using an information data base architecture strategy. Such organizations are often characterized by:

- Production systems that have evolved over time in a fragmented and uncoordinated fashion and are not going to be restructured to conform to the enterprise data model. These production systems do not have the capacity to meet the need for online end-user queries without major hardware upgrades.

- Management's need for an executive information system (EIS) fed from current production systems; management frustrated in its ability to quickly access decision support information stored in production systems directly; and management that has bought into the concept of EIS and the data feeds from production systems.
- Data created by production systems that is transactional in nature and may not be organized for decision support purposes. When analysis is performed, transactional data must be arranged in a chronological sequence so that trends can be discovered. This means that production data must be collected and summarized to provide a stable amount of data for analysis.
- An executive who can obtain the funding for the information data base effort. Because data and processing is duplicated, it is likely that additional hardware investments must be made. A divisional executive may want product line profit-and-loss statements to discover which products are causing excessive service efforts. In many cases, the IS executive would be chartered to develop this data base as a corporate effort.

Benefits

Many benefits accompany using an information data base as a data architecture implementation strategy. For example, the information data base project can be implemented in parallel with routine IS activities supporting existing production applications. In this manner, existing projects are not adversely affected. Also, decision support personnel and executives get involved in the process of defining the information data base because they have a vested interest in the result; therefore, their support for the data architecture effort that precedes the information data base effort can be sustained.

In addition, end users and decision support analysts use data from different production data bases created from an enterprise data model that provides a cross-organizational or functional view of information. Finally, the information data base is a cost-effective way to deploy data base technology to support the needs of a large number of end users.

THE INFORMATION DATA BASE

The information data base consists of data from existing production applications and other external sources, organized to meet the requirements of decision support personnel and executives. Exhibit VIII-1-1 depicts where the information data base lies in the traditional data hierarchy found in most organizations. The information data base is often referred to as an information utility and sits on top of the production systems that are mainly transaction oriented.

Modeling tools are most commonly associated with decision support systems, and the results obtained from executive information systems are referred to as the briefing book. In a simple implementation, a data base of extracts from production systems are front-ended with such end-user tools as

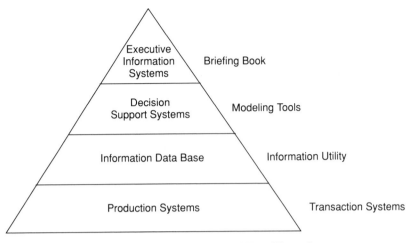

Exhibit VIII-1-1. Organizational Data Hierarchy

4GLs. In the typical case, the data extracts are subjected to further process-ing or scrubbing to prepare the data for the information data base. For more real-time access and to save on storage, the data extracts can be obtained from production systems by servers so that duplication of data is minimized. Only the data requested most often is kept in permanent storage—the rest is maintained in temporary storage and refreshed from the production data base whenever a request is made.

The organization of data in an information data base differs from the way it is organized in a production data base for the following reasons:

- Only a transaction summary may be required, as opposed to a detailed record of all transactions.
- Only data that is critical to day-to-day performance of the business may be required.
- Data may be required in a different order than that of the production data base. For example, transactional data is generally identified by the customer or activity identifier that initiated the transaction. In an infor-mation data base, it may be desirable to maintain a historical or chrono-logical record by activity identifier. It may also be necessary to hold data for lengthy periods of time.
- Data may have to be reconciled into a single ordering scheme before it is put into the information data base. Organizational changes are a case in point. If business activities are associated with a particular organiza-tion structure, any changes would be tracked with the original structure so that the user gets a coherent view of the data.
- The structure of the information data base must be consistent with the enterprise data model for it to be considered a data architecture imple-

mentation strategy. This requires the enterprise data model to be developed before the information data base is implemented.

Information Data Base Components

The information data base can be represented in terms of the information flows shown in Exhibit VIII-1-2. Three major components are involved: data input and formatting, data storage and integrity, and the data access mechanism.

Data input and formatting deals with extracting data from existing production systems with the right level of detail. Extracts must contain data within the right time frames, possess consistent coding schemes, and maintain accurate relationships with other extracts on which there may be dependences. Data may also be sourced from external sources and integrated into the warehouse.

Data storage and integrity is concerned with ensuring that the stored data fits into the proper scheme and adds value to the warehouse. Audit trails, internal checks to ensure that the data in the warehouse is consistent, and security controls are important. Finally, the data access mechanism provides the ability to deliver the data that is requested from the warehouse in the format that the user can use directly in the tool.

Data Structure Design

The first step in the data structure design of the information data base is to understand the existing information resource (i.e., the production systems). In most companies, production data bases have not had consistent naming conventions applied to them. Therefore, the existence of a data element dictionary that cross-references existing structures to a standard set of data element definitions is a prerequisite for conducting user requirements anal-

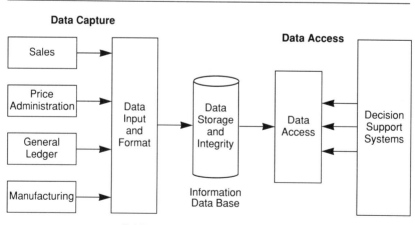

Exhibit VIII-1-2. Information Flows

ysis. The major benefit of having a data dictionary is that it sets a baseline for data requirements discussions and minimizes unnecessary misunderstandings and conflicts.

The starting point of the requirements analysis is to identify the kinds of information needed by users. A data model representing the major information groups and the business rules (i.e., relationships) needed to support the requirements is determined from examining existing reports, manual decision analysis output and input, and the types of extracts that have been requested in the past. If the application is new, interviews with key users can help obtain the data that is needed. The data required may occur in a derivative form (i.e., an aggregate or a combination of primitive data).

The development of the overall data model is accomplished by interviewing key decision makers and finalizing the data elements that are required to support their decision-making needs. The data elements are organized into groups using the rules of normalization. This results in a model of the information as seen by the end user. The data required by the end user may exist in several production systems.

The next step is to identify the extracts to be produced from the various production systems and the interrelationships between the extracts, scheduling, and timing issues. The extracts may or may not be in third normal form. In addition, not all informational needs may be known as of the first iteration. The focus of the initial iteration should be to identify the major decision support activities. It is also recommended that the analysis and planning phase be carried out in a workshop setting so that the issues are handled in a nonthreatening atmosphere.

VALUE OF THE INFORMATION DATA BASE

With the tremendous growth in mission-critical production applications needed by users, most centralized IS organizations are not able to fulfill decision support and executive information needs expeditiously. End-user computing functions may provide extracts of production data bases, but this tends to ameliorate the situation and is not an entirely satisfactory solution for the following reasons:

- Extracts used in one analysis may not be the same ones used in another analysis, which can lead to inaccurate comparisons.
- The lack of a stable information base makes it difficult to conduct the kinds of analyses that are important to support key decisions. A case in point is profit-and-loss analysis by product line. Unless this kind of data is available, decisions would be made on the basis of hunches rather than concrete data.
- By separating reporting systems from production systems, the IS function can concentrate on important mission-critical production systems and associated data bases. Because reporting can be obtained from the information data base, incorporating individual reporting requirements does not become the most important part of IS development work. Instead, attention can be focused on implementing the data architecture.

- Applications are being created at the departmental or individual level at which the expertise to perform data analysis does not exist. In such instances, the user is unaware of the benefits of complying with data architecture standards. Therefore, more and more applications are created that may not be consistent with the enterprise data model.

By addressing these problems, the information data base provides a common foundation for data sharing, data standardization, data synchronization, and other data management goals. It also provides a mechanism for realizing the data architecture.

For example, the users of an information data base may require information on contract revenue by product code on a monthly basis. The data about contract terms and conditions is maintained in the contracts administration system by customer account number. The billing and accounts receivable system sends out the invoices and tracks the payments against those invoices. Between the two, the billing and accounts receivable system would be considered a more accurate source of information.

In this specific example, the billing and accounts receivable systems are transaction oriented, whereas the contract system uses a data base. Exhibits VIII-1-3 and VIII-1-4 illustrate the high-level models implemented in the contract system and the billing system. The model of information in the information data base that can satisfy the users is shown in Exhibit VIII-1-5. It is possible to maintain more detailed information in the information data base and let the user aggregate the information required. By keeping the data at a more detailed level, the usefulness of the data is broadened to multiple users at the expense of additional storage. An example of a broader model of information is shown in Exhibit VIII-1-6. Both models conform to an overall data model and do not conflict with the data model or with each other.

The preceding iterations enable management to come up with the optimal solution to the problem. Whether the data is sourced from one system or two

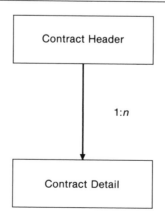

Exhibit VIII-1-3. Contract System Data Model

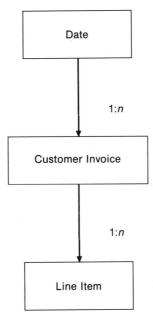

Exhibit VIII-1-4. Billing System Data Model

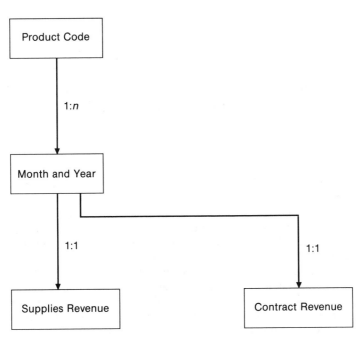

Exhibit VIII-1-5. Information Data Base Model I

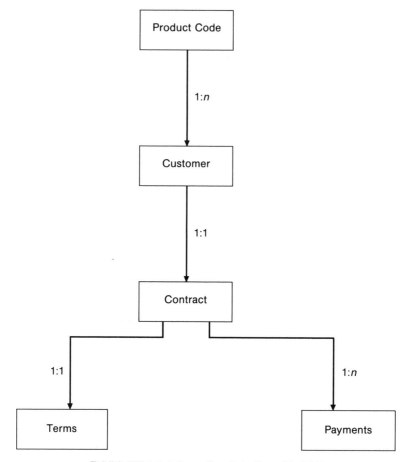

Exhibit VIII-1-6. Information Data Base Model II

is a problem in logistics. This specification, when combined with other such specifications, moves the organization toward the data architecture. An important aspect of this type of analysis is that the model developed at any iteration belongs within the data architecture. If the enterprise data model is the ideal target model, the models from the information data base project should conform. The fact that many models are available confirms the premise that the information data base can be structured in many ways and still conform to the data architecture of the organization. The models that have been derived can be subjected to what-if analysis to see if they can handle future scenarios. The mission-critical production systems and data bases can continue to address current business transaction processing requirements, whereas the information data base has a futuristic slant.

BUILDING THE INFORMATION DATA BASE

Development of an information data base involves several activities. From interviews with the users, the data requirements for decision support and executive needs must be identified. A rough-cut data model for the information data base must be developed. This sets the direction for the effort and offers guideposts in making decisions about including or excluding data and process. The data model does not have to be detailed; a high-level data model is sufficient, with the data model including entities and their key attributes.

Integration Issues. The scope of integration that the information data base will provide must be identified. This requires the development of a high-level business model of the enterprise that identifies the processes that are going to be included in the effort. This model provides a boundary for the information data base project. For example, an organization may wish to include only the financial reporting aspects of all transactions being performed in support of the business. In that case, it would identify the key processes and systems that generate financial information as the starting point of the analysis.

Data Elements. The data elements that form the input values of the information data base must be defined. These are often referred to as primitive data elements as opposed to derivative data elements, which are obtained by combining the primitive data elements by algorithms. Derivative data elements should be examined carefully to see if it would not be better to let users perform the aggregations from the primitive data. In many cases derivative data elements are stored in the information data base as a result of the scrubbing effort or in situations in which only summary data is required.

Support. The major information groups (i.e., entities) needed to support the high-level needs must be determined. During this analysis, some critical properties of the data elements and their relationship to the primitive data elements become evident. The results of the data analysis effort are documented in a data dictionary that makes it visible to everyone on the network. From this analysis, the source data (both the conversion algorithms that must be applied and the source data bases) are identified. Existing systems should be considered first as a feasible source before separate input streams are developed. It is better to source from an existing imperfect system than to create a separate system and maintenance interface.

Migration Strategy. The migration strategy must be developed so that the information data base can be populated with data from the production data bases on a regularly scheduled basis. Because many sources must be reconciled and interdependences in the timing of the loads may exist, it is important to schedule the loads to minimize interruptions. Also, the scheduling of these runs must consider the effect on production data bases. Most DBMSs allow concurrent read operations. When an update job is running concurrently, however, DBMSs behave differently in that they can provide either before-update images, after-update images, or retries.

Changes in the Data Bases. Finally, it is extremely important to plan for changes that occur in the production data bases. In some cases, the accuracy of tracking changes may not be necessary. In those instances, changes to certain fields are not replicated in the information data base; however, these decisions must be documented, because if one user sources data directly from the production data base and another user sources information from the information data base, they will not get matching results. Disclaimers must be documented so that the IS staff does not become the scapegoat.

By following the preceding steps, IS management is in a position to answer the following questions:

- What file format will the data be in when it is released to the information data base?
- What record format will the data be in when it is released to the information data base? If the record description is not in standard data definition format, it must be mapped to a standard data definition.
- How much data will be released? How frequently?
- Who are the people responsible for the data? Who is the business person responsible for the quality of the data? Who is the technical person responsible for the physical transmission of the data?
- Where is the data coming from? Where is the physical location of the data producer or supplier?

SECURITY ISSUES

Security of the data is an issue because varied users are now able to access the data. Questions regarding data ownership must be addressed before implementation. Written policies on data ownership should be created. One of the questions that arises is who provides the approval to access the data. The data administrator should not accept this role because of the conflict of interest. It is preferable to have a person from a user organization delegated for this purpose. This person would have the responsibility for updating the matrix of authorized users and the data elements that they have access to.

If a relational DBMS is used for the implementation of the information data base, views can be defined for individual users or even for categories of users. The views can be designed to exclude the data that a user does not have access to—a process that involves some technical administration. Another important aspect of security is to install audit trails on the activity against the information data base. This lets the administrator know which users are accessing the information data base.

DEVELOPMENT PROBLEMS

Getting senior management to commit the time can become a problem unless IS management can tie the project to a result desired by the CEO. Once the project is under way, however, various problems may emerge during the development of the information data base.

Handling data redundancy in existing production files becomes an issue in cases in which redundant copies of the data are inconsistent. A choice between the copies must be made, and the problems resulting from that choice must be dealt with.

Timing of extracts can become a problem in cases in which the extract criteria cannot be matched between any combination of production data bases. Sometimes arbitrary decisions must be made regarding the cutoff times for the intervals to be considered comparable, such as when some information may be collected on a transactional basis and other data is available on a weekly or monthly basis.

Reconciliation of data pertaining to the same entity in different files becomes important if different pieces of data pertaining to an entity exist in several files. For example, the order entry system may contain some information about a customer, the contracts file may contain other information, and the shipment system might contain still other information. For all this information to be combined to the same customer, customer naming and numbering conventions must be consistently applied. If this is not the case with existing production systems, a certain amount of reconciliation must be done. An interesting situation arises when companies change names because of a merger or divestiture. To furnish the information data base with reliable information, the changes must be tracked by a date and time stamp.

Many transaction systems do not maintain history because it detracts from the response time and throughput. The information data base, however, may be required to provide a historical view of information. This can be done by adding data elements that track status changes in the production systems so that transactional records can be organized into a historical format.

The storage of summary records versus detail records is a classic problem. Storing detail requires vastly larger disk capacity; however, because not all uses of the data can be predicted in advance, data administrators usually take the easy route and include detail just to be on the safe side. The use of summary data must be promoted during the requirements discussion and the trade-offs considered before detail records are allowed into the information data base.

Other situations that must be dealt with during the development of the information data base include the following:

- Business areas must confront and resolve conflict in data terminology; this process encourages end-user cooperation and helps address ownership issues.
- The platform for the information data base implementation can introduce new technology (e.g., relational DBMSs, data sharing, and con-

current access). Although users need not know about the details of these technologies to get the work done, they must know that the complexity of the technologies demands greater technological and management skills and that their project expectations should be moderated accordingly.

* The dilemma of adapting to local needs versus corporate needs is faced by all IS managers and reflects the need to store data for one particular end user versus focusing on data that benefits all users.

CONCLUSION

The advantages of implementing an information data base include the following:

* It enables IS management to enhance credibility with the business manager as well as the IS staff.
* It enables data administration to develop the enterprise data model in conjunction with business users.
* It obtains the ongoing support of senior managers.
* It enables IS management to concentrate resources on only those business processes that are important to the business.

The use of the information data base as a foundation to implement a data architecture across one or more business processes can be to the advantage of both IS management and the business itself.

VIII-2

Data Classification Concepts

Martin E. Modell

FOR ALL PUBLIC, private, government, and commercial enterprises, the typical course of doing business generates numerous forms and other business records. These records reflect business transactions, the actions of personnel, and the information collected and stored for current and future reference. The collective data and information contained in these records constitute the organization's base.

If not properly and consistently organized and cross-referenced, the sheer number, complexity, and interrelated aspects of these business records could easily inundate the organization. All organizations therefore have created systems that can organize, categorize, classify, and store business records for easy retrieval, later reference, and use. All of these systems began by segregating the records by major category or group. Data organization methods exist in all organizations, regardless of whether their business records are stored manually, electronically, or some combination of both. Often, the systems used to organize business data use a personal or local perspective in some areas and a common, centralized, or partially centralized perspective in others. A given set of records may be used by a relatively small group of persons or a relatively large group of employees. Unless its record storage method is centralized and uses a corporate perspective, a given set of records is rarely used by all personnel within the organization.

Many organizations are working to reduce data acquisition and maintenance and storage costs, increase productivity, and improve information access by centralizing the storage of commonly used records, such as those contained in central account files and those used for central reference. Centralization ensures that the same set of records can service the largest group of employees possible. This process must accommodate the many diverse business perspectives and data retrieval needs of large groups with differing needs for the same records. This process can be simplified with entity-relationship (ER) modeling, which facilitates the development of a categorization and classification scheme for data storage. The data model is developed using an analysis of an organization's data requirements, the characteristics of its data, and the integration of the various views and perspectives of the functional areas of the organization that collect, maintain, or rely on this data.

The ER approach uses three basic constructs: the entity, the attribute, and the relationship. This chapter assumes a basic knowledge of the ER model and focuses on applying the concepts from classification as an aid to a more comprehensive understanding of that modeling approach.

ENTITY-RELATIONSHIP MODELING LANGUAGE

The term *entity*, as used throughout this chapter, refers to any group of persons, places, things, or concepts about which an organization must collect and maintain records (in this case, business records). The term is used as a surrogate, linguistic symbol, or linguistic convenience in place of a more specific reference. Entity does not refer to any kind of thing in specific, and is usually a surrogate until an analyst determines its true identity.

In the data model, the term *entity* refers to the central components of the model, as opposed to the supporting components of attributes and relationships. Difficulties occur because in data modeling the term has as much meaning and definition as the term X has in mathematics. X has meaning when used as part of an equation, but is meaningless by itself. X is almost always defined in terms of other symbols and numbers. *Entity* is the data modeling equivalent of X.

Because of the inherent vagueness of the term in unqualified form, the term *entity* is often used:

- As both a group and singular term, sometimes within the same context.
- To refer to the whole group and a portion of the same group, sometimes within the same context.
- As a general term when it is impractical or cumbersome to use the phrase person, place, thing, or concept.
- To refer to many levels of aggregation and conceptually different components at the various design levels (i.e., conceptual, logical, and physical).
- By physical designers and by CASE tool vendors who borrow the term to refer to the records in the data base structure models.

Because of the ambiguity of meaning, the term *entity* should always be qualified in some manner with an adjective or other noun to make clear the kind of entity or group of entities being referred to.

The term *attribute* represents a property, aspect, descriptor, data group, data element, identifier, qualifier, or characteristic of an entity or a relationship. This definition creates difficulties, however, because these terms are not synonymous and, therefore, the term *attribute* is used:

- As both a group and in singular form, sometimes within the same context.
- To refer to a group of data elements, a portion of a group of elements, or a single element, sometimes within the same context.
- To refer to many levels of aggregation and to conceptually different components at the various design levels (i.e., conceptual, logical, and physical).

- By physical designers and by CASE tool vendors, who borrow it to refer to the data elements in the data base structure models.
- To refer to the properties (i.e., descriptors) and the characteristics of entities and of data elements.

In addition, within some data models, attributes have been elevated to the status of entities. In general, however, many models and most CASE tools have only two constructs: the entity and the attribute. The attribute is a single data element and the entity is anything that has more than one attribute.

As a further complication, the classification of a model component as either an entity or an attribute is subjective and based on perception, organizational emphasis, and contextual use. Simply put, whether something is an attribute of an entity (or relationship) or whether it is an entity (or relationship) in its own right is in most cases a design choice. In the same manner, the treatment of many components as either an entity or a relationship is also a design choice.

DATA ORGANIZING TECHNIQUES

All processing, whether automated or manual, can be divided into two categories: processing of every record and processing of selected records. In most procedural systems, the selection of records for conditional processing (i.e., each kind of record is processed differently) is based on tests that are performed on the values of the data contained within the records. Usually, each discrete value tested corresponds to a specific type of processing. Based on the results of these tests, certain records are selected, others discarded, and specific processing performed.

Records can be sequenced by the contents of a data element, and specific processing takes place when the contents of the data element change: this is another variation on value testing. The values of certain data elements can be used to indicate the presence or absence of other (i.e., dependent) data elements. All of these procedures represent uses of classification.

CLASSIFICATION DEFINED

Things or entities are distinguished from one another to form groups to facilitate management or understanding. To classify is to organize, arrange, or group things according to family, class, or category. These terms refer to various levels of specificity or generality when discussing sets, groups, or collections that contain members with common characteristics. One of the best examples is found in taxonomic charts for biology—the origin of modern classification—to categorize flora and fauna and each implies a group that ranges from the general to the specific. The level of specificity of a group is determined by the number of characteristics the members of the group have in common.

Because the term *entity* must always be qualified by some adjective or noun, because a data model must distinguish between groups of entities in the same general to specific manner, and because it is necessary to distinguish between a whole group and a portion of that group, the following terms will be used in the remainder of this discussion:

- *Entity family.* The largest, most general group.
- *Entity group.* A subdivision of the entity family.
- *Entity occurrence.* A single entity.

Such taxonomic terms as *type* are unsuitable as a qualifier, because although it means a group, it has been so widely used with so many definitions that it has become meaningless. Data classification is not just a general-to-specific decomposition; therefore, it might be misleading to use terms that imply that it is. Although many taxonomic terms refer to level of specificity and commonality of characteristic and have specific meanings when used in relation to each other, the simple term *entity group* conveys sufficient meaning.

The use of the terms *family, group,* and *occurrence* is more significant than the use of *class, type,* and *subtype* because the latter group of terms implies a hierarchic decomposition of an entity in much the same context as the hierarchic decomposition of function and process. The term *family* has been chosen primarily because it has no specific usage within the current data modeling language. In addition, although the data model concentrates on the identification of groups within groups (i.e., decomposition), it must also account for overlapping groups and multiple groups that are decomposed from the same population and share some characteristics and not others.

ENTITY FAMILIES VERSUS ENTITY GROUPS

An entity family is composed of members with at least one characteristic in common. The fewer characteristics that the members of a group have in common, the more members the group can potentially have. Of all the components in a data model, an entity family has the largest possible membership. Entity families are identified in the first phase (i.e., the enterprise or conceptual phase) of data model construction and are the components of the conceptual or highest-level data model.

With few exceptions, each entity family becomes the subject of a data base. When there is a one-to-one correspondence between an entity family and a data base, the term *subject entity* may be used instead. The entity families of a data model are general groups of things that are often only loosely related. Organizational business processes usually deal with families and selected (i.e., specific) entity groups within those families and they need both general (i.e., familywide) data and specific (i.e., group) data. The identification of both family and group and the relationship between the two becomes critical to the effectiveness of the data model.

A data entity family represents a collection of records—each containing data that is common to all family members. For each distinct entity group within the family and each business user perspective, the data also includes:

- Characteristics that distinguish all entity groups from each other at every level of categorization.

- Details of the general-to-specific progression of the characteristic sequence or string for each characteristic of the entity group.
- Attributes of interest for the entity group that are beyond the characteristics used to form the group.

CHARACTERISTICS AND ATTRIBUTES

An attribute is some aspect or descriptor of an entity and many contain one or more highly interrelated data elements. Attributes have no meaning, existence, or interest to an organization, except in terms of the entity (or relationship) they describe. An attribute may be abstract or general information, a specific data element, or some piece of information in between these two extremes. In a data model, most attributes are clusters of highly interrelated data elements that together describe some aspect of the entity. The values of most data elements are not critical to the data model and in most cases are unique to an entity occurrence. A data model, however, must document the valid ranges of the values for each data element as well as its format.

A *characteristic* is a multipurpose, multivalued attribute whose discrete values identify or describe entities, families, and entity groups or distinguish one entity group or family from another. Within the data model, all valid values of each characteristic must be identified and documented. These values then form the basis of entity classification, which controls processing, data grouping, and entity identification. Both the characteristic and its values are of interest to the data model. Characteristics are best diagrammed as a T-list. An example of the standard form of a T-list is illustrated in Exhibit VIII-2-1.

The most definitive characteristic within any model is the *identifier*, or key, whose values distinguish one member of a family or group from another. In other words, the unique range of values of the identifier creates the smallest, most restrictive group—a group with only one member. All entity families and entity groups must have an associated characteristic. Each entity occurrence must have a specific set of characteristics for correct identification, processing, and data grouping.

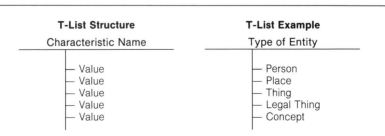

Exhibit VIII-2-1. Diagramming Characteristics Using T-Lists

THE USE OF CHARACTERISTICS IN DATA MODELING

The primary goal of data analysis is to identify the data requirements of the company (or a portion of it) and to identify the data elements needed to satisfy those requirements. The primary goal of data modeling is to assist the data analyst in the requirements definition and to provide a means for determining the most effective method for organizing that data.

The ER approach states that companies require data about people, places, and things (and concepts) and that data should be organized around those entities. The ER approach also states that there is a difference between analyzing entities and determining requirements for data about them, and analyzing data to determine how best to organize that data into records for storage and processing. Data organization must be centered around entities. The concept of normalization organizes data around primary keys and into functional dependency groups. The same concept as incorporated into the ER approach organizes data around entities and into attribute groups. The success of both approaches depends on effectively determining how to group the required data. In effect, a data model attempts to organize and group data, and each approach attempts to describe how to accomplish that task.

Extensional and Intensional Characteristics

Classification is the science of organizing and grouping. Classification techniques, when properly applied, can be highly effective when used to organize and group data. Classification techniques can be most effective when first applied to the real-world entity models and then translated to data models. Classification science uses characteristics to group like entities. Data modeling uses attributes to describe entities and uses characteristics to group both entities and attributes. Data modeling uses two kinds of characteristics: extensional and intensional.

Extensional characteristics are developed from organizational policies, business rules, and the organization's perception of the entities that it deals with. Extensional characteristics are largely fixed by policy and are subjective in that they are what the organization deems them to be. Extensional characteristics determine the criteria for entity family creation and membership. In other words, organizational policies determine what entity groups are to be treated the same and how these groups are to be identified.

Extensional characteristics define the boundaries around a group, in this case an entity family. Extensional characteristics are multivalued, as are all other characteristics, but by definition, each member of the family must have the same value of a given extensional characteristic. If family membership is defined by multiple extensional characteristics, then each member must have the same value of each selected extensional characteristic. All members of a given entity family must have the same extensional characteristics because possession of those characteristics is the criterion for family membership.

Intensional characteristics are used to determine the differences between the members of an entity family, to determine how the members should be grouped, and as an aid in processing. Intensional characteristics also determine data grouping requirements, and data content. All members of a given group within an entity family have the same intensional characteristic values.

Intensional characteristics define the various types of members, their identifiers, and their relationship to each other. Intensional characteristics make up the majority of the characteristics of interest for an organization and are used to construct the entity family model. Unless otherwise noted, all characteristics that are discussed in the remainder of this chapter are intensional characteristics. Characteristics are value dependent. The presence or absence of a characteristic is the presence or absence of a specific value. Group (and family) membership is specified in the form of a series of equations (e.g., something is a contract if there are at least two parties, there is an agreement between the parties, and there is consideration).

Dependent and Independent Characteristics

Intentional characteristics may in turn be dependent or independent. Independent characteristics do not depend on each other for definition and use. Characteristics may be together, or chained, to form sequences where characteristics qualify other characteristics. All characteristics between chains and at the first level (i.e., below the family) within a chain must be independent of each other. (Characteristic chains are discussed in detail in the latter part of this section.) Examples of independent characteristics include contract price terms (i.e., fixed price or variable price) and contract payment type (i.e., lump sum or installment).

Dependent characteristics are those whose values qualify the values of another characteristic. The value of a dependent characteristic depends on another characteristic for its definition and use. At a specific level, however, dependent characteristics must be independent of each other. An example of a dependent characteristic is type of price variability (i.e., incentive, discount, or indexed), which depends on the variable price value of the characteristic contract price terms.

A characteristic chain is similar to the leg of a hierarchy, only a chain is a sequence of values, not data fields. More specifically, a chain is a sequence of characteristic values that is headed by the value of an independent characteristic and is followed by one value from each of its dependent characteristics. The extensional characteristics that identify an entity family and distinguish its members from other families' members are also, by definition, intrinsic or intensional to the entity. Exhibit VIII-2-2 is a diagrammatic representation of the classification chain of a contract entity family by the intensional characteristic price terms, with further price term classification by type of price variability.

As a matter of diagrammatic convenience, characteristic chains are assembled from most specific to least specific, or bottom-up. The following is an example of characteristic chains:

```
Contracts
    fixed-price contracts
    variable-price contracts
        incentive variable-price contracts
        discount variable-price contracts
        indexed variable-price contracts
```

Each chain consists of one or more characteristics, and the indentation level of each chain represents a specific type of contract. Each indentation level also represents a more restrictive group than that of the group at the preceding level. Each characteristic chain begins with an independent characteristic followed by one or more dependent characteristics.

Levels of Characteristics

A first-level, or base, characteristic must be capable of grouping all members of the entity family population independently of any other grouping of the same population. Second-level characteristics are dependent because they group only within a first-level characteristic. This representation of

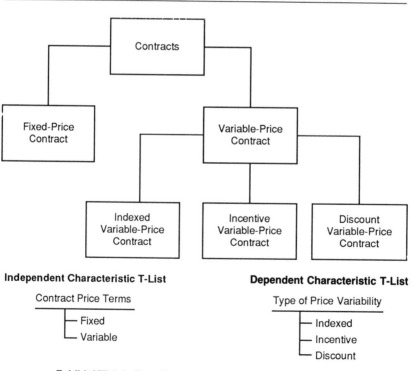

Exhibit VIII-2-2. Classification of the Entity Family Contract

qualification levels (i.e., the length of qualifier chain) and the entity groups that are determined by these qualification levels give rise to the notion of entity decomposition—the idea that entities can be decomposed in the same manner as functional area activities.

Exhibit VIII-2-3 uses the concurrent classification of employee entities by both employee type and pay status to demonstrate two first-level entity family classifications. Within the exhibit, both *employee type* (full-time, part-time) and *pay status* (nonexempt, exempt) are considered independent first-level characteristics because all employees work full- or part-time and are either exempt or nonexempt. If, for example, all part-time employees were paid weekly but full-time employees had a choice of pay cycle, the *pay cycle* (weekly, biweekly, semimonthly, monthly) would depend only on the full-time value.

Rules Governing Characteristics

The values of a characteristic must be exhaustive and mutually exclusive—that is, they must cover all possible conditions, and two values of the same characteristic cannot apply to the same entity. Each entity occurrence within a given entity group must have only one value from the values list used to identify the group; each entity must have the same value, and every entity in any other group must have some other valid value. For example, the *sex of employee* characteristic is both mutually exclusive and exhaustive. The concept of mutual exclusivity can be further illustrated by the term *French language proficiency* (reading, writing, and speaking). This term is exhaustive, but its components are not mutually exclusive, because an individual can have proficiency in reading, writing, speaking, or any combination.

The values *both, other, all others,* and *unknown* are not valid values for a characteristic. An individual characteristic value cannot include the connectors *and* or *or*. Characteristic values should, whenever possible, be a single word or, at most, a two-word phrase. The list of characteristic values should not have an explicit or implicit "*and*" between individual terms. A list of characteristic values must, however, always have an implicit "*or*" in the list of terms (male *or* female).

Each first-level intensional characteristic must completely divide up the entire family population. Each value of every first-level intensional characteristic forms the name of one of the divisional groups and heads its own independent chain. The use of additional dependent intensional characteristics further groups the members of the value-dependent entity group represented by each chain.

Characteristics in Action

Characteristics serve three distinct purposes. First, their values distinguish one entity family from another (i.e., extensional characteristics) and, within an entity family, one entity group from another (i.e., intensional characteristics). Entities may be grouped for the following reasons:

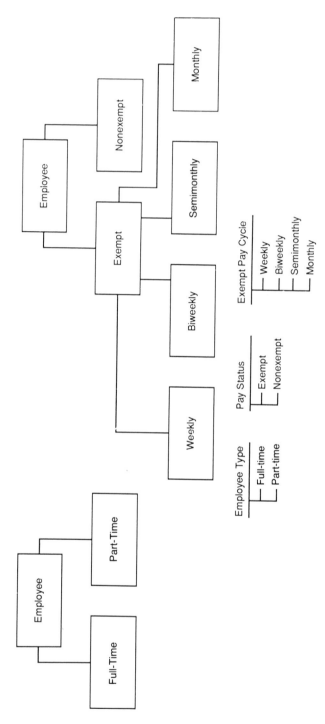

Exhibit VIII-2-3. Employee Family Classified by Two Characteristics

- When each individual value represents a different kind of processing, a characteristic determines which entity occurrence should be processed and in what manner. For example, the characteristic *pay status* has two values: exempt and nonexempt. Employees who are coded exempt do not get paid for overtime; those coded nonexempt are paid for overtime.
- The entire family or a group within the family must be sequenced for reporting purposes, based on the values of one or more characteristics. Characteristics separate entities into groups and, as an extreme case, separate one entity from another.

Second, characteristics are used to name entity groups. Although characteristics are usually manifested as coded attributes, these codes represent some condition, state, or test result that has an English-language word or phrase associated with it. The word or phrase that is associated with each characteristic value, alone or together with the value name of one or more other characteristics. It also provides the name of the entity group that contains the members with that particular set of characteristic values. For example, two named groups from Exhibit VIII-2-3 are exempt employees and nonexempt employees.

Third, characteristics are surrogates for, and usually the keys or identifiers of, larger data groups that depend entirely on the presence of those characteristics. In many cases, each characteristic value implies the need for one set of attributes or group of data elements that is unique to it—one specific data group per characteristic value. These data groups are also known as records or functional dependency groups.

As illustrated in Exhibit VIII-2-4, the business data required for nonexempt employees must include data that determines how overtime is to be compensated (e.g., according to an agreed-on work week, agreed-on work hours per day, agreed-on work start and end times, rates per overtime hour, and rates per shift). Generally, these groups of data items (elements) are associated with the characteristic value itself or on a unique sequence of characteristic values.

Defining Characteristics

Data models group entities by characteristics to form families and groups within families. Each entity must have a set of distinguishing characteristics

---

Nonexempt   =
- Pay status—nonexempt
- Agreed-on work week
- Agreed-on work hours per day
- Agreed-on start time
- Agreed-on end time
- Rate per overtime hour
- Rate per shift

Exhibit VIII-2-4. Characteristic Value Used to Identify Additional Data

that determines its family and group membership. These characteristics form a data equation:

entity = f (characteristic 1, characteristic 2, . . ., characteristic n)

The definition of each characteristic describes its function, its role in identifying family or group membership, and the aspect of the entity it represents. The definition describes the reason for the characteristic and where its values originate. A suggested form for the definition of a characteristic follows:

The values of the characteristic (*name of characteristic*) delineate the (*item being delineated*) aspect of the entity (*name of entity*). The list of values of the characteristic (*name of characteristic*) are:

1. Code value—English equivalent.
2. Code value—English equivalent.
3. Code value—English equivalent.
4. Code value—English equivalent.

.

.

.

n. Code value—English equivalent.

The following statement should be added when the characteristic is dependent on another characteristic:

The characteristic (*name of characteristic*) further qualifies the characteristic (*name of characteristic*),

where

(*name of the characteristic*) is the English name of the list of values,
(*item being delineated*) states the aspect of the entity that is being
described, and
(*name of entity*) is the name of the entity family.

The following is an example of a characteristic definition:

The values of the characteristic *pay cycle* delineate the frequency of the exempt employee paycheck issuance aspect of the entity employee. The list of values of the characteristic *pay cycle* are:

1. w—weekly paycheck.
2. b—biweekly paycheck.
3. s—semimonthly paycheck.
4. m—monthly paycheck.

The characteristic *pay cycle* further qualifies the characteristic *pay status*.

CONCLUSION

Many techniques have been developed to organize data. Entity-relationship data modeling is such a technique for organizing and grouping data. To use this method effectively, however, familiarity with the concepts of classification, entities, and entity characteristics is essential. The terminology adapted from classification science is highly specialized, but when used to define and apply these concepts it can be clearly understood. By becoming thoroughly conversant with this terminology and these concepts and by using them when creating and discussing data models, an organization can begin to understand and take the necessary steps that are involved in classi-fication and data modeling.

Section IX
Data Center Management

TOP MANAGEMENT in most organizations today insists that each and every department justify its continued existence. IS managers have to demonstrate their contribution to the organization's bottom line. They must illustrate the efficient performance of the data center function so as to demonstrate their management capabilities and to counter the company's arguments for outsourcing.

One way of documenting the performance of the data center is by developing a data center reporting system. These reports provide IS managers with the information they need to highlight the strengths and weaknesses of the department and to keep track of the critical resources the department needs to operate properly. Chapter IX-1, "Data Center Reporting Systems," describes a reporting system that can, with a little work, be extended to the entire IS department.

One task that is increasingly falling to the IS management team is that of maintaining computer equipment in user departments—that means microcomputers and the peripherals attached to them. Although the mission of all IS departments is to help clients use microcomputers productively, they may also be assigned the responsibility of ensuring that the computers themselves work effectively. A hardware maintenance program helps the IS department guarantee that its clients, the business users, will not be interrupted by frequent or inconvenient hardware failures. Chapter IX-2, "Microcomputer Hardware Maintenance," provides the IS support professional with an overview of the available hardware maintenance options to choose from depending on the individual organization's needs and budget.

One area ripe for productivity improvement is tape management. This area is often labor-intensive compared with other parts of the data center. In many organizations, tape operations have not changed in 20 years.

The opportunity to address the issue of productivity emerged with the availability of cartridge tape technology. Automated cartridge loaders and robotic storage and retrieval systems have increased efficiency but they require a substantial capital investment. Chapter IX-3, "Tape Workstation Management," presents a software-based methodology to further capitalize on the benefits of tape technology.

IX-1

Data Center Reporting Systems

John P. Murray

THE IS MANAGER faces an ongoing challenge in managing the data center as a business function; changing business conditions have caused that need to become more urgent in recent years. There are two reasons for this increased urgency. First, the available processing hardware and software options have proliferated dramatically. Second, the move to reduce—or at least control—data center expense as effectively as possible has become a primary issue in many installations.

To respond to the pressure to manage more effectively, the IS manager must become a more adept business manager. In addition to increasing their business skills, all managers must demonstrate the success of their management. The manager's ability to prove that effective management is in place must be backed with factual data. The management of the function must identify instances of improved performance and use that information to strengthen the position of the department. Managers who do not have this ability or who are not willing to begin the process of moving to such an environment are in a vulnerable position.

DEVELOPING A REPORTING SYSTEM

The purpose of a reporting system is to document what is occurring in the data center. These reports are used to highlight areas of strength and weakness and to lay the basis for changes to improve the environment. The reports should:

- Document current data center resource use and develop a historical record of what occurs with resource use for a period of at least a year.
- Develop additional material that can be used as the basis for forecasting anticipated changes in the processing environment. This process should provide the ability to make estimates for at least 18 months with a high level of confidence and for up to 36 months with a reasonable level of confidence.

The intention should be not to provide definitive answers for the future but to provide information for considering the various options as the requirements of the business and the technology change. No one can completely forecast what will occur. However, having a clear understanding of where the data center is at a given time provides the basis for making reasonable judgments about the future.

Developing and using a reporting system effectively (i.e., the appropriate reports are in place and are regularly produced and distributed) has an immediate positive effect by enabling the IS manager to move to factual rather than emotional assessments of the service provided by the data center. So many people throughout the organization depend on the services of the data center that any disruption in service can create considerable difficulty. When problems arise, the actual degree of the difficulty can, however, become distorted. Unless the manager can produce accurate information about the performance of the system, it is almost impossible to counter criticisms that the system is always down or too slow. Even if the reports show that the service levels are unacceptable, it is far better to work from facts instead of emotion.

Baselining

Reporting systems should be designed to generate reports that are consistent, timely, and structured toward the development of a historical data base. The data base is used to track performance and to provide material for the development of forecasting models. Those models can eventually be used to manage the growth of data center hardware requirements over time.

The first stage in the overall process should be to assess the current performance of the data center. The assessment should consist of identifying the current use of the installed hardware resources as well as the level—if any—of excess processing capacity available. Then, the requirement for a reporting system can be addressed.

In identifying the current use of installed hardware resources, the idea is to develop the processing baseline—that is, the current level of demand on data center resources. This is the basis for identifying any usable excess capacity in the system. This process can be used to find a realistic processing level—that is, the highest level of processing load the system can accommodate before being adversely affected. The material developed should enable the IS manager to plan for and provide increased processing power as required and before the demand becomes critical.

If there is no reporting system currently in place, the task is to build a system that meets the needs of the installation. If a system is in place, it should be reviewed to determine whether the data is correct and whether it is sufficiently comprehensive. Circumstances change, and what may have been an adequate or even a useful reporting system several years ago may not be appropriate today. If the data center already has such a system, the first step should be to identify what, if any, of the existing system can be incorporated in the new system.

Data center reporting systems should be implemented with the needs of both the data center and the organization in mind. The system should be designed to provide sufficient detail to adequately inform anyone with an interest in the information. However, there should not be so much detail that the reports become difficult to understand and use.

Two sets of reports are necessary. One should be a set of nontechnical reports that can be readily understood by data center customers as well as by senior management. The second set should contain more detail and have a technical orientation. These reports are used by the IS management and the technical support group. These reports can then be used to analyze current resource use to establish a basis for the development of the forecasting models. The intent is to be in position to present well-documented, factual cases for increasing the data center hardware resources when the need arises.

The second set of reports also provides details that are used to fine-tune or optimize the performance of existing hardware. In addition, the reports provide information the manager needs to make the adjustments required to meet changing processing demands. Those demands can include increased resources to accommodate new applications or for increased transactions in existing systems.

WHAT ITEMS TO MEASURE

Reports should be comprehensive and practical. Effective mainframe measurement packages can produce extensive data about use of a variety of resource components. Initially, it is advisable and usually more effective to capture as much data as practical, because it is likely that at least some crucial questions will not be apparent in the beginning of the process. Having plenty of data from the start provides the ability to answer questions when they arise. Over time, the amount of data required and the number of reports produced can be reduced as appropriate.

The data required depends on the particular requirements of a given installation. However, a basic set of reports is necessary for most installations. The following sections describe these core reports and their functions. In addition, an example of each report, currently being used to manage a medium-sized data center in an insurance operation is included.

Mainframe Use

This report is illustrated in Exhibit IX-1-1. A basic tenet of any data center operation must be to ensure adequate processing resources. The term *adequate* is understood to mean sufficient resources not only to handle current processing demands without stress but to allow for temporary increases in the processing load.

Many data centers work to maximize the use of all resources. These installations routinely operate as close to 100% of capacity as possible. Although this may seem a sound business practice, it can be a shortsighted approach. Because the expense associated with managing such an installation is inordinately high, the time employees spend trying to juggle resources offsets any savings gained from delaying the acquisition of appropri-

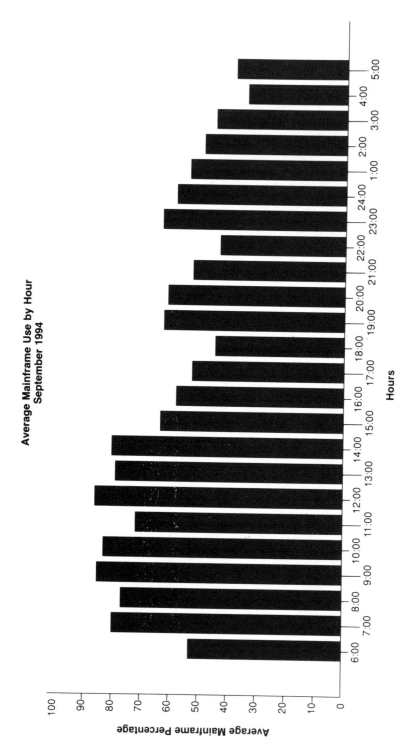

Exhibit IX-1-1. Sample Mainframe Use Report

ate hardware. The problems of scheduling, reruns, shifting disk storage loads, and poor service levels usually exceed any savings in hardware expense.

Because the expense associated with an increase in hardware is easily calculated, avoiding that cost can be seen as controlling expenses. However, the cost of operating too close to maximum capacity generates unnecessary additional effort and perhaps some overtime costs. These costs can have a substantial effect on the data center.

These reports focus on the total availability of the system. The availability of the system should be reported monthly. Current hardware is sufficiently sophisticated that the mean time to failure for most components is measured in years. Although hardware failure should no longer be an important availability issue, it does occur.

Other items that affect the availability of hardware resources include operating software failures, operator error, applications program difficulties, and power failure. Even though sound data center management can go a long way toward mitigating these failures, they do occur occasionally, even in the most effectively managed installations. They should be addressed when they occur. Recognition and acknowledgment of these failures enables the IS manager to present an accurate picture of what has occurred as it relates to established service levels and to the availability of hardware resources. In addition, highlighting these problems helps to ensure that they receive appropriate attention.

Online Processing Environment

Reports here indicate online system response times (see Exhibit IX-1-2) and overall online system availability (see Exhibit IX-1-3). Consistent processing response times should be maintained across the entire online network. Like hardware availability, the response times must fall within the agreed-upon service levels. Establishing and maintaining online response-time standards should be mandatory, and a reporting system can summarize these times to enforce or demonstrate compliance with the standards. Response-time requirements should weigh the legitimate concerns of the departments that will use the system against the expense associated with increasing the speed of the system. The goal should be to meet the actual needs of the users in the most cost-effective manner possible.

Usually, the affected departments attempt to obtain the fastest response times possible. Should a standard response time of less than two seconds 80% of the time be established when three seconds would be adequate? The issue may seem minor, but the consequences can be significant. First, there may be a considerable expense associated with the delivery of faster response time—it may, for example, require a CPU upgrade.

Another concern is the data center's ability to maintain fast response times as the processing load grows. Less than two seconds response time at least 80% of the time may be easily accomplished at the moment, but what about six months from now? Once the user community becomes accustomed to a certain level of response time, it will be less accepting of anything slower.

Region	Transactions	Average Second	Less Than 1 Second	Less Than 2 Seconds	Less Than 5 Seconds	Less Than 10 Seconds	More Than 10 Seconds
California	682,254	1.2	54.2%	90.7%	99.5%	99.9%	0.1%
Freeport	1,137,683	1.0	65.8%	93.5%	99.6%	99.9%	0.1%
Indiana	214,999	1.5	56.5%	85.4%	98.4%	99.3%	0.7%
Northwest	683,365	1.0	67.0%	93.8%	99.4%	99.9%	0.1%
Southwest	490,749	1.9	32.9%	65.0%	92.5%	97.1%	2.9%
Midwest Claims Park Center	197,861	1.1	64.5%	91.0%	99.2%	99.8%	0.2%
Midwest Premium and Home Office	428,721	0.3	94.5%	98.0%	99.6%	99.8%	0.2%
Total	3,835,632	1.1	62.7%	89.5%	98.6%	99.5%	0.5%

Exhibit IX-1-2. Sample Online System Response Time Report

Online System Availability Summary
September 1994

Region	Claims		Premium	
	Weekdays **Goal = 98%**	**Weekends** **Goal = 75%**	**Weekdays** **Goal = 98%**	**Weekends** **Goal = 75%**
California	99.83%	100.00%	99.83%	100.00%
Freeport	99.92%	100.00%	99.92%	100.00%
Indiana	99.94%	100.00%	N/A	N/A
Northwest	99.94%	100.00%	N/A	N/A
Southwest	96.69%	100.00%	N/A	N/A
Midwest Claims Park Center	99.94%	100.00%	N/A	N/A
Midwest Premium and Home Office	99.94%	100.00%	99.94%	100.00%
	Weekday Claim Average 99.38%	Weekend Claim Average 100.00%	Weekday Premium Average 99.90%	Weekend Premium Average 100.00%

Availability Standards
Weekdays Monday–Friday 6:00 AM—8:00 PM CST
Weekdays Saturday–Sunday 6:00 AM—7:00 PM CST

Exhibit IX-1-3. Sample Online System Availability Report

Transaction Rates—Batch and Online

Reports on transaction rates must distinguish between batch and online processing because the demands and management techniques for each are different. In addition, the interests of those who rely on the different production environments are not necessarily the same. Because of its higher level of visibility and the continuous increase in its use throughout the IS community, the online processing environment usually gets the most attention in many data centers.

Transaction rate reports should help the manager determine whether the applications development group is receiving sufficient processing resources. The two aspects of online processing that require attention are the immediate, daily entry of data and production of reports to operate the business and the longer-term concerns of the work carried out by the members of the applications development group.

Concern about meeting the demands of the applications development group should involve both the online and the batch processing environments. In many installations, a large portion of the testing for development is carried out in batch mode. However, although the batch environment is usually the more stable and therefore easier to manage, the IS manager must ensure that a reasonable portion of both the online and the batch processing resources are consistently available to the development group.

Jobs Processed

Both batch and online jobs processed should be addressed by the reporting system (see Exhibit IX-1-4). Growth of the mainframe processing load often occurs subtly. Although there may be little noticeable growth from day to day, over time the processing load is likely to grow considerably. The reason is that activities that affect mainframe resources occur simultaneously in many areas. In this circumstance, attempting to identify and monitor all occurrences without some automated system is all but impossible. The assistance of an automated system cannot obviate all surprises, but the system can provide the ability to track the areas of growth and measure what is occurring.

Growth in the processing load can come from any number of sources. Online transaction rates can rise as business increases or as new or enhanced versions of existing systems are implemented. The testing load from the applications development group may increase. Data base processing systems require increased hardware resources compared to non–data base systems. That circumstance is even more severe in installations that allow substantial user department inquiries.

The trend toward data base processing, coupled with the increased use of data center hardware resources by people in other departments, will continue to grow. A manager cannot afford to be forced to request an unplanned increase in hardware resources. The effective monitoring of the hardware resources can help the IS manager avoid such an unpleasant circumstance.

Batch and Online Jobs Processed by Month

	January	December	November	October	September	August	6-Month Average
Production	6519	4301	3930	4263	3734	3978	4454
Model	1480	1138	1371	1792	1556	1388	1454
Test	811	268	291	224	159	139	315
Online Processing	5340	4902	4505	5022	4264	4574	4768
Programmer Testing	6134	4673	4816	5302	4651	3527	4850
Production Control	—	—	—	670	278	435	—
Systems Software	4314	3140	3258	3648	2632	1875	3144
Nonconforming Job Names	701	915	2785	1517	2728	4376	2170
Totals	25,299	19,337	21,477	22,438	20,002	20,292	21,474
Production Reruns	147	153	108	111	101	99	119
Production Rerun Percentage	2.3%	3.5%	2.7%	2.6%	2.7%	2.4%	2.7%
Abnormal Termination	1563	1406	1780	1637	1390	1392	1528

Exhibit IX-1-4. Sample Job Accounting and Reporting System

| | September 1994 Production Reruns | | |
System	Number of Jobs	Elapsed Time (HH:MM:SS)	CPU Time (HH:MM:SS)	Lines Printed
Premium	38	19:13:29	03:10:10	219
Claims	77	00:54:03	00:02:31	384
Underwriting	11	00:14:53	00:00:15	636
Stats	02	01:39:40	00:13:95	0
Commissions	15	01:27:12	00:01:42	27641
Accounts Payable	06	00:24:07	00:01:12	0.
Agency	02	00:24:45	00:02:00	138
Loss Ratios	02	00:02:49	00:00:00	0
Total	153	24:20:58	03:28:35	29018

Exhibit IX-1-5. Sample Report on Job Reruns

Application Program Tests and Compiles

Two aspects of the capture and recording of data associated with the applications testing environment are of interest to the IS manager: the capability to identify the amount of resource being used to meet the demands of the development section and to decide whether the demands are growing, and the capability to provide the development manager with data about the testing and compiling activity in the section. In many installations, it becomes a habit to use the data center resources to debug source code. The programmer compiles a program, corrects the identified errors, and recompiles again until the code is clean. Spending time desk-checking the program before compiling saves machine cycles and provides the programmer with an improved understanding of the code.

Jobs That Must Be Rerun

The primary purpose of the job reruns report (see Exhibit IX-1-5), unless the incidence of reruns is high, should not be to address the area of the resources used to accommodate those reruns but to address other issues. The first issue concerns the cause of the reruns. The IS manager should question why those applications are being rerun. As that question is pursued, such topics as job control language (JCL) errors, inadequate operator instructions, incorrect dates, or other management issues arise. As those issues are recognized, the appropriate steps can be taken to make the necessary corrections.

The topic of production reruns is one that must have more than a cursory examination. There are several pragmatic reasons for paying attention to the issue. The place to begin is with a precise definition of what constitutes a rerun. For the purpose of this chapter, reruns are production jobs processed more than their scheduled number of times in any given period of time.

Once the guidelines for the recording of reruns have been established, a monthly examination of the details of the rerun reports should be conducted. The examination may reveal rerun patterns; some jobs create substantial problems. The more likely causes for the reruns include:

- Incorrect data entry.
- Weak or nonexistent program edits.
- Programming errors.
- Inadequate operating documentation.
- Incorrect JCL or operator actions.

With the detail from the rerun reports, the causes of those reruns that are creating processing difficulty can be found and corrected. Not only does this improve the data center operation, it can in time provide the basis for an improvement in the quality of the IS department's products. The IS manager should develop a process to track and correct those production jobs that consistently create rerun problems.

Presenting the Data

Once the required data has been identified, a process can be established to capture that data. The next issue is the method of presentation of the data. It is advisable to move the raw data from the job accounting system to a microcomputer-based system (e.g., Lotus) that allows for the presentation of the material in graphic form. Using this approach puts the material in a format easily understood by nontechnical personnel. It also provides an opportunity for the data center to be seen as taking a businesslike approach to the issue.

DEVELOPING SERVICE LEVELS

When managers are confident that the resource use data is accurate, they should then focus on the issue of service levels. Working with the use data the IS manager can decide on a set of reasonable service levels to which the department can make a commitment.

Obviously, care is required in this area. The agreed-upon service levels must be readily attainable under typical working conditions. As part of the agreement, the IS manager must be willing to take responsibility for the service levels that are not met. When that occurs, the manager has to identify the cause of the problem and take the required steps to keep the circumstance from recurring.

When agreement on the content of the service levels has been reached, the performance of the IS department concerning those levels must be published monthly. In an operation as vulnerable as the data center, that circumstance must be anticipated. The goal is not to overemphasize levels that are missed occasionally. The issue is that management is willing to acknowledge the problem when it arises and to show the commitment to rectify it.

Those who use the services of the data center are sometimes skeptical about the data center's concern with issues that bear upon their work. The effective use of service levels can help to improve that aspect of the data center services.

CONCLUSION

Too often IS managers find themselves caught in a trap when it comes to providing the resources required to maintain the necessary level of processing power. The management of the installation may know—or have a strong feeling—that increased power will be required. However, it sometimes happens that there is little substantial evidence upon which to base that feeling.

IS managers thus become caught in the unfortunate position of pleading for increased processing power, not realizing that current hardware resources may be completely consumed. When this occurs, there is an immediate need to take some action. The IS manager must maintain appropriate control of the hardware resources at all times. Providing a continuing analysis of the use of the resources, and sound estimates of when the requirement for additions is likely to occur, is simply efficient business practice. A well-developed data center reporting system is imperative for this reason.

Having kept the appropriate management informed of the status of data center use does not, of course, ensure support. The important point is that IS management has fulfilled a responsibility to report on the data center through the production and distribution of these reports.

Successful management of the data center is contingent upon having sufficient information to understand events as they occur. The use of that information to monitor the progress of the function and to plan for future growth improves both the actual management of the IS department and its image.

IX-2

Microcomputer Hardware Maintenance

Gilbert Held

FOR MOST IS DEPARTMENT clients, the microcomputer has become an indispensable tool for getting their jobs done effectively. Some organizations use microcomputers to provide access to customer billing records, sales, and marketing data. Other firms extend the use of microcomputers to the execution of accounting and payroll programs. Still other uses of microcomputers range in scope from terminal emulation for minicomputers and mainframe access to computer-aided design. A hardware failure that results in an inability to use a microcomputer can therefore have a negative impact on the well-being of the entire organization.

In many organizations, it is—at least to some degree—the responsibility of the IS department to ensure that its clients' microcomputers are operating efficiently. The key to microcomputer availability is hardware maintenance. When problems arise with an organization's microcomputers, the support department should be able to react quickly and effectively. The IS department should have in place a well-thought-out methodology or contractual agreement for repairing or replacing defective equipment. Several hardware maintenance options are available, and knowing the advantages and disadvantages of each option can help support professionals select the approach that best satisfies the requirements of their particular organization. This understanding will in turn enable the department to provide a high level of microcomputer operational capability consistent with client needs and budgetary constraints.

Two hardware maintenance options are available for repairing or replacing defective microcomputers: local or third party. Within each general type of hardware maintenance, the support professional can consider several specific methods then select the one that is most appropriate for the organization's operational requirements and budgetary constraints, as well as for the technical knowledge of its end users. This chapter examines the following categories of hardware maintenance and the methods used in each category:

- Locally performed maintenance:
  —Diagnostic analysis and component replacement.
  —Repair by return.

- Manufacturer and third-party performed maintenance:
  —On-site service.
  —On-call, on-site service.

LOCALLY PERFORMED HARDWARE MAINTENANCE

Two methods are used to perform hardware maintenance at the local level. The first method, diagnostic analysis and component replacement, requires that the organization have both trained personnel as well as either an inventory of spare parts or access to sources that can provide required components within a reasonable period of time. The second method, repair by return, may require that the organization have an inventory of spare computers or major components.

Diagnostic Analysis and Component Replacement

Although many microcomputer failures are easily identified (e.g., a hard disk crash), the cause of other failures may not be easy to isolate. For example, a disk controller failure may appear to be a hard disk failure, and a memory parity failure on an adapter card may be noticeable only when software accesses the memory location at which there is a failure. Although a client may report a problem to the support department or help line, the cause of the problem may be unknown and the use of diagnostic software may be required to identify it.

Both computer manufacturers and third-party vendors market a number of diagnostic software programs that support staff personnel can use to isolate failed components. Some programs are limited to providing an analysis of diskette and hard disk drives. Other programs are more comprehensive and can test disk and video controllers, monitors, and on-board and adapter memory, as well as examine the settings of board-level interrupts to detect the presence of any interrupt conflicts resulting from the use of a mixture of hardware products. This type of sophisticated diagnostic program enables technically trained support personnel to isolate hardware problems down to the chip level.

Once the problem has been identified, a predefined policy should govern how repairs are conducted. If the organization either stocks spare parts down to the chip level or is capable of ordering parts at that level, chip-level component replacement can be considered, provided trained personnel with a background in electronic component replacement are available. Otherwise, the support department may elect to repair by replacing major components; for example, some would replace an entire adapter board even though the problem was determined to be a faulty chip on the board.

Repairing boards by replacing defective chips requires identifying the failed chip and replacing it with a functionally equivalent chip. Otherwise, microprocessor access to memory may result in a slowdown of information retrieval from memory or, more seriously, in random read failures. If the IS department decides that repairs should be conducted at a board replacement level, it is not necessary to determine which chip on the board is faulty. The board that contains the defective chip—or more than one faulty chip—would simply be replaced with a new board. In general, board-level replacement is commonly referred to as component replacement.

In deciding whether to replace parts at the chip or component level, the support professional must also consider the mixture of equipment at the particular location.

Many organizations have purchased microcomputers on a piecemeal basis. This purchasing practice may have resulted in, for example, 20 IBM PCs, 30 AST Bravos, 50 IBM PC ATs, 50 Compaq DeskPro 386s, and 50 IBM PS/2 Model 55s being installed. Each of these microcomputers uses different memory chips, and four of the five types of computers use different video and disk controllers. In this situation, the decision to perform either chip- or component-level replacement would require stocking or obtaining a large number of spare parts. If the microcomputers were used for critical operations in which minimizing downtime is a crucial issue, the support department should probably consider carrying an inventory not only of spare parts but of replacement computers as well.

Stocking one or more spare computers provides several options for the selection of maintenance methods. For example, the need to stock spare parts may be reduced or eliminated by stocking one or a few spare microcomputers. The decision to do this should depend on a comparison of the cost of stocking spare parts for a number of different microcomputers with the cost of stocking at least one spare microcomputer for each type in use in the organization.

Because most organizations experience a ½%-to-1% microcomputer failure rate, one spare computer should be stocked for every 100 to 200 installed microcomputers in the organization or at least one of each type of installed microcomputer. The cost of stocking those spare computers should be estimated on the basis of a configuration that would satisfy the minimum needs of the maximum configuration in use. For example, if some microcomputers have 100M-byte hard disks but only 60M bytes are typically used, it would be necessary to stock only a spare computer with a 60M-byte hard disk. In actuality, because spare computers are to be used only on a temporary basis, it may even be feasible to stock spares that provide a level of support below what clients are used to. However, doing so may not be politically expedient, especially if a manager's 386-based computer with a VGA monitor is replaced by an old IBM PC XT with a CGA monitor.

Stocking spare parts or components and stocking spare computers can also supplement each other. This approach is usually more practical in organizations that have a large installed base of microcomputers. In any case, even organizations that do not have skilled technicians on staff should consider stocking external computer components that are easily interchanged with failed devices. Such external components include video displays, keyboards, printers, plotters, external modems, and external disk drives. Stocking such major components enables the solution of many problems without necessitating the installation of a spare computer.

Repair by Return

The second method of locally performed hardware maintenance is often referred to as box maintenance. This is because the repair of inoperative equipment is accomplished by boxing or packaging the failed computer and shipping or transporting it to a computer store or to the manufacturer. Because most IS clients cannot afford to be without the use of their microcomputers for the extended time required to have repairs made by the manufacturer or by a third party (in this chapter, the term *third party* refers to maintenance performed by a vendor other than the manufacturer of the equipment), it is typically necessary to keep a larger number of spare computers on hand with this approach to hardware maintenance. However, stocking spares for major external components that are easily replaced (e.g., keyboards, video displays, and similar devices) enables the client to continue to use the microcomputer and not tie up a spare computer while the component is out for repairs.

Exhibit IX-2-1 compares the major activities associated with both the diagnostic analysis and the repair by return methods of locally performed hardware maintenance. Most of the entries in the exhibit are self-explanatory, but two areas require elaboration and are discussed in the following sections.

Stocking Spare Components. Stocking spare components can be accomplished at three levels: chip, internal component, and external component. Chip-level components require skilled personnel with an electronics background to isolate a failed chip, remove it, and replace it with a spare. The internal component level refers to adapter boards, diskette drives, hard disks, and internal modems. Such devices can be removed and replaced with spares by staff members who know how to open the system unit of a microcomputer, remove adapter boards and disk devices, and insert their replacements. The external component level refers to such external components as keyboards, display units, external disk drives, modems, printers, and other devices that are cabled to a connector at the rear of the system unit of the

Activity	Diagnostic Analysis and Component Replacement	Repair by Return
Trained Technician Required	Yes	No
Spare Component Stocking:		
• Chip level	Optional*	No
• Internal component level	Optional*	No
• Major component level	Optional*	Optional but recommended
Stock Spare Computers	Optional	Yes
Spare Computer Stock Rate	½% to 1%	1% to 2%

Note:
*At least one of the three starred options must be implemented.

Exhibit IX-2-1. Comparison of Hardware Maintenance Methods

microcomputer. Replacing external components involves the disconnection and connection of cables and does not require the system unit of the micro-computer to be opened. In many cases, therefore, clients themselves are capable of replacing external components.

Spare Computer Stock Rate. The repair by return method of hardware maintenance requires that a greater percentage of spare computers be stocked than for the diagnostic analysis method—in Exhibit IX-2-1, this is noted as the spare computer stock rate. This is because repairing by boxing and shipping can result in a delay of several days to a month until the repaired computer or computer component is returned. If the organization performs repairs by return, a second computer could malfunction while the first computer is outside the organization. This would not happen if the first computer were repaired by chip-level or internal component-level replace-ment. Because the computer would be back in operation faster when repairs are performed on site, the spare computer stock rate could be reduced as compared with the rate required when repairs are made by shipping com-puters to a vendor.

One important area that must be considered if the support department decides to stock spare computers is the time required to tailor the computer to the specific requirements of a user. Preloading a core set of software that represents the word processing, data base, communications, and spreadsheet programs used by the majority of clients can substantially reduce the time required to make the computer operational. However, it is still more than likely that the client will require some help transferring backup copies of data files to the new system. Therefore, in addition to determining a spare computer stock rate, the IS department must also consider the support re-quired to make a spare computer operative with respect to the requirements of individual clients.

MANUFACTURER AND THIRD-PARTY MAINTENANCE

When the identification of a failed computer and its packaging for ship-ment is performed by members of the support department, it is usually clas-sified as locally performed maintenance—even though another organization actually performs the repairs. Third-party maintenance in general refers to either on-site service or on-call, on-site service. Both of these methods of hardware maintenance involve an employee of an organization other than the manufacturer working at the organization to repair or replace equipment.

On-Site Service

On-site service refers to a computer manufacturer or a third-party em-ployee being assigned to work at an individual organization. This method of hardware maintenance was established by hardware vendors to support large data processing installations that could not tolerate any significant amount of downtime. On-site service was justified by the large investment in equip-ment and the necessity to rapidly repair or replace computer components by vendor-trained technicians.

In a microcomputer environment, the use of on-site service is limited to organizations that have a large amount of microcomputers at one location or at several locations within a city or suburban area. Companies with 200 or more microcomputers can justify the expense associated with paying a manufacturer or third-party vendor for the services of a full-time employee. Some vendors may charge a flat yearly fee for on-site service; others may base their fee on the number of computers and other equipment requiring support.

A service and support contract may offer a wider degree of support. This type of contract can be issued to expand the on-site support of contractor personnel to nonmaintenance tasks. Such personnel are usually assigned the job of loading and configuring new hardware, moving local area network workstations, and repairing failed equipment.

The key advantage of on-site service is the immediate availability of a trained and knowledgeable specialist at the client site. This can be extremely important if the organization is located in a remote area in which it is difficult to hire appropriate personnel. In such instances, an on-site service contract may enable a contractor to rotate personnel to the remote location to provide direct support during the life of the service contract.

Although the rotation of employees is usually not desirable because of the time required for an outside employee to become familiar with the organization, in certain situations it may be the only practical method of obtaining on-site service. For example, one government agency has several hundred computers in a record processing facility located in a cave more than 60 miles from the nearest city. To satisfy its requirement for on-site service, the agency agreed to accept a new service technician every 30 days because the vendor providing on-site support could not find an employee willing to relocate to such a rural area. In this situation, the vendor sends employees on a 30-day per diem temporary assignment.

The primary disadvantage of on-site service is its cost. A person hired by the organization at a salary level of $30,000 per year would probably cost more than $100,000 per year when obtained on a contractual basis from a computer manufacturer or a third-party vendor. Because of the high cost of on-site service, most organizations that require the use of technical expertise contract for on-call, on-site service.

On-Call, On-Site Service

In comparison to on-site service, in which a computer manufacturer or third-party employee is assigned to work at the organization on a permanent basis, on-call, on-site service results in manufacturer or third-party support arriving within a predefined period of time after receipt of a service call. Another difference between on-site and on-call, on-site service concerns the expenses associated with each type of service. On-site service is usually billed at a fixed monthly or yearly rate regardless of the actual amount of work performed by the computer manufacturer or third-party employees. On-site, on-call service is billed on an hourly basis, reflecting the number of hours spent by computer manufacturer or third-party employees traveling to the site, fixing a reported problem, and returning to their home base.

The actual hourly rate charged can vary, depending on the type of on-site, on-call service contracted for. For example, a service contract that guarantees response within four hours of receipt of a service call would probably be billed at a higher hourly rate than an agreement that requires the arrival of service personnel within 24 hours of receipt of a service call. Here, the specific type of on-call, on-site service selected should depend on the criticality of the functions performed by the microcomputers in the organization and on budgetary constraints. In many organizations, the stocking of a few spare computers can considerably reduce the cost of on-call, on-site service. This is because spare computers mounted on carts can serve as mobile backup to other computers and permit the required time for on-call service to be extended, reducing the hourly charge for service.

CONCLUSION

In summary, there are two major categories and four major methods of hardware maintenance available for the repair or replacement of inoperative personal computers. Some methods require the use of trained employees, while other methods rely on third-party support.

In selecting a method, the IS department manager and staff should first determine the level of service support required by the organization, the experience of the clients, and the funds available for hardware maintenance. Once this has been accomplished, each method should be matched against these requirements and the most appropriate approach chosen. In many instances there may not be one best method but a combination of methods that will provide the organization with the ability to maintain microcomputer hardware with a minimum of interrupted service to clients.

IX-3

Tape Workstation Management

Daniel F. Schulte
George W. Zobrist

THE SPEED AND RELIABILITY of magnetic tape processing has increased considerably over the years. For all practical purposes, a tape library can operate at one of three levels of efficiency: the standard environment, the working tape library, and the workstation. The standard environment offers the lowest level of efficiency because the tape media and hardware are stored in physically separate locations. The working library—the middle level of efficiency—is an additional library located near the tape drives. The workstation concept—the highest level of efficiency—subdivides a consolidated tape media and hardware environment into separate entities that have exclusive media and hardware resources. This chapter discusses the tape library in terms of these scenarios.

STANDARD TAPE LIBRARY AND OPERATIONS ENVIRONMENT

Although organizations may differ in their strategies for maintaining tape resources, tape processing tasks and problems are very similar. These similarities permit the definition of a standard tape library and operations environment.

The logical structure of a tape environment includes several separate entities. The two major items are the tape library and the tape drive area. Usually, the library and the tape drive area reside in different sections of the building. In addition to the main tape library, one or more off-premise library vaults might exist, mainly for backup and disaster recovery purposes.

A smaller entity of the logical structure of tape operations is the tape cleaning and evaluation area. This area handles tapes that have caused I/O errors or become otherwise unusable. In most operations, tapes must be transferred to areas outside the data center either because they must be stored in an off-premise storage vault or because information on the magnetic tape must be communicated to persons outside the organization. The data center also receives tapes returning from off-premise storage, satellite processing centers, and outside organizations. To effectively manage the movement of tapes, a shipping and receiving area usually acts as a go-between for the data center and outside sources.

Tape Operations Tasks

The daily routine of a tape operations environment includes many tasks. The primary responsibility of tape operations is to satisfy tape-mount requests so that the data on tape can be processed. Keeping track of what data is on each tape and which tapes are eligible for output is usually handled by an automated tape management system. This system may have hooks in the operating system that obtain control when a data set is created on tape, or it may be part of the operating system itself. At the point of control, all pertinent characteristics of the data are logged in a tape management catalog. A catalog inquiry can identify the contents of any tape in the library at any time.

Another daily task of tape operations is determining which tapes can be used for output. These scratch tapes contain either no data or data that has expired. The automated tape management system saves much time in this area because the tape management catalog contains the expiration date of each tape in the library. A common activity in many data centers is the prestaging of tapes. In some cases, advance notice is given that a certain job requires the use of specific tapes.

Many support tasks affect the time required to mount a tape; this chapter outlines a method to improve productivity by tuning tape operations. The emphasis is on minimizing nonproductive activities so that the tape operations environment becomes a highly tuned process.

THE WORKING LIBRARY

Practical experience has shown that after a data set has been created or accessed on tape, it is likely to be reused as input within the next 24 hours. Considering the overlap of automated applications, this is a reasonable assumption. Many applications have grown so large and complex that it is not uncommon for one application to use data created by another.

To accommodate this need, it is possible to create an additional tape library that resides very near the tape drives. This working library would be comparatively small in relation to the main library and would house only tapes that have been created or read within the last 24 hours. Under this scheme, a considerable percentage of the tapes requested for mounting would reside in this library. Because the working library is located next to the tape drives, less time is required for an operator to retrieve and mount the tape. Any reduction in tape mounting time enhances the efficiency of the entire data center.

To create a working tape library, operators must log the date and time of last use for each tape in the library. For environments without an automated tape management system, the manual effort required to track the date and time of last use would probably offset any potential gains in efficiency. On the other hand, most tape management systems feature the ability to post the last-use date and time after a tape is mounted.

With this feature, an operator immediately files a tape in the working library instead of in the main library after removing the tape from the drive. When a particular tape is requested for mounting, the operator tries to locate the tape first in the working library and then in the main library. Each day, a reverse pull is required to move any tapes not recently used back to the main library. A simple program can be written to identify these tapes in the tape management catalog.

After the initial installation, two actions are necessary to retain an efficient working library environment. First, each tape must be filed in the working library after removal from a tape drive. This allows faster access to the newly created data if the tape is requested within the next 24 hours. Second, the reverse pull must be run daily to purge the working library of older tapes. If this is not done regularly and punctually, the working library becomes an unwieldy second library. With daily tape movement between the two libraries, the working library should remain small and should increase the efficiency of tape operations.

THE WORKSTATION ENVIRONMENT

In medium- and large-scale tape environments, media and hardware are usually housed in separate areas of the data center because of building space constraints and security considerations. The introduction of cartridge tape technology to a data center, however, offers an opportunity to abandon the concept of separately housed media and hardware.

Compared with previous tape technology, the overall size of cartridge media and hardware is vastly reduced. This reduction allows most data centers to house both tape media and hardware in the space that previously contained only the tape hardware. The working library concept partially brought media and hardware together, but the cartridge technology allows full exploitation of this concept (in addition to improved tape processing reliability and performance). The benefits obtained from consolidating media and hardware are substantial; the most obvious is the time reduction for tape-mount requests.

Productivity Implications

The consolidation of media and hardware (i.e., libraries and tape drives) allows the formation of a new operations environment that was previously impractical for large tape operations. This new environment uses the concept of separate and independent tape workstations within the overall tape operation. The goal of the use of workstations is to reduce the nonproductive activities associated with mounting tapes. For example, in most operations, the majority of tape operator activity consists of walking to and from the tape library to search for requested media. The reduction of walking and searching results in lower mount-pending times and increased efficiency.

Another benefit is that the use of workstations addresses the problems involving the size of the tape library. Implementation of tape workstations can overcome the degraded efficiency resulting from consistent growth of the tape library. The workstation environment divides a consolidated media and hardware operation into distinct entities, each functioning as an independent tape operation with separate media and hardware resources. As a result, a large tape operation is broken down into two or more smaller tape operations.

Each operation division is assigned a number of tape drives and a range of tapes. The objective is to assign a tape attendant to a workstation and eliminate the need for that attendant to leave the workstation. In theory, a tape-mount request will never be issued for a volume that does not reside in the same workstation as the allocated tape drive.

Of paramount importance is the transparency of this scenario to both the user and the workstation attendant. There are no job control language requirements for the users and the attendant's productivity is increased because most tape-mount requests can be satisfied with a volume located within the workstation.

The benefits obtained from workstation implementation are substantial. First, tape volume retrieval and refiling time are reduced. Instead of the original large tape library, a tape attendant works with a smaller, personal library. The number of volume serials (volsers) that an attendant is responsible for is smaller, which reduces the time required to locate a volume.

Second, all volumes are housed within a short distance of the tape drives. This reduces the amount of walking required to retrieve a tape; in addition, the library becomes the easiest place to store a tape when it is not on a drive, decreasing the number of lost tapes and simplifying the identification of scratch tapes. Most important, workstations promote productivity and improve the quality of work life for tape attendants. These factors are no longer mutually exclusive.

Workstation Implementation

The implementation of workstations for a tape operation assumes that the required systems software packages are in place. (This software is discussed later in this chapter.) After installation of the required software, the workstation parameter library members must be created and maintained.

Creation of the parameter library members requires visualization of the tape operations area as logical clusters of tape drives and cartridges. Standard editing techniques are used to create the parameter library members that describe these clusters to the control software. An example and description of these members (e.g., TMOSCR00, TMONSM00) is provided later in this section.

In creating parameter library members, the first item of concern is the number of workstations required for a particular tape operation. The number of workstations depends on the amount of productivity expected from a tape attendant. This could vary greatly among organizations, depending on the emphasis placed on efficient tape activity. In addition, productivity levels vary among tape attendants, so the IS manager must exercise care when determining the number of workstations. After an appropriate number is determined, the IS manager simply divides it into the total number of volumes in the tape library to arrive at the number of volumes within a workstation.

The resulting physical environment should be arranged as follows:

- Each workstation should be arranged so that the average walking distance from any volser in a workstation to any drive in the same workstation is minimized.
- The number, length, and placement of media racks should remain consistent from one workstation to another so that an attendant who is moved to another workstation need not learn a new system.
- Workstations should be conveniently positioned so that one attendant could easily cover two workstations during slow periods or breaks.

These three concepts should guide the physical placement of resources to achieve the lowest possible mount-pending times.

When the IS manager has established a mental picture of the workstation environment, the parameter library members representing this picture must be constructed for each system CPU. At initialization, these parameters are scanned and a map of the environment is built in each CPU. In this way, each system has invisible boundaries defined for each workstation and will attempt to prevent tape activity from crossing those boundaries.

Example. The tape operations of a particular data center might have 32 tape drives and 20,000 tape volumes. After studying tape attendant productivity, the data center manager might decide to divide operations into two workstations.

To define this environment for the system, two parameter library members are required. The first member (TMOSCR00) defines the volser ranges for tape pools, and the second (TMONSM00) defines the mount rules to be used. The TMOSCR00 member separates the tape library into pools 1 and 2, ranging in volsers from 000000 through 009999 and from 010000 through 019999, respectively. This has basically divided the library into two entities, with 10,000 tapes each. The TMONSM00 member has divided the pool of tape drives into two sections containing 16 drives each. In addition, the rules have indicated that tape pool 1 belongs to the range of drives with addresses of 240 to 24F and that tape pool 2 belongs to the range of drives with addresses of 250 to 25F.

As discussed earlier, the allocation of tape resources is based on device priority for scratch tapes and volser priority for input tapes. For example, using the workstation assignment rules given for the sample environment, if a scratch tape were required for a job using drive 243, the system mount request message would be modified to indicate that a scratch from the pool 1 range should be mounted (i.e., a scratch tape with a volume serial in the range of 000000 through 009999). After a tape is mounted, checks are initiated to ensure that the tape was indeed available for scratch and that its volser was in the requested range. If the checks fail, the mounted tape is rejected and the modified system mount request message is reissued. In the same manner, scratch-mount requests are processed for the other 15 drives within workstation 1 (i.e., pool 1). Scratch requests for drives 250 to 25F are handled similarly, except that the mount request and mount verification are done from the pool 2 range (i.e., volsers 010000 through 019999).

A volser priority scheme is used for input tape requests. If a job required the use of volser 015000, drives 250 to 25F would have preference for allocation. Before allocation, the system scans the TMOSCR00 member parameter to determine which volume pool the volser belongs to. In this case, the volume pool is 2. A scan of the TMONSM00 member reveals that drives 250 to 25F are to be used for this pool of tapes. An attempt is then made to allocate a drive from this range. If no drives are available in this range, a drive outside the range is allocated. This is known as workstation crossover, which is discussed later in this section.

An operational option is required to increase the flexibility of workstations. This option deals with scratch tape availability. In the sample data center described, the tape library was divided into two pools. If a scratch tape from pool 1 were requested and one from pool 2 were mounted, the volume would be rejected and the mount message reissued. This check is valid for accidental mounting but does not address the possibility that no scratch tapes remain in pool 1. A quick resolution is needed to prevent the delay of tape activity on the 240 to 24F range of drives.

The solution is a system command that can enable or disable the volume serial range check for scratch mounts. In this situation, the check can be disabled to allow scratch mounting from any workstation. The volume serial check can remain disabled until scratches are available from pool 1. This option also permits a smaller data center to direct input tapes to the nearest drive without being required to manage multiple scratch pools. The option is most important to the tape librarian, who sees the potential catastrophe of depleting scratch tapes within a particular pool.

Workstation Crossover. In some situations, a tape volume must be mounted outside its own workstation. This is known as workstation crossover and must be minimized to ensure the highest possible efficiency. One source of crossover is tapes received from outside vendors or satellite data processing centers. This type of crossover is unavoidable, and it poses no major problem because such outside tapes usually represent a very small percentage of the total number of tape mounts.

Another source of crossover is the unnecessary extended use of the volume serial check disable. This permits scratch tapes from any workstation to be mounted and causes crossover later for multivolume files. If a file is created and spans multiple volumes that reside in different workstations, crossover occurs when this file is called for input. The first volume of the file will be requested from the proper workstation, but subsequent volumes may reside in other workstations because of the volume serial check disable when the file was created. With the volume serial check enabled, all multivolume files should reside on volsers from the same workstation.

The final type of crossover results from unit affinity and prevents the allocation of unneeded tape drives. If a user wishes to process multiple tape files serially, only one tape drive is needed at any given moment, so only one is allocated. This prevents idle drives from being unavailable to other users. Because of unit affinity, the first tape is requested from a drive in its workstation, but subsequent tapes could reside in any other workstation on the floor. Although unit affinity can cause crossover, it is a useful technique.

Systems Software Packages

CA-1/MVS (Tape Management System from Computer Associates International, Inc.) and MIM (Multi-Image Allocation Component of Multi-Image Manager from Legent Corp.) are established systems software packages that interface with the operating system to provide a mechanism for workstation capability. If either MIM or CA-1/MVS is absent from the operating environment, any substitute software or operating system user modifications that have been applied to achieve workstation capability must interface with the operating system in a similar manner.

CA-1/MVS, as distributed by the vendor, supports the pooling of tapes through data set name or job name. By modifying the CA-1/MVS source code, management can establish the capability to pool tapes by tape drive device address. When CA-1/MVS is initialized on each system, the workstation boundaries are mapped out in each system. These mapping tables are then referenced by CA-1/MVS and MIM for each incident of tape activity.

The extent of the CA-1/MVS role for workstations appears very simple. Each time a scratch tape is requested on a particular drive address, CA-1/MVS scans the workstation map to see which pool of tapes corresponds to that drive. After a pool is determined, the system tape-mount request message is modified to reflect the proper pool of tapes. CA-1/MVS also ensures that multivolume data sets reside on volumes that all belong to the same pool. Any subsequent tapes mounted for a spanned data set must belong to the same pool as that of the first volume of the data set.

The role of MIM in the workstation environment is more complex. An optional user exit controls the allocation of tape drives. The exit receives a list of devices eligible for allocation and is permitted to trim the list, if desired. When a request for an input tape is issued, the exit scans the workstation mapping tables and uses the specified input volume serial number to determine which tape drive addresses are applicable. The eligible device list is then trimmed to exclude those that are not applicable for the specified volume serial number. The trimmed list is then returned to MIM so it can select one of the remaining devices for allocation. If the list has been trimmed to nothing (i.e., if no drives are available in that workstation), MIM allocates a drive from the original list that was passed to the exit.

For drives that are requested for output, the exit does not modify the original eligible device list. In this manner, regular system device selection occurs for output tapes. The eligible device list is modified only when an output data set requires multiple tape drives. The first drive is chosen by system device selection, but the exit attempts to select subsequent drives from the same workstation that the first drive resided on.

The final component of workstation software is TDS (Tape Display System written by Southwestern Bell Telephone Co.). The use of TDS is optional, but the features provided can further enhance the benefits of workstations. Usually, an attendant views tape-mount messages on a system console. These messages remain highlighted on the screen until the mount is completed. One difficulty is that the attendant sees mount messages for all workstations and must ignore the mounts that are the responsibility of other workstation attendants. TDS can monitor the status of as many as 42 tape drives on a single terminal screen. Each TDS terminal can be defined to display the status of a selected number of tape drives (e.g., those in a given workstation). At any instant, an attendant can scan the current status of all drives within a particular workstation. Each drive entry on the screen displays the system and job name of the drive allocated as well as the volume serial number of the tape. Drives that have mounts pending are highlighted to provide easy readability.

The objective of TDS is to allow quick and easy reference, which tape attendants can use to determine what outstanding tape-mount requests are in their areas. The less time attendants use to determine tape activity in their areas, the more time they have to satisfy tape-mount requests.

CONCLUSION

Aside from the obvious benefit of minimizing the walking distance required to mount a tape, other benefits are obtained from implementing a tape workstation environment. With the consolidation of tape media and hardware, the only two places that an active tape can be located are on a tape drive or in its storage rack slot. Workstation implementation also reduces the distance traveled to refile a tape after it is used. In addition, multiple-volume files are localized in a smaller region than before, making it easier to retrieve the entire data file when it is required. In an environment that does not use workstations, the multiple volumes could be scattered anywhere in the tape library.

All of the potential benefits of workstation implementation serve to achieve the overall objective, which is to reduce the nonproductive tasks associated with mounting tapes. The higher productivity level attained affects not only the efficiency of tape operations but the entire data center, resulting in better service for end users, at a lower cost.

Section X
Security and Control

WITH THE TREND TOWARD increased use of technology among corporations, academia, and nonprofit groups, it is as important as ever that the security and control of information processing technology receive high visibility. To remain competitive in a global economy, many enterprises are seeking to develop more flexible organizational structures and the more adaptive information systems that go with them. In this environment, traditional security approaches can actually make it more difficult for organizations to respond quickly to market changes. Chapter X-1, "New Approaches to Information Security," proposes new strategies the IS manager can use to accommodate the decentralization of IS technology.

Chapter X-2, "Application Systems Change Control," details the need to provide control during the systems development life cycle. Organizations have traditionally adopted stringent systems development controls to ensure that new application systems are efficient and reliable in meeting the needs of the organization and its business users. Application change controls have been neglected, however, despite the fact that large firms generally spend between 60% to 80% of their application software dollars on maintenance activities. A new breed of application change control system is emerging that ensures that all changes made to application systems are properly authorized, tested, and approved for implementation. Chapter X-2 examines the design and implementation of such a control system.

"Protecting and Controlling Information in Complex System Environments," the topic of Chapter X-3, is a challenge to the IS manager. This chapter offers readers ideas on how to provide a secure environment for enterprisewide information systems.

Although the centrally controlled mainframe is far from obsolete, it is no longer solely responsible for fulfilling the information processing requirements of an organization. IS managers need to reassess the protective strategies for the multiplatform, interoperable information systems that are becoming commonplace in many organizations. An information protection architecture can be a major help in planning and implementing a secure enterprisewide information system.

X-1

New Approaches to Information Security

Richard Baskerville

IN A GLOBAL MARKETPLACE, large organizations find that they must compete against smaller, more limber firms that are often better able to quickly adapt to new market conditions. In responding to this challenge, these large organizations must develop more flexible forms of organization as well as more adaptive information systems. In turn, IS managers must rethink traditional approaches to designing and implementing security controls.

In fast-changing, competitive environments, rigid, centralized controls may actually threaten the ability of the organization to respond to change. Managers must therefore understand the conflicts that can arise in using traditional security controls. They must take an active role in developing new control mechanisms that support rather than hinder the organization's ability to adapt to change.

Innovative security measures can provide an essential element in the battle for organizational survival in an increasingly competitive world. This chapter explores why organizations are changing, how these changes challenge the fundamental assumptions of information security, and how security managers can develop new strategies to cope with these changes.

MORE FLEXIBLE SYSTEMS

The target of security—information systems—comprises more than just computers and programs. Information systems also include people and procedures. In broad terms, the purpose of information security is to constrain the behavior of people using information systems to legitimate activities. Security controls must operate to prevent or mitigate the effects of illegitimate system use.

It is assumed that the organization benefits by limiting the system to allowed action through the use of controls. However, this belief is based on two underlying assumptions that are increasingly anachronistic in competitive organizations. The first assumption is that it is possible to predict allowed behavior for a reasonably long time period. The second assumption is that the organization can change in an orderly fashion. In both cases, experience has shown that the opposite is true.

Pick up any article on the struggle of large mainframe manufacturers to compete with small technology companies. Inevitably, blame is laid on inflexible organizational structures that are incapable of responding quickly to market changes. Security controls and other structures are criticized for contributing to the cost and inertia that retards adaptation to change.

The problems confronting information systems managers spring from the basic principles of security management. Security controls and other structures are intended to provide a framework for organizational activities. But when the organization experiences stress caused by a change in its environment, these controls can actually make it more difficult for the organization to function. When controls no longer match the real environment in which an organization functions, the organization must work harder to process its input and output through mismatched channels. At some point, this additional work becomes intolerable; the structures and controls have to change to better align with the new environment.

This disruptive process may have been acceptable when firms dominated relatively stable markets with long-range product development cycles. But in today's climate of unstable, competitive markets, it creates an intolerable drag on the organization, creating a level of internal disorder that can destroy competitiveness. An entirely new approach to information security controls must be developed for adaptive organizations.

ADAPTIVE ORGANIZATIONS

The organization must be able to change its own form in response to the opportunities and challenges created by rapid shifts in its economic and political environment. Adaptive organizations accomplish this by establishing loose and shifting internal structures in which autonomy is diffused. In adaptive organizations, strategic plans evolve from within the organization rather than being dictated from above; boundaries with trading partners, governments, and support services are intentionally fuzzy.

Although some of the most difficult challenges posed by the trend toward adaptive systems affect information security management, most security practitioners seem to be unaware of the consequences of these trends. The following review of current business practices—in marketing, strategic planning, and management—is intended to challenge that complacency.

Marketing in a Global Economy

Traditional goals for market domination in specific geographical regions are giving way to the exploitation of market niches to capture worldwide market share. Manufacturing and service firms of all sizes are competing in a world where trade, communications, and transportation barriers are rapidly dissolving. For example, communications barriers are dissolving between companies and their suppliers (e.g., through just-in-time inventory systems) and between companies and their customers (e.g., through direct order entry systems). The dissolution of these boundaries poses unique security risks, especially with respect to intercompany and transborder data flows. The tendency of security professionals to implement rigid controls is in opposition to the organization's need for a flexible and adaptive marketing capability.

Strategic Planning

Planning strategists value organizations that can respond rapidly to changing market forces. For example, shortened product development cycles enable companies to respond quickly to market opportunities. Successful product-driven organizations cannot tolerate functionally oriented management hierarchies; firms must break down at least some of the internal boundaries that inhibit the ability to adapt. Effective strategies must include high-performance communications technologies. Often, however, information security is ignored in planning, being relegated to merely an implementation issue.

Management

The trend in management is to develop a culture that emphasizes cross-specialization and innovation rather than compartmentalized dedication to a limited functional area. This requires employees who are highly qualified, well trained, and trustworthy. Power is dispersed downward so that the organization can respond quickly to environmental changes. Problems are quickly resolved where they occur to promote continued innovation.

Traditional models of information security rely on a centralized model of organizational control. Dispersion of power within the organization is viewed as a threat to the lines of authority on which controls depend. The problem is perhaps best illustrated by looking at the unique questions of security in virtual organizations.

Virtual Organizations. A virtual organization is a type of adaptive organization that has no established boundaries, fixed assets, or permanent staff. Virtual organizations often spring up in response to a crisis, usually from within one or more real organizations. Typically, a group of people team up to develop an innovative design, product, or strategy, borrowing the resources they need on the basis of their personal authority in the organization. In some cases, one virtual organization may comprise parts of several real organizations. For example, competitors may need to cooperate to develop an industrywide response to an environmental problem or to a government initiative.

Such virtual organizations pose a particular challenge to security managers. Traditionally, security managers are charged with preventing industry competitors from gaining access to corporate information. But in virtual organizations that require information sharing, the security specialist may actually be responsible for protecting the information of a competitor while it is being used by the virtual organization. If the security manager were to follow the traditional approach to establishing access controls, senior management of the companies involved would have to approve policy statements, legal opinions, and even contracts governing system access. This would have the effect of destroying the spontaneous, innovative culture of the virtual organization.

Computing Flexibility

Information systems are a key element in these new organizational forms. Organizations need to create systems that are fast, flexible, and responsive to change; these systems must be capable of being quickly developed and changed to support different processing requirements and data structures. Firms increasingly rely on rapid prototyping to quickly develop systems without extensive preliminary analysis and specifications, as well as on end-user computing techniques, in which users develop their own applications using various development tools linked to existing spreadsheets and data bases. These small-scale projects are often poorly organized. In this environment, security specialists can no longer expect to receive hard specifications on which to base their design of security controls. New methods of systems development require new methods for developing controls.

In addition to new development methodologies, advances in technology are producing more flexible, adaptive systems. Downsizing to smaller computers, the drive for easily reconfigured open systems that support connectivity of dissimilar platforms, use of highly flexible client/server architectures, and the integration of hypertext and hypermedia all contribute to increased computing flexibility. When these technological developments are coupled with the trend toward rapidly adaptive organization forms, it becomes clear that the traditional, centralized management of security controls is dangerously outdated.

A NEW BASIS FOR INFORMATION SECURITY

This section presents a new approach to information security, based on the key assumption that change is the essence of organizational success. From this single tenet, there are a few surprising conclusions—for example, in a fast-changing, competitive environment, risk analysis is irrelevant as a basis for establishing security controls. This section also examines how to implement flexible, adaptive controls, and is followed by specific guidelines for managing the security function in adaptive organizations.

Is Risk Analysis Relevant?

Risk is typically evaluated according to the formula for risk (R) as the product of probability of a threat occurrence (P) and the cost associated with that threat (C) (i.e., $R = P[C]$). This tired formula is usually interpreted as the question, "What risk is the organization confronting?" But perhaps this is the wrong question. Another question is more to the point: "Does the risk to the organization justify investment in the control?" (That is, the cost of the control should be less than, or at least equal to, the potential risk faced by the organization.)

In grappling with this question, its complexity becomes apparent. In an unstable environment, risk probabilities and costs become unstable. More important, the cost of controls becomes immeasurable. This is because the positive value of any control must be weighed against its potential for damaging the organization's ability to respond quickly to change; this can be impossible to clearly evaluate in truly adaptive environments.

Example. Network engineers at University X extol the benefits of the TCP/IP LAN protocol; this protocol is open and easily configured and expanded to help the university remain innovative and competitive. However, TCP/IP is difficult to control; encryption is difficult and turnkey security solutions few. The network engineers feel that controls would inhibit the network's flexibility and require extensive modifications; yet without such controls, passwords and other confidential information could easily be compromised.

In this complex situation, risk analysis is incapable of reaching a clear decision; it simply cannot account for the cost of controls. Do the potential losses that could result from using a flexible but poorly controlled technology really outweigh the benefits that can be achieved from organizational innovation and adaptiveness? For University X, a secure network may well be suicidal.

Security professionals must take a balanced view in evaluating the impact of security controls on corporate survival. Focusing on the potential losses for a given system exposure without considering the overall needs to the organization is both narrow-minded and misguided.

The Need for Flexible Controls

New forms of controls must ensure safe computing, regardless of how quickly systems processes might change. Traditional controls limit systems to only authorized forms of behavior. Adaptive controls must actually interpret what constitutes authorized behavior in a changing environment. Controls must be able to make correct decisions about allowed forms of behavior in an unpredictable context. This requires a move away from large-scale, physical, technology-based controls to small-scale, logical, people-based controls.

Technological controls may be reliable and simple to maintain, but they are also rigid and unresponsive to change. Controls based on human behavior are more subjective, but they are also flexible.

It has always been said that people are the key to effective information security, but this has usually meant getting people to use technological controls effectively. In an adaptive setting, the objective is to get people to be the effective controls. To maintain such people-based controls, continuous training and tight management is required.

To understand how that might work, consider the example of virtual organizations. When a virtual organization forms, the security manager or a staff member of one of the participating real organizations would join the virtual organization. In this position, the security specialist is now responsible for security of the virtual organization. This specialist is entitled to recommend proper security measures within the virtual organization, including training of other members of the virtual organization in security policies and controls created by the virtual group. The virtual group can ensure that the controls it establishes do not inhibit innovation.

The participating real organizations may have to take measures to protect information elements that are now shared among several companies; conversely, data may need to be temporarily stored and processed within a real organization's computer system dedicated to the virtual organization. The security manager may even need to temporarily protect confidential data of a competitor and provide such assurances to the competitor's management.

In the case of University X's network, the security administrator might choose to distribute authority across the network rather than controlling it centrally. For example, a security administrator could be assigned to each subnetwork of LANs that is routed to the backbone of the campuswide network. These subadministrators would focus primarily on training users, not only in careful system operation but in detecting abuse. Administrators and users share the task of monitoring LAN sessions for suspicious activity.

In essence, control is pushed downward in the organization. Because network monitoring is localized, it becomes easier to differentiate activity that may appear unusual in the system at large but that is appropriate given changes in the local network environment. In fact, given the commitment of large segments of users to enforcing security, the overall system may actually be more secure than if purely technological controls were used.

MANAGING RISK IN ADAPTIVE ORGANIZATIONS

This section examines steps the IS manager can take to reduce information risk in adaptive organizations. Many familiar forms of controls are employed in adaptive organizations; differences reflect changes in the priorities and management of these controls.

The discussion of the security management process begins with details regarding implementation of adaptive controls and moves toward broader issues of security management. This is done because the general management process stems from the detailed control mechanisms. In practice, however, management should begin by settling the broader issues of security organization and management before tackling the more specific problems associated with implementing controls.

Relying on People for Control. Wherever possible, manual procedures and policies should form the basis for security controls. These procedures and policies give people a greater front-line role in protecting information assets. Proper controls on human behavior can effectively protect against such threats as:

- *Privacy violations.* For example, browsing is discouraged and reported.
- *Virus infections.* Foreign executable code is monitored and reported.
- *Fraud.* Separation of duties is enforced.
- *Denial of resources.* User passwords are carefully managed. Such manual controls can be effective without unduly limiting system capabilities.

To succeed, security based primarily on manual procedures requires a highly qualified, well-trained, and trustworthy staff. This is a requirement of any adaptive organization.

Increasing the Role of Logical Controls. Data-oriented, logical controls are more flexible than physical controls and are less easily circumvented when the processing environment changes. For example, embedded control fields and check digits often remain effective even when data procedures, technology, or personnel change. Logical controls can include data classification schemes, file encryption (i.e., not just communications encryption), and password enforcement.

For all new systems designs, logical controls should first be considered before consideration is given to physical controls. For existing systems, a thorough analysis should be performed to determine the impact on security of removing all physical controls.

Promoting Temporary Security Measures. Where possible, small-scale control technologies that can be easily modified and reconfigured should be used. Software-based controls are preferred to hardware-based controls for encryption, communications control, user identification, and access control. Because the investment in these small-scale controls is smaller than with more highly structured security mechanisms, they can also be discarded or redeployed more readily when they no longer serve their purpose.

Corporatewide security schemes should be rejected in favor of loosely integrated networks of diverse security elements. This is done because security requirements may differ within the organization depending on where the security measures are to be implemented. The security manager must ensure that no incompatibilities exist between the various nodes of this integrated security network that might expose the network to compromise.

Assimilating Security Staff from Other Departments. Because of the need for human involvement, the security organization should be broadened to include a network of persons throughout the enterprise. Even the smallest user group should have a designated security manager responsible for protecting the information assets controlled by the group. In this network, the professional security staff serves as a resource to the assimilated staff members, training them in effective security techniques and procedures. Each security manager of an end-user group should be taught that the users' actions make the difference between a secure system and one that is dangerously vulnerable.

Dispersing Authority for Security. Centralized control is impractical and ineffective in adaptive organizations. Authority for security should be dispersed throughout the organization, using a diverse set of network-based security controls and a decentralized security staff. In a fast-paced, adaptive environment, the authority for security changes must be as close as possible to each control element. The security managers in each functional area must have the authority to change or enhance controls; the centralized security authority is responsible for coordinating and facilitating implementation of dispersed controls.

Increased reliance on decentralized controls and on proper human behavior requires close supervision of users. The centralized security authority cannot evaluate every user; instead, authority to change and enforce security policy or to retrain users must reside at the level of end-user groups and their security managers.

Reorganizing the Professional Security Staff. The major role of the professional security staff shifts toward internal consulting and training in the adaptive organization. Such functional specialties as communications security or data base security are not as useful as are specialties that reflect the structure of the organization—for example, marketing security or accounting security. Because loss of functional specialization can result in reduced efficiency, the overall security staff may need to be increased. The size of the security staff depends, in part, on the security organization's ability to co-opt staff from other departments.

Revising and Expanding Security Training. Increased reliance on behavior-oriented controls must be supported by a program of routine training and retraining for professional security management and staff, assimilated security managers, and affected end users. Because information systems staff will be given greater control over systems resources (including responsibility for deciding how to protect information), they must be taught how and why information assets are important to the organization. The training program must be revised and expanded to support end users and assimilated security managers who have final authority over particular system resources. Training should serve to both expose staff to protection techniques and remind them of the consequences to the organization of improperly protected assets.

Developing an Adaptive Framework for Security. A more flexible security planning process must be created, reflecting the need for adaptive security controls. Planning should therefore be based on behavioral controls and low-cost technical controls, as discussed previously.

Reviewing Organizational Trends. IS and security management should evaluate whether the organization exhibits characteristics of an adaptive organization. These characteristics might include cross-functional teams, downsizing, product specialization, or use of virtual organizations. Because the organization may bypass the structures defined in its own policies, it is better to actually observe how information assets are used in the organization, looking for patterns of rapid change in processing techniques or procedures. It is also useful to discuss trends in adaptive organizations with the CEO and CIO as well as managers in planning, finance, marketing, and production.

If the organization does not exhibit adaptive characteristics, it may not be prudent to change the traditional security structures that are in place. There is no reason to believe that an adaptive security framework will be effective in a traditional organization. However, consideration should be given to implementing adaptive security as a backup for traditional protection mechanisms. This may have the effect of facilitating a transition to more adaptive forms of organization. In any event, the IS manager should continue to evaluate the pulse of the organization for signs of adaptive behavior.

CONCLUSION

To remain competitive in increasingly globalized markets, many organizations are seeking new forms that support rapid change. Even not-for-profit organizations and government agencies are realizing benefits from adopting more flexibile characteristics.

This trend challenges the nature of both existing information systems and their related systems security controls. Current systems controls are designed to impose structure on processing activities, which may make it more difficult for the organization to quickly respond to market changes.

The information systems manager must consider a new set of assumptions about how to operate in today's competitive environment. If the organization's ability to change is a key to its success in the marketplace, security controls must be capable of changing in response to organizational change. In this context, risk analysis is less relevant in making decisions about implementing and managing controls.

The IS manager can take the following steps to protect information while enabling the organization to be adaptive:

- Review overall organizational trends.
- Develop an adaptive framework for security.
- Revise and expand security training.
- Reorganize the professional security staff.
- Disperse authority for security.
- Assimilate additional security staff.
- Promote temporary security mechanisms.
- Increase the role of logical controls.
- Rely on people for control.

These steps may simply require reorganizing or reassigning the priorities of information systems controls that are already familiar.

X-2

Application Systems Change Control

H. Van Tran
Cynthia D. Heagy

NEW APPLICATION SYSTEMS are typically developed by in-house programmers in a development environment and then transferred into a production environment to be used to support daily business operations. After being placed in production, however, the systems frequently must be changed to improve the efficiency of the applications, adjust the applications to changing business conditions, or correct defects in the applications. Application changes affect computer programs, screen and file definitions, and job control language instructions, with the bulk of the changes being made to computer programs.

In-house applications systems development and maintenance have different control objectives. Systems development controls provide assurance that application systems are efficient and reliable and meet the organization's and the users' needs. Application change controls ensure that all changes to application components are properly authorized, tested, and approved for implementation. If application change controls are adequate, business users can be confident that the application system being used is the one that was initially developed but with known and approved changes.

In general, large firms spend 60% to 80% of their application software dollars on maintenance activities and the remainder on systems development activities. Each new large systems development project generally is expensive and highly visible; in contrast, each application system change usually is small and low-key. The high visibility and costliness of large systems development projects have compelled firms to adopt stringent systems development controls; however, they have neglected application change controls.

Large systems development controls are grounded in a defined systems development life cycle methodology. The development project is subdivided into phases with tightly controlled milestones, deadlines, coding and testing schedules, and budgets. Moreover, the roles and responsibilities of both programmers and system owners are clearly defined.

However, substantial systems development controls would yield little value if subsequent modifications to application systems were to undermine these expensive systems development controls. Thus, the integrity of an application system could be in jeopardy without adequate control over application changes. This chapter describes an emerging breed of application control systems.

TRADITIONAL APPROACHES TO APPLICATION CHANGES

Traditional approaches to application changes are used by many large mainframe computer centers. Firms that do not use contemporary application control procedures store computer programs in common libraries on secondary storage devices. For example, all COBOL source programs are stored in a common production source program library. All COBOL load or machine-executable programs are stored in a common production load program library.

When creating a new program, the programmer initially codes a source program and then uses a compiler to generate its load program equivalent. Both programs, after being fully tested, are moved into the common production source and load program libraries, where the load program is executed by the computer to support the organization's daily business operations.

The program change process consists of a series of tasks. When a program change is requested and authorized by the system owner, a programmer copies the source program from the common production source program library into the programmer's development source program library. Development libraries are private libraries that can be created, deleted, read, or written to by a particular programmer and no one else.

After the source program is in the private development source program library, the programmer modifies the program, compiles the program to produce a load program, links the program with all essential compiled subroutines, tests the program by executing the load program using test data, and informs the system owner of the successful change. Typically, the system owner approves the change without any additional testing and authorizes the copying of both source and load programs to the common production source and load libraries. The newly generated load program is now used for daily business operations.

Traditionally, organizations have taken two approaches to application changes. One approach provides hundreds of maintenance programmers with update access to the two common production libraries (i.e., source and load) so they can copy programs directly from production to development and back to production at any time. After being given update access, a programmer can read, modify, and delete any program stored in common production libraries.

The main advantage of this approach is efficiency, because programmers can move changed programs to production libraries in a timely fashion without any red tape, burdensome paperwork, or time-consuming bureaucracy. However, this is a dangerous approach to application changes. Because hundreds of maintenance programmers have update access to common production libraries, intentional errors and fatal attacks by disgruntled programmers are difficult to prevent.

The other traditional approach to application changes uses a librarian to perform the task of copying programs from development libraries to production libraries. In this approach, only the librarian has update access to common production libraries. As a result, the risk of attacks is greatly reduced. After a program has been modified successfully and tested by a programmer, forms must be completed authorizing the librarian to move both the source and the load programs from the development libraries to the production libraries.

One disadvantage of this second approach is that moving the changed programs into the production libraries can take several days under this procedure. For emergency changes, the use of a librarian hinders the timely update of production libraries. Therefore, daily business operations that depend on the successful outcome of these changes may be disrupted.

Risks Associated with the Traditional Approaches

In addition to the unique inherent risks in each of the two traditional approaches to application changes, they share several other risks. For example, use of common production libraries causes information privacy problems, because a programmer who has read access to the production source library can read and copy any program in this library. Disgruntled or dishonest programmers can engage in industrial espionage by copying proprietary programs for sale to the competition.

In addition, if only the programmer tests changes, erroneous program instructions can slip into production and the system may fail to meet the needs of the organization and the users. Moreover, having the programming staff perform such incompatible duties as testing changes and moving the changed program to production creates an opportunity for errors and irregularities to occur.

Another risk is that programs are subject to accidental loss if there is no strict version control. Both programmers and the librarian can accidentally copy one program over another and thereby destroy the first program. Moreover, conflicting changes may be made to the same program when two or more programmers concurrently modify the same program without being aware of the other's activities.

In addition, the source program and its corresponding load program may not be compatible if the load version is copied into the load production library but the source program is not. Incompatibility between the source and load programs makes future changes to a program much more difficult and expensive.

Because of the risks associated with the traditional approaches to application changes, organizations should consider more effective methods. The following section discusses the design of an improved system for managing application changes.

DESIGN OF AN APPLICATION CHANGE CONTROL SYSTEM

New application change control systems are emerging that mitigate the risks associated with application system changes, thereby protecting the application system's integrity. A common change control system design has also emerged. This section presents an overview of such a design to guide information systems personnel and auditors through the development and implementation of this type of control system.

Application change control systems typically are developed by a joint effort of four groups: system owners from various user departments, application change control administrators, programmers, and auditors. Although control requirements are defined by both system owners and auditors, ease-of-use and efficiency requirements are defined by system owners, change control administrators, and programmers.

A typical application change control system consists of several data bases, libraries, and subsystems (see Exhibit X-2-1). Among the data bases, the control and security data base serves as the backbone for defense against unauthorized access to application source program components. It contains the names of the application systems, the name of the owner of each application system, and the names of the programmers who are authorized to make changes to components of each application system.

The historical source data base contains all source components of all the application systems. All authorized programmers have access to this data base; therefore, it is referred to as a common data base. However, read and write privileges are restricted to only those application systems for which certain programmers are authorized.

An activity log data base stores the audit trail. Because all programmers, system owners, and application change control administrators have read access to this data base, it also is called a common data base.

This application change control environment requires three groups of libraries:

- Programmer private libraries.
- System owner acceptance libraries.
- Production libraries.

Management of application system changes is supported by two major subsystems: the user interface subsystem and the administrator interface subsystem. These two subsystems and the other system components are discussed in further detail in the following sections.

Control and Security Data Base. The control and security data base contains the application ownership structure of the organization (i.e., the system owners who can authorize changes to be made to their application systems and the programmers who are authorized to make the changes). The top layer of the structure consists of the names of organizational area systems (e.g., accounting, manufacturing, and marketing) and the names of each area's management.

In the middle layer are the individual application subsystems that constitute each organizational area system. The responsibility for keeping each subsystem fully functional is vested in a system owner, who must have an intimate working knowledge of the system. At the bottom layer of the structure are the system owners and authorized maintenance programmers who make changes to application systems on behalf of the system owners.

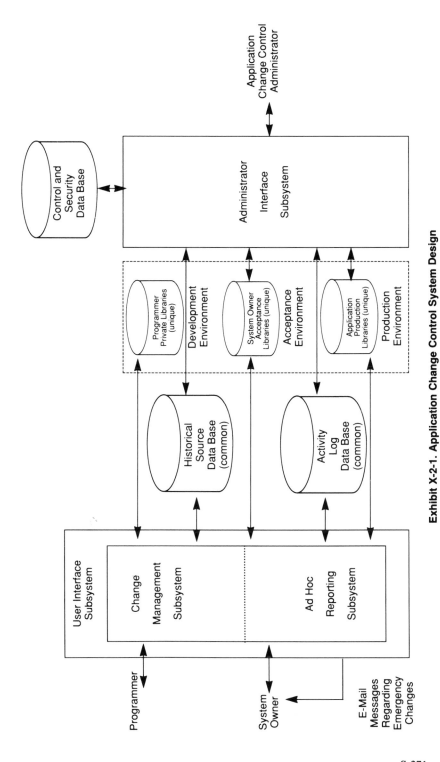

Exhibit X-2-1. Application Change Control System Design

This application ownership structure governs who can assign system owners and programmers to (or remove them from) an application subsystem. Therefore, update access to this data base must be limited to a few trusted administrators.

Administrator Interface Subsystem. The administrator interface subsystem, which is available only to application change control administrators, is used to perform several controlling tasks. These tasks include:

- Adding application systems to (and removing them from) the application change control system upon management's request.
- Creating and deleting application production and acceptance libraries when application systems are added to or removed from the application change control system.
- Adding maintenance programmers to (and removing them from) an application system upon the system owner's request.
- Deleting application components erroneously added to an application system, upon the system owner's request.
- Increasing disk space for application production and acceptance libraries when they become full.

Historical Source Data Base. All source components for application systems are stored in a historical source data base, which consists of two distinct data bases. One data base stores the original source components, and the other stores incremental changes made to the original components. From the two data bases, all prior versions of an application component can be restored quickly by combining the original component with its incremental changes.

The data bases should be fully protected by means of encryption and compression. Furthermore, access to an application component should be restricted to programmers whose identification codes are attached to the application in the control and security data base. Audit trails are logged automatically when these two data bases are updated.

Activity Log Data Base. The activity log data base is used to log all change activities, including:

- Movement of a version of an application component from one environment to another (e.g., production to development, development to acceptance, and acceptance to production).
- Changes made to the historical source and the control and security data bases.
- Actions taken by the system owner of an application (e.g., freeze, approve, or reject).

Programmer Private Libraries. Programmer private libraries contain the application components being changed by individual programmers. Only one programmer can create, delete, read, or write to each group of private libraries. In addition, for each application system, there exists a group of system owner acceptance libraries. These libraries contain both source and machine-executable application components that have been tested by programmers and will be tested again by the system owner. Finally, for each application system there is a group of production libraries that contain only machine-executable application components. Thus, there are hundreds of groups of production libraries in this application change control environment, as opposed to just one in the traditional environment.

System Owner Acceptance Libraries. System owner acceptance libraries consist of unique groups of libraries for each application system. They contain the application components that have been changed and tested by programmers. These libraries are provided so that testing can be conducted by system owners to reduce the risk of accepting erroneous program instructions inherent in the traditional approaches to program change. As shown in Exhibit X-2-1, the system owner acceptance libraries are sandwiched between the development and production environments.

Application Production Libraries. A large organization has hundreds of application systems that are composed of hundreds or even thousands of individual application components. To achieve better control over application changes, the old common production libraries must be replaced by hundreds of sets of unique application production libraries.

Each set of libraries is used to store the current executable components of a unique application system. Each library within a set is used to store similar components (e.g., all COBOL programs in one library and all PL/1 programs in another library). Access to a set of unique application production libraries should be restricted to authorized programmers, as defined in the application ownership structure.

User Interface Subsystem. Programmers work through the user interface subsystem to invoke the change management subsystem to perform the following tasks:

- Copy application components from the historical source data base to private libraries for making changes.
- Copy changed application components from private libraries to acceptance libraries for acceptance testing conducted by the system owner.
- More approved, frozen, and changed components from acceptance libraries to the historical data base and production libraries.

System owners can use the user interface subsystem to invoke the change management subsystem to approve and freeze application components being stored in acceptance libraries. Once an application component has been frozen, a programmer can no longer make changes to it. Both programmers and system owners can use the ad hoc reporting subsystem to investigate change activities that have taken place.

Because the user interface subsystem allows programmers and system owners to issue instructions to the change management subsystem and the ad hoc reporting subsystem, it should be tailored to the needs and preferences of programmers and system owners. The user interface subsystem must provide for:

- Segregation of duties.
- Source and load program compatibility.
- Elimination of conflicting changes.
- Emergency changes.

Segregation of Duties. Duties in the user interface subsystem should be segregated between programmers and system owners to prevent errors and irregularities from being both perpetrated and concealed. The user interface subsystem should permit a programmer to instruct the change management subsystem to perform the following tasks:

- Copy a program from the production to the development environment.
- Copy the changed program to the acceptance environment.
- Move the approved, changed program to the production environment.

The user interface subsystem should permit the system owner to instruct the change management subsystem to perform the following tasks:

- Freeze the changed program.
- Approve or reject the changed program.
- Document that acceptance testing has been conducted.

Exhibit X-2-2 shows the proper segregation of incompatible duties. When a requested change to a program is authorized by the system owner, a programmer copies the appropriate source program from the production environment to the programmer's private development library, where the change is made and tested to the programmer's satisfaction. Next, the programmer copies the changed source program to an acceptance library to allow the system owner to conduct appearance testing. When the changed source program is in an acceptance library, the system owner should freeze the changed program to prevent any unexpected modification; the system owner then can test the modified program.

The acceptance testing may have one or two outcomes. If the acceptance testing results are not satisfactory, the system owner can reject the changed source program and send it back to the programmer. If the acceptance testing results are satisfactory, the system owner can electronically approve the changed program and authorize its movement to the production source program library.

To achieve total control, the task of moving the changed program should be given to a librarian. However, the use of librarians hinders the timely update of production libraries, as discussed for the second traditional approach. In an application change control environment with many compensatory controls, it is safe and efficient to have the programmer move the changed program.

First, the use of the control and security data allows the programmers to update only programs for which they are authorized. Second, all prior versions of a program can be quickly restored because the original program and

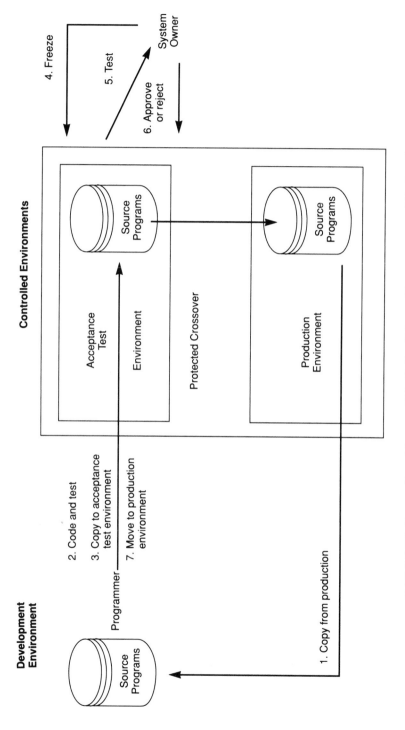

Exhibit X-2-2. Segregation of Incompatible Duties Between Programmers and System Owners

its incremental changes are retained separately in the historical source data base. Third, audit trails are logged automatically when the historical data base is updated. Finally, each application change may affect many components, and it is more difficult to have programmers move the changed program because they have the most knowledge about all the changed components.

Source and Load Program Compatibility. Moving low- and high-level programs to production requires special care to ensure source and load program compatibility. To maintain this compatibility, the user interface subsystem must perform the final compilation of a program when the source program is copied from the development environment to the acceptance environment. Then, when a program is moved from the acceptance environment to the production environment, the frozen source program and its corresponding load program are moved simultaneously. Thus, source and load program compatibility is ensured, and accidental loss of programs is prevented.

Elimination of Conflicting Changes. To eliminate conflicting changes in the same program, the user interface subsystem should provide a locking capability to lock a program when it is copied from production to development for modification. The lock should remain in place until the first change has been completed or until a programmer removes it. This control procedure ensures that only one programmer can make a change to a program at a time.

Emergency Changes. When a defect in an application brings a system down and the system owner is not available to authorize program changes electronically, a programmer must correct the defect quickly to bring the system back into operation. In such emergency situations, the user interface subsystem should permit a programmer to bypass the system owner's electronic authorization to move the changed component to production. The system owner should be notified of the change through electronic mail. Because this type of change is an exception to the normal change control procedure, it must be carefully monitored.

Change Management Subsystem. The change management subsystem, which is accessed through the user interface subsystem, performs various updating activities to five groups of data bases and libraries: the historical source data base, the activity log data base, the programmer private libraries, the system owner acceptance libraries, and the production libraries.

Ad Hoc Reporting Subsystem. The ad hoc reporting subsystem, which is accessed through the user interface subsystem, consists mainly of a series of canned parameter-driven programs to permit programmers, system owners, and management to investigate change activities that have taken place. The system must provide the following information, at a minimum:

- The system owner of each application.
- A list of all programs that constitute an application.
- A list of programmers authorized to make changes to an application system.
- Programs being changed at a given time.
- Actions (e.g., freeze, approve, or reject) taken by the system owner of an application.
- Movements of programs from one environment to another (e.g., production to development).
- A list of approved, changed programs that have not been moved to production.
- A list of the users who have received electronic messages regarding emergency changes.
- A log of emergency change attempts made by programmers.
- A list of changed programs that have not been tested by system owners.

IMPLEMENTING AN APPLICATION CHANGE CONTROL SYSTEM

Because implementation of a new application change control system affects all application systems, care must be taken to avoid disruptions of business operations. The main steps involved in implementing a complex application change control system are:

- Development of forms and procedures.
- Purchase or development of software.
- Determination of a library naming convention.
- Conversion.

Development of Forms and Procedures. Two forms are needed for an application change control system. One is used by management to add or remove system owners, and the other is used by system owners to add programmers to (or remove them from) the application ownership structure. Next, change control procedures must be developed in detail to define roles and responsibilities of all involved parties, which include programmers, system owners, application change control administrators, and management.

Purchase or Development of Software. An application change control system of the type described can be purchased from change control software vendors. Vendors that market change control management products include LEGENT (Westborough MA) and Softool Corp. (Goleta CA). Organizations can buy a system in its entirety or buy portions of it—namely, the change management subsystem and the administrator interface subsystem—and then build the user interface and ad hoc reporting subsystems to reflect the tastes and preferences of the programmers and system owners.

Determination of a Library Naming Convention. In the traditional environment, all machine-executable application components of the same type

Code	Description
ASM	Assembler Program
COB	COBOL Program
DBD	IMS Data Base Layout
FOCEXEC	FOCUS Program
FOCMSTR	FOCUS Data Base Layout
FOCSQL	FOCUS/DB2 Table Layout
FOR	FORTRAN Program
JCL	Job Control Language
PL1	PL/1 Program
SAS	SAS Program

Exhibit X-2-3. Examples of Application Component Types

from all application systems are stored in one common production library. In the contemporary environment, they are stored in many unique libraries in addition to the common historical source data base. Because there are hundreds of application systems, hundreds of groups of unique production libraries must be created. Furthermore, acceptance testing requires hundreds of additional groups of acceptance libraries.

To manage the sheer number of acceptance and production libraries, a library naming convention is essential. Each library name must be unique and must consist of a series of the following codes:

- An organizational area code (e.g., MKT for marketing).
- An application system code (e.g., SALES or INVOICE).
- A code indicating whether it is the acceptance or production library.
- The application components type (see Exhibit X-2-3 for a list of types).
- A code indicating whether it is the source or load library.

Exhibit X-2-4 shows two groups of unique libraries (acceptance and production) of an application system. In this exhibit, the organizational area code is MKT, the application system code is SALES, and the acceptance and production indicators are ACPT and PROD. Application component types are FOCEXEC, FOCMSTR, FOCSQL, JCL, SAS, and COBOL. The source and load indicators are SRC and LOAD, respectively.

Conversion. Moving components of all application systems from a traditional environment to a contemporary environment is a substantial undertak-

Acceptance Library	Production Library
MKT.SALES.ACPT.FOCEXEC.SRC	MKT.SALES.PROD.FOCEXEC.SRC
MKT.SALES.ACPT.FOCMSTR.SRC	MKT.SALES.PROD.FOCMSTR.SRC
MKT.SALES.ACPT.FOCSQL.SRC	MKT.SALES.PROD.FOCSQL.SRC
MKT.SALES.ACPT.JCL.SRC	MKT.SALES.PROD.JCL.SRC
MKT.SALES.ACPT.SAS.SRC	MKT.SALES.PROD.SAS.SRC
MKT.SALES.ACPT.COBOL.SRC	MKT.SALES.PROD.COBOL.LOAD
MKT.SALES.ACPT.COBOL.LOAD	

Exhibit X-2-4. Libraries of an Application System

☐ Clearly identify the application ownership structure (i.e., management of broad application areas, individual application systems, system owners, and authorized maintenance programmers).

☐ Obtain management's authorization to define system owners, and obtain system owners' authorization to define maintenance programmers.

☐ Store the application ownership information in the control and security data base.

☐ Clearly identify all components of each application system.

☐ Identify all required libraries for each application system.

☐ Adopt an effective library naming convention for the acceptance and production libraries of all application systems.

☐ Create the historical data base and new acceptance and production libraries.

☐ Develop and implement new access control rules to allow maintenance programmers, system owners, and application users to access the appropriate acceptance and production libraries.

☐ Document the way the new application change control system works and the way maintenance programmers, system owners, and application change control administrators use it.

☐ Train system owners to operate in the new environment (i.e., to seek authorization to become a system owner; to authorize maintenance programmers to maintain specific application systems; to test, approve, and reject changed application components; to closely monitor emergency changes; and to generate audit trail reports on the history of all changes to specific application systems).

☐ Train maintenance programmers on how to operate in the new environment (i.e., to seek authorization to maintain an application system, to check application components for modification, to copy them to acceptance libraries for system owner approval, and to move components from acceptance to production libraries after the approval).

☐ Schedule individual application systems for transfer to the new environment. Simple and less critical application systems should go first to flush out both technical and procedural bugs from the change control system. Experience gained from moving small systems will help avoid major disruptions to business operations supported by big and complex application systems.

☐ Develop acceptance testing facilities for all application systems so that system owners can test changed components. This may be a major expense for application systems without any formal testing facilities. Additional training must also be provided to system owners with limited experience or knowledge of their application systems.

☐ Modify job control language components and online regions to identify new and appropriate production libraries for all application systems.

☐ Use the application change control system to move all of the application components into the historical data base and appropriate production libraries. Maintenance programmers and application change control administrators should be responsible for this task.

☐ Test all application systems in the new environment before turning them over to business users for actual use.

☐ Retain the old environment (by copying old source and load production libraries to tape) until all application systems function well in the new environment.

☐ Clean up the old environment by scratching old source and production libraries and deleting old access control rules from the security system (e.g., ACF2 and RACF).

Exhibit X-2-5. Checklist of Conversion Tasks

ing for a large computer center. Hundreds of thousands of application system components that are stored together in common libraries must be stored separately in hundreds of unique production libraries. A massive conversion effort entails a series of tasks. A checklist of conversion tasks is provided in Exhibit X-2-5.

CONCLUSION

Traditional approaches to application changes are inadequate, inefficient, and full of serious exposures to risk. One of the traditional approaches allows many programmers to read or modify programs stored in common production libraries, thus allowing fatal attacks, mishaps, or espionage to occur. Another approach restricts programmers so much that it can hinder business operations when emergency situations arise. Other risks associated with the two traditional approaches to application changes are:

- Inadequate program security.
- Erroneous program instructions.
- Failure of the system to meet the needs of the organization and the users.
- Difficulty of detecting errors and irregularities.
- Accidental loss of programs.
- Source and load program incompatibility.
- Conflicting changes made to the same program at the same time.

The new application change control system described in this chapter mitigates the risks associated with application changes. Management can build this type of system to be used along with others so that computer-related risks can be reduced to an absolute minimum.

X-3

Protecting and Controlling Information in Complex System Environments

Harry B. DeMaio

AS INFORMATION SYSTEMS environments become increasingly distributed, IS managers must address how to implement an information protection program that fits the needs of diverse user groups within the organization. Special problems arise if the information protection program was designed for a relatively small staff of technically oriented specialists or an end-user group accustomed to mainframe-based transaction systems. Expanding the information program can be further complicated if the information resources to be protected run on different platforms or under different communications protocols.

Despite these and other obstacles, the manager must develop a consistent and comprehensive protection program that balances protection objectives with other constraints and requirements (e.g., performance, function, capacity, cost-effectiveness, and ease of use). Furthermore, the information protection program must be capable of growing and adapting along with the organization.

The information protection program described in this chapter is centered on an information protection architecture. This protection architecture provides a common basis for the design, development, and implementation of a coherent and consistent audit and security program. The architecture is developed as part of a comprehensive, business-oriented process of defining audit and security requirements and objectives.

OVERVIEW OF INFORMATION PROTECTION

Information protection can be defined as the preservation of the integrity, confidentiality, and availability of information resources. This definition goes beyond the more traditional views of information security by including availability. Most business and organizational managers regard disruption (i.e., unavailability) of information resources as a more serious threat than unauthorized modification and disclosure. This reaction simply reaffirms the pivotal role that information processing plays in most enterprises. Although a certain amount of unauthorized access and even corruption of information may be considered tolerable, the loss of information is not. The loss of data or process integrity can directly result in loss of service.

In addition, security breaches involving viruses and hackers have created significant availability problems as the result of destruction of software and data. Logically induced outages are taking their place along with fires, power losses, and floods as major sources of lost business continuity.

Information resources include the information itself on all media, the computing hardware and software, the communications equipment, and the buildings or facilities and all related infrastructure elements (e.g., electricity and heat, ventilation, and air conditioning). In most information processing environments, however, the most important information resource is people.

In this context, it is important to note that the information protection program must be directed toward managing both technical activities and people. The administrative components of the protection program are often more important and more difficult to implement than the technical elements. The program should not be developed solely by technicians; the full participation of business managers throughout the entire process is a critical success factor.

AN EFFECTIVE INFORMATION PROTECTION PROGRAM

To be effective, an information protection program must be continually and consistently driven by the requirements of both the technological and the nontechnological information systems of the organization. Information systems, in turn, must be driven by business requirements. Although sound protective practices must not be ignored, the unique requirements of the organization should occupy center stage in establishing the priorities and objectives of any information protection program.

It is especially important to determine, early in the design process, what operating characteristics, priorities, and constraints drive the organization's information systems and, more important, whether these factors will continue to prevail in the future. Elements to consider include the information system's completeness, consistency, cost-effectiveness, expected growth, adaptability, responsiveness to users and management, performance, simplicity of design, stability, and ease of use. The information protection program must address all of these issues; how they are balanced and what priority each is given will vary from organization to organization.

The operating climate of the enterprise, as it relates to information use and protection, is best determined through direct workplace observation; policy manuals and even executive interviews can be misleading. For example, on receiving consultant reports based on observations of workplace practices, managers at several organizations initially refused to believe the accuracy of the reports. Later, they reluctantly accepted the reports after discovering that their policy manuals only implied certain procedures.

It must also be determined whether the current operating environment is expected to change. For example, during a period of layoffs, employee satisfaction often plummets, so management may need to reexamine the level of trust it currently grants its information users. In other situations, a tight but poorly communicated security program may be interpreted by the work force as a sign of management distrust. The impact of an information protection program must be carefully considered before the design process gets very far.

ARCHITECTURE-BASED INFORMATION PROTECTION

Several principles should govern the development of any information protection process. First, the information, not the technology, should be the focal point. Many protection programs have been designed to protect the computer, the information stored in the computer being protected only as a side effect. In interconnected systems, it is critical that every information resource be given appropriate protective treatment. This can be accomplished only by relating the protective measures directly to the information.

Making information protection the focal point may require expanding the information protection policy, standards, and procedures to include information in all forms and on all the media. It may require organizational changes, such as extending the role of the security and continuity administrators beyond the computer center. It definitely requires much deeper involvement on the part of business and technical management.

A second principle that should govern the development of the protection process is that information protection is a dynamic process, not a one-time event. Given the nature and speed of current technological and organizational changes, the information protection program must be flexible. The term *architecture* in this context is meant to suggest a set of characteristics and objectives to be attained through continual reevaluation and modification of the protection program.

Third, the protection process should encompass the entire organization. In fact, the process often extends beyond the organization to partners involved in information exchange (e.g., electronic funds transfer or electronic data interchange). Although resource constraints typically require that the program be developed and implemented in increments, the design should reflect the entire scope of the program from the outset, with provisions for modifications as new elements come into play.

Components of the Information Protection Program

Exhibit X-3-1 illustrates the relationship among the following components of an effective information protection program:

- The business impact analysis.
- The information protection policy.
- The information protection strategy.
- Technical and management requirements.

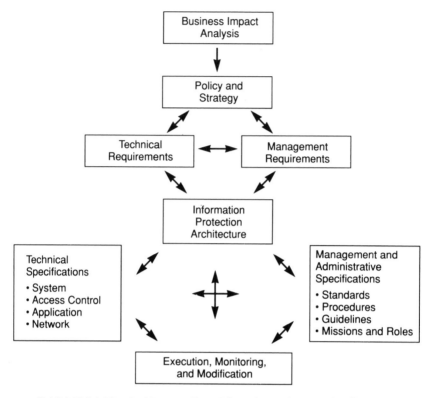

Exhibit X-3-1. The Architecture-Based Security Implementation Process

---

- The information protection architecture.
- Technical and management specifications.
- Execution, monitoring, and modification of the information protection program.

At first view, the diagram might suggest a straight-line developmental sequence among components, but the relationships are more complex. Although each component is important in its own right, it is also part of an ongoing activity that affects the other components in the process. For example, the protection strategy and policy provide information needed to develop the technical and management requirements. The bidirectional arrows shown in the exhibit indicate that each component influences the development of other components in an iterative fashion.

Business Impact Analysis. The business impact analysis provides the basis for justifying the information protection program and assigning priorities to the security measures to be implemented. The business impact analysis differs from more traditional risk analysis approaches because instead of concentrating on threats and their likelihood, it addresses such basic questions as:

- What are the critical business functions of the organization?
- To what extent do they depend on information processing?
- What applications and systems are critical to sustaining those business functions?
- If those applications were lost or compromised, how would the organization be affected?

Risk analysis should focus on those areas of the organization that have a significant impact on business operations. Too often, risk analyses do not garner much attention from management because they focus on relatively inconsequential areas. By focusing only on the likelihood of threats to significant areas of the organization, the business impact analysis addresses a smaller and more manageable group of issues.

Information Protection Policy. This policy is a relatively brief and high-level document that outlines management's objectives for the organization's information protection program. The policy's principal functions are to give guidance and to establish responsibilities and authority for the more detailed technical and administrative activities (e.g., classification, risk management, authorization, incident reporting, awareness programs, and the development of procedures, tools, and practices for implementing security and maintaining program continuity). The policy should outline the responsibilities of managers, employees, and outside participants in the enterprisewide information system. It should lay the groundwork but not substitute for standards, procedures, and guidelines; it should not contain detailed and specific instruction.

Information Protection Strategy. This document provides the general approach to be followed in implementing the information protection policy. The strategy's level of formality will vary with the organization, but the strategy should always establish the program's priority and the required level of organizational participation. The responsibilities outlined in the policy are further defined in the strategy and, when possible, given specific schedules for completion.

The primary output of the information protection strategy is a set of direction statements, which helps determine the technical and management requirements of the protection program. These requirements, in turn, help determine the information protection architecture.

Technical and Management Requirements. These requirements should be stated in terms of results to be achieved rather than required procedural steps. They should cover both technical and administrative aspects of the program and must be tightly coordinated to ensure consistency, appropriateness, and effectiveness. Need-to-know and single sign-on classifications are examples of requirements. The information protection architecture and the associated technical and management specifications stipulate how the requirements are to be attained.

Information Protection Architecture. The architecture is a statement of the desired design characteristics. It provides the basis for developing detailed technical and management specifications, which in turn determine the implementation process.

The architecture must be commonly understood and accepted by all of the participants in the design, development, and implementation process, including any entities outside the organization. The greater the number and diversity of the participants, the more important an explicit architecture becomes.

The architecture is developed on the basis of the technical and management requirements. For example, if a requirement exists for single sign-on, the architecture should address such issues as whether there will be multiple or single points in the system from which user and transaction authorization can be granted.

The architecture identifies and describes the security, control, and continuity services and functions to be supplied by the system, application, data base, and network subsystems. Perhaps most important, it describes the security, control, and continuity interface structures between subsystems. For example, it would describe the controls used when passing authorization characteristics from one subsystem to another to ensure that critical information is not lost in the transfer between systems.

Technical and Management Specifications. The specifications describe in detail how a process or function should behave. They are the basis for the development of standards, procedures, measurement programs, training, mission statements, and job descriptions and for the design and selection of hardware and software.

The format and structure of the specifications should correspond to those already in use by the organization. To the greatest degree possible, the entire information protection program should have a familiar appearance to the technicians, managers, and users responsible for designing and implementing the program. This familiarity helps eliminate confusion.

Execution, Monitoring, and Modification. Although the flow of the process diagram in Exhibit X-3-1 is directed toward creating a working protection program, the program must be sufficiently flexible and modifiable to reflect changes in the business environment, to accommodate phased implementation, to rectify mistakes, to provide opportunities for improvement, and to propagate those changes all the way back through the process. Program execution, monitoring and feedback, and modification are therefore integral to the information protection process.

It is extremely important that monitoring and audit mechanisms be incorporated into the process from the start. This should not be confused with incident reporting or handling of violations. Although the gathering of such statistics is important, there are other design objectives—such as ease of use, consistency, cost-effectiveness, and adaptability—that also require observation, measurement, and reporting. At every level of design and development, the methods of measurement to be used should be established and agreed on by all functions in the organization that are charged with monitoring system use and performance (e.g., internal audit, IS, and information protection administration). Measurement programs should be designed and implemented along with, not after, the information protection program.

DETERMINING NEED

It may be unnecessary for every organization to develop an information protection architecture in its full, formal sense, though every information processing system has protective architectural characteristics—even if they are the defaults supplied by the vendors. Certain reliable indicators that can help determine when the development of an architecture is warranted.

Multiple Technology Platforms. Multiple platforms can include hardware, software, or both. The connectivity and interoperability of multiple platforms can pose significant security and control problems. Systems compatibility, consistency, comprehensiveness of function, and control are all subject to greater variation, even among hardware and software products that subscribe to the same standards.

For example, protocol converters, bridges, routers, and gateways are commonly used within and between networks. Their primary jobs are to direct message traffic and to convert message format and coding to fit the different environments the messages travel through en route to their destinations. How these devices carry out these functions and the degree to which control is preserved in the process are architectural issues.

Multiple Logical Networks. A logical network is defined as a group of network nodes and facilities that support common business functions and applications. A single physical network may support several logical networks, and a single node or workstation may be part of several logical networks.

Although the security of the physical network is a common denominator, the controls and security requirements of each logical network may be vastly different. Designing these controls and security functions in the most cost-effective way is a significant architectural concern. For example, if only a small number of applications require encryption, it may be more cost-effective to structure encryption around selected logical networks rather than the entire physical network. As another example, certain logical networks may not require password protection, provided they do not allow backdoor entry to other networks.

Shared Data. In a shared environment, the requirements for data classification and the authorization of access to data must be reevaluated. Ownership rules must be reexamined. The data administrator or data base administrator may be the only individuals who can reliably produce the information necessary for auditing where and by whom data is used and determining by whom the authority was granted.

Consistent classification of all views and copies of the same data must be ensured. If the same information is being shared by multiple users on different systems and applications, it is highly possible that the same data element may be logically known to each system and application by a different name or identifier. Consistent and appropriate classification of data must start with consistent identification of that data. Close coordination of design and implementation of such fundamentals as data descriptions, naming conventions, and aliases is absolutely necessary.

One of the primary purposes of an architectural approach is to bring the control and security issues in data design, administration, and use to the surface for early resolution. It is important that the data architecture contain within it the applicable security and control architecture characteristics; neither should be developed in isolation.

Interoperable Systems and Applications. Interoperable systems and applications are those that can be run on different types and scales of hardware and operating system platforms. For example, UNIX-based applications are interoperable.

Interoperable systems and applications must be able to identify, process, and transmit security and control transactions in a consistent and effective manner. This is not the same as passing transactions or messages across different platforms to programs written for those specific platforms. With interoperable systems and applications, the objective is for the same program to run on different platforms.

For protection to be complete in an interoperable environment, there cannot be any independent or rogue subsystems or applications with their own individual security processes or without any security functions at all. Through gradual development and implementation of design standards in accordance with the architectural view, even widely diverse systems and applications can be reengineered to fit a common security design. The architecture provides the basis for establishing priorities for reengineering.

Integrated Business Functions. If all members of the same business function are to be connected and share the same data and application sets, regardless of location or platform, the security and control rules for that function should be consistent, relevant, and cost-effective. The business function may constitute a logical network or a hierarchy of logical networks within the enterprise.

External Users. External users include those involved in electronic funds transfers, electronic data interchanges, and other exchanges between organizations. Generally, the relationship between organizations should be governed by explicit, formal security interfaces and procedures as well as agreed-on recovery activities. Incidents in which one partner transfers a virus infection to another highlight the need for mutual protection between partner organizations.

Distributed Processing. To be effective, distributed processing relies on consistent treatment of shared information and other resources, and consistent security and recovery processes are part of that treatment. The principles of consistent protection apply just as strongly regardless of whether the information is transferred within a network or by means of portable tapes and disks.

Outsourced Systems Development and Management. In any outsourcing arrangement, security and continuity requirements must be explicitly agreed on by all parties. Data service organizations often commission a third-party information security review, which is typically performed for the benefit of their customers' auditors. Instead of each customer performing its own audit of the controls, customers rely on the third-party review. A similar relationship should exist for reviewing the design and development of security controls.

Although it is seldom the case, security specifications should be included in all software contracts and procurements as well as in all processing management contracts. Similarly, it is essential to have a common set of protection design, development, and operating procedures for all outsourced activities.

Differentiated Access Control. A prevalent approach to access control is to have one authorization permit access to the entire system and its resources. Most organizations, if they intend to differentiate and classify resources, require finer granularity in controlling access. An architectural approach can help consistency, effectiveness, and appropriateness in applying differentiated access rules and technologies throughout the organization.

DEVELOPING AN INFORMATION PROTECTION ARCHITECTURE

An information protection architecture should not be developed in isolation. If it is, its chances of approval and successful implementation are minimal. It is important to recognize that information protection architectures are derivative, because many of their functions and characteristics are based on system, application, and network processes. For example, in some platforms, access control is integrated into the operating system design. Furthermore, such an architecture is dependent on the implementation of system, application, and network functions and administrative procedures for its execution. Therefore, not only must control procedures be developed as independent processes, but integrated control characteristics must be developed in system, application, data base, and network functions.

Finally, the architecture is subordinate, in the sense that controls are seldom developed before or even along with functional processes. One of the reasons for the architectural process is to introduce control considerations as early as possible in the development cycle.

For these and similar reasons, any approach to developing an information protection architecture must integrate the planning, design, development, implementation, and operational tools and approaches to be used by the organization. This is an important exercise that should be performed early in the system life cycle.

If the organization uses a systems development life cycle methodology, the methodology should integrate security and continuity control mechanisms into overall systems planning, design, and development. The organization should determine the control, security, and continuity implications (positive, negative, or neutral) of the use of a specific CASE technology and should determine how to protect the CASE resources themselves (e.g., repositories and encyclopedias). This is only a small sample of areas that the organization must explore. It is important to determine to what extent the organization's methods and tools facilitate or inhibit development of protective measures and establish a plan for dealing with the realities.

System Access Issues

Assuming the organization has classified information resources and, as part of that process, determined how each level of information is to be protected, the next objective is to control system access by individuals and processes. To accomplish this, five basic functions must be addressed:

- Authorization (by user, process, and resource).
- Identification (by user, group, device, program, and transaction).
- Access control (by system, application, action, resource, or value).
- Accountability (by user, action, and resource).
- Auditability (to facilitate monitoring, reporting, and reconstructing processes and events).

Each of these functions is the subject of a set of architectural statements that will in turn lead to more detailed specifications, standards (as necessary), and procedural guidelines to ensure effective design, development, and implementation.

In developing an information protection architecture, these five functions must be examined in each processing environment, application, and procedure. First, the requirements for each of these functions must be determined for the environment, application, or procedure under study. The tools, techniques, and procedures currently used to support these functions must be evaluated to determine whether they are adequate for the proposed design. If they are not adequate, the requirements for additional tools and procedures must be established. In addition, it must be determined whether any conflict exists between these functions and such other system or procedural objectives as cost, speed, capacity, or ease of use.

The second step is to pinpoint the areas that have top priority for implementation, as established by the strategic priorities of the organization. If these implementation priorities conflict with any other information-related plans and priorities, the affected areas must be reevaluated and the conflict resolved.

Third, specifications must be developed for the required hardware, software, and procedures. These specifications should describe the desired process steps and results in detail, but they should not attempt to actually design or determine the hardware or software—that is the developer's responsibility. The specifications should include methods for measuring the design and evaluating levels of performance and function.

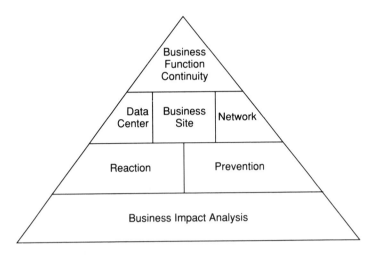

Exhibit X-3-2. Enterprisewide Continuity Planning

ENTERPRISEWIDE CONTINUITY PLANNING

Any comprehensive protection program must also ensure the continuity of system operations throughout the enterprise. Exhibit X-3-2 outlines a program for such enterprisewide continuity planning.

Beginning at the base of the triangle shown in the exhibit, the first step is to conduct a business impact analysis to identify the critical business functions that must be protected by the continuity plan. The next higher level of the triangle presents two types of strategies for ensuring the continuity of critical business functions: preventive strategies and reactive strategies. Preventive mechanisms help to minimize the likelihood of system failure by enhancing the robustness of the system, network, and business site. This is the appropriate level of protection for business activities that cannot tolerate any outage. In cases in which some level of outage can be tolerated, reactive measures are established to respond to an outage after it occurs (e.g., using backup and recovery techniques). In most business environments, an optimal continuity strategy involves a mixture of preventive and reactive techniques and controls.

The third level of the triangle identifies three areas that are the primary targets for prevention and recovery: the data center, business site, and network. It is no longer sufficient to plan for recovery of the data center alone; in fact, in certain businesses, the data center may not be the most critical area to be recovered. For example, in such applications as telemarketing, recovery of the network and the business site where orders are taken may take precedence over recovery of the central computer center. After all, it is possible to process orders without a computer, but not without a functioning business site and communications network.

The prevention and recovery plans for these three areas constitute the business function continuity plan, shown at the top level of the triangle. This continuity plan can be expanded into an enterprisewide protection plan.

Recovery and prevention plans affect how information systems are designed and built. Especially when prevention is a primary strategy, the rigorous implementation of controls during software design and development reduces the potential for serious system failure.

IMPLEMENTING THE PROTECTION PROGRAM

An architecture-based information protection program is designed to be implemented over a relatively long time period—usually from three to five years. However, the iterative nature of the process allows the enterprise to meet objectives for enhanced systems security and continuity at each stage of development. For example, such benefits as improved data classification and access authorization can be achieved relatively quickly.

Many types of organizations have used this approach, including manufacturing and financial enterprises. Technically, most organizations share such common traits as the use of multiple platforms in networked environments. However, there are often great dissimilarities in terms of the developmental stage of their security programs. Some organizations implement the protection program in an already highly developed, policy-driven security environment, whereas others are just beginning to develop a formal security program.

Organizations may also differ with respect to the development of the system security architecture. Some enterprises may already have a mature system and network architecture in which protection rules and constraints are already in place. This provides the advantage of a formal management approach to systems design and development that is accustomed to architectural concepts and methods; in such an environment, it may be easier to implement an architecture-based protection program. However, if design rules and constraints are already firmly established, it may be difficult to implement new protection mechanisms. Of course, this is only a problem if the original controls were not well designed.

Organizations do not necessarily follow the same set of procedures in implementing a protection program. For example, if management has already determined the organization's critical business functions and applications, it may not be necessary to perform a business impact analysis. This caveat aside, however, most successful implementations of an information protection program follow a three-stage process.

Stage One. During the first stage, key members of such control-related functions as security, internal audit, and quality assurance should review existing controls. (A facilitator can be used to keep the group focused and on schedule.) Information can be obtained by reviewing current systems management practices and tools, audit comments, incidents of computer error and failure, and planned and existing control objectives and policies. The point is simply to obtain as clear a picture as possible of the status of controls, without judging their adequacy. This process should attempt to determine the availability of information that pertains to each component of the information protection program. For example, such information may include the data needed to perform a business impact analysis or the technical requirements needed to build controls.

Stage Two. During the second stage, the adequacy of existing program components is evaluated. For example, if there is an existing protection policy and strategy, does it accurately reflect the current controls environment? This evaluation will help determine how the enterprise should implement the protection program. If policy, strategy, and requirements are found to be already well defined, it may be sufficient to focus on developing detailed technical and managerial specifications and control mechanisms. On the other hand, if policies and requirements have not been adequately defined, it may be necessary to take a more comprehensive approach, starting at the beginning of the protection process summarized in Exhibit X-3-1.

Stage Three. The third stage involves gathering organizational support for implementing the protection program. The group convened during the first two stages should now be expanded to include representatives from all areas of the organization that will need to be involved in building the program. These include the CIO or IS director, network managers, data administrators, department managers, application owners, and concerned staff. The objective at this stage is twofold. First, it is necessary for this group to validate and accept the recommendations developed in the preceding stages and to demonstrate a willingness to commit to the selected approach. Second, participants must reach a common understanding of how security requirements affect current and planned projects in each of their areas of responsibility. The group should identify, and assign relative priorities to, the preparatory actions that must be performed in order to begin implementing the program.

CONCLUSION

The success of this process depends, in large part, on the degree to which participants believe in the importance of information protection to the enterprise and in the need for implementing a consistent, cost-effective protection program. It is less important that they agree on the specific means to a given security objective; after all, the program is designed to develop such agreement.

Participants must, however, recognize the value of designing and implementing effective controls as systems and applications are built, not after the fact. Retrofitting security controls to existing systems is the least effective and most expensive way of implementing a security program. The purpose of an enterprisewide security process is to ensure that no single processing characteristic—speed, capacity, ease of use, function, or protection—dominates the design of the system. Compromise is therefore an essential element of a successful program. It should also be recognized that administrative and managerial controls are as important to the success of the protection program as are purely technical controls.

In implementing an information protection program, the organization must make a substantial commitment of both time and resources. This commitment will be repaid by a cost-effective, coordinated approach to information protection.

Section XI
Auditing

IN MANY CASES the IS management team and internal auditors share the responsibility to ensure that information processing resources are properly used and protected in the enterprise. This applies in business, government, and not-for-profit organizations. Another experience management of the IS and internal auditing groups share is the need to improve productivity within their respective organizations.

One way to improve productivity is to integrate the audits that were formally conducted separately. This approach has implications for the IS manager, because auditors need training and experience in IS topics in order to perform effectively. For the auditing manager it means that a new and very different approach to audits must be introduced and implemented.

The internal audit function faces a number of challenges. Companies are cutting staff; microcomputers and electronic communication are becoming standard means of doing business. The use of information engineering is spawning enterprisewide data bases and integrated applications. The internal auditor can no longer afford to be somewhat familiar with IS technology. Internal audit staff must make the transition to total integration, developing IS and financial audit skills. Chapter XI-1 examines "The Integrated Audit Approach" with emphasis on practical ways to make the transition.

Chapter XI-2 is a broad discussion of "Developing and Testing Business Continuity Plans." Contingency plans often address only mainframe operations. This chapter describes the necessity to extend this specialized planning to the full range of IS installations.

Because businesses depend on their information, planning for the recovery of an interruption to data processing functions has become a top priority. With information spread throughout the organization, a more comprehensive form of recovery planning and testing is essential. Comprehensive business recovery solutions must include not only large systems but midrange systems, networks, and work groups. Chapter XI-2 presents steps for developing and testing a comprehensive business resumption plan. The discussion covers specific plan development stages, testing objectives, and actual testing approaches. Basic guidelines and recommendations are given for a test plan that helps ensure business continuity.

XI-1

The Integrated Audit Approach

Jack B. Mullen

INTERNAL CONTROL SYSTEMS have traditionally been reviewed by separate IS and financial staffs, with the overhead of two separate management teams and the production of separate audit reports. Separate audits, which have one budget for the review of non-IS activities and another for those related to IS, consist of separate audit programs, audit management teams, time schedules, testing, and audit reports.

The IS application audit evaluates computer processing controls by analyzing transaction origination, input, processing, and certain output controls performed in the manual environment. However, some of these controls are also examined during the financial audit, resulting in redundancy. Data integrity controls are the user's responsibility during input and output phases, which require coverage in both audits.

The separate audit approach does not address the timing of the two audits, often resulting in inconclusive testing or redundancy. Input, processing, and output control reviews are performed by separate staffs during different periods. Procedural changes in user operations implemented after the first (usually financial) audit but before the second (application audit) may either correct or exacerbate control weaknesses previously detected. This requires repeating certain audit steps.

If compensating controls in the manual or automated portions of the system are not found, audit findings may be invalid. The separate approach creates an environment in which the IS auditor's knowledge and experience become one-sided from concentrating on the IS aspects, and although some review of the manual system is required, the IS auditor is often unfamiliar with the manual operation, accounting framework, or business activities within which computer systems must operate. Supervision of the separate audits requires more time and duplicates effort, because both audits require separate management teams. Separate audits produce redundancies in preliminary surveys, internal control questionnaires, compliance testing, and administration.

THE ONE-TEAM APPROACH

To improve on separate audits, some organizations have tried to share resources and use one management team with a mix of both IS and financial auditors to audit the complete system. Financial and IS auditors were assigned to the audit under the supervision of one manager, one supervisor, and one in-charge auditor, who planned the audit and designed the testing for both sides of the audit. However, a single audit program was not always developed, and the management teams did not usually have sufficient training to prepare proper IS testing or to review IS audit work papers.

An additional change involved the development of a technical support group consisting of high-level IS audit specialists skilled in advanced IS topics to handle data base systems, online systems, systems software, and other audits. They provided technical consulting to the audit staff and conducted systems development reviews.

TOTAL INTEGRATION

The final evolutionary phase of the audit function is total integration. The internal audit industry is currently moving toward this goal. All management team members are trained in IS and financial audit disciplines, and little crossover consulting is needed. Staff auditors are trained in both audit disciplines and use a single audit program. An IS audit technical support group handles the high-tech IS audits, and a single audit report is issued that covers the total system, including compensating controls and problems. Audit efficiency is at its peak with this approach.

Total integration is designed to analyze the complete control environment with one scope and audit program, evaluate results, and present an audit report covering the total control environment. This approach permits evaluation and testing of the manual and automated systems from a data flow perspective.

Total integration does not suggest total elimination of IS audit specialists. There will always be the need for IS audit technicians to review the highly technical areas of IS, because the entire audit staff cannot be cost-effectively trained to keep up with the rapid technological changes of online, operating, data base management systems, and other IS environmental areas. The high-level technical IS audit specialist, however, is only a small segment of what is needed; therefore, integration can reduce overall audit staff requirements and costs.

The In-Charge Auditor. Familiarity with system details decreases in higher levels of the audit management organization, regardless of the audit approach. The focal point of the audit work under the integrated organization structure is the staff auditor, because both the automated and manual portions of the system are observed by one single auditor. The knowledge gained from preliminary survey and testing is passed up from this level. All audit team members above the focal point, therefore, have more knowledge of the total system.

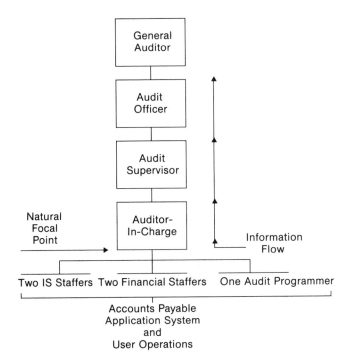

Exhibit XI-1-1. One-Team Audit Approach Job Organization Structure

---

The focal point under the one-team structure is the in-charge auditor, because the automated and manual portions of the system are observed by separate auditors and passed to the in-charge auditor. Therefore, although the level of detailed knowledge decreases at higher audit management levels, a more extensive knowledge now exists among the audit staff as a whole. Exhibit XI-1-1 depicts the one-team organization structure.

Testing. Compliance testing is designed to test the controls throughout transaction processing instead of in separate segments using separate tests. The test programs are designed by a single team on the basis of a preliminary survey of the entire system. The transactions subject to review are completely flowcharted, from transaction origination to report output. The testing of a transaction flow is designed to include the effects of the entire system. Therefore, all input, processing, and output controls (manual or automated) are reviewed for each selected transaction, which prevents inconclusive testing. This allows for continuity of testing and documentation of the control weaknesses and permits the issuance of a single report.

One auditor, under total integration, observes the entire flow and all control points associated with that transaction in place of two separate auditors with two objectives observing two distinct and separate portions of the system that actually relate to each other. The testing is more efficient and effective and provides greater probability of isolating all true errors in control techniques. This testing design permits formation of an opinion of the total control environment, reduction in time to perform the audit evaluation of the manual operations flow relating to computer processing, and reduced scheduling and interface problems.

Most programming of automated testing should be left to experienced technicians to permit its timely completion. Simple audit software programming, if closely supervised, can be performed by an inexperienced auditor as a training exercise.

Timing. The timing of audit work is totally controlled by one management group and is more easily managed as staff members become available. As information-gathering phases give way to testing, staff size can be altered without regard to coordinating test results with a separate team or another auditor. With the one-team approach, the auditor leaving one audit must advise the rest of the testing team, the in-charge auditor, and possibly the supervisor and manager of any test results, perceptions, and opinions they have accumulated during their work. Written documentation is not sufficient; spoken communication is necessary to convey the proper message because someone else will complete the test. With total integration, one auditor is assigned to test a given transaction. When the audit is completed, this person communicates the completed test results, perceptions, and opinions to the in-charge auditor by way of standard audit documentation. The auditor is then free to move on to another task or audit.

Budget Considerations. Initially, the budget of the one-team audit remains close to the subtotal of the two separate audits. As experience increases, the hours to complete the one-team or integrated audit decrease, becoming less than the sum of the two parts.

Productivity. Productivity management constantly searches for methods to reduce cost without reducing quality. The separate audit approach, although necessary in some circumstances, requires more time to complete the extra administrative and functional audit activities.

Through persistent effort in implementing total integration, reductions in hours will be gained slowly in the evolutionary process from separate to integrated audits. The exact reduction is difficult to determine, because it depends on the organization's requirements. Generally, a 20% decrease in chargeable time is reasonable. Administrative time reductions are the most obvious; however, other time improvements can be gained by more efficient test design and work assignment.

User and IS Exposure. The separate audit approach induces the auditor to hold postaudit conferences with the user for the manual portion and IS personnel for the IS portion. Although IS personnel share certain insights into manual operations, they do not always completely understand the effect of internal control weaknesses on the total system. With the integrated approach, user and IS representatives are usually invited to a single postaudit conference, exposing both parties to the audit results. This technique gradually increases the understanding of IS and user personnel of the total control system.

Career Pathing. Traditional audit approaches require a certain degree of specialization for each business unit and IS situation. College graduates entering the internal audit profession view it as a stepping stone, because of the wide exposure obtained. These people are willing to work for overall IS and business unit exposure, but few are willing to commit to specialization early in their careers. Integration, system flow evaluation, and staff pooling permit broad exposure, providing more auditors with a broader understanding of the total system.

Training. The training necessary depends on the overall job mix, IS audit experience of the management team, and existing level of experience. For example, an IS audit manager may need accounting training or education about the business area. The financial audit manager may need IS audit technique training or consulting assistance. Managers, supervisors, and auditors-in-charge must eventually gain sufficient experience to manage, design, and control technical IS audit aspects; these management techniques can be learned. During the learning period provided by one-team pilot audits, design, implementation, and control of the technical aspects can be achieved through use of the IS auditors on a direct assignment or consultant basis until sufficient experience is gained by the management team. Most important, the manager should possess strong management skills.

CHECKLIST AND SYSTEM FLOW EVALUATION TECHNIQUES

System flow evaluation is a controversial technique because of the extended time required to prepare flowcharts and analyze the control system. Some auditors prefer to concentrate on control points and exposures provided by the checklist technique, but this requires specific training and experience in the subject area, control objectives, techniques, and risks to permit an adequate review so that key points are not omitted. The system flow evaluation technique brings the audit of the manual system more in line with IS application audit techniques. The use of the checklist technique does not prohibit use of the integrated approach.

Checklist Technique

The checklist technique uses standardized audit programs and internal control questionnaires developed through experience and aimed at specific control exposures. It concentrates on specific areas within an auditee's function but does not always examine the complete transaction flow. In an accounts receivable audit, for example, the checklist approach typically reviews controls governing charges, credits, cash receipts, credit and collection activities, and reconciliation to general ledger. The risk of missing compensating controls, or the lack of them in other areas, is increased.

System Flow Evaluation

System flow evaluation is a technique for review and documentation of a business area that is accomplished by focusing on the flow of information created to complete business activities. Because each business area uniquely defines its activities and functions, the auditor must have a general control evaluation technique that is easily adaptable to and considers the individual characteristics of an area. A common denominator among all business area activities is the transaction, an event recognized as affecting the organization's financial statements.

The system flow evaluation technique is a detailed analysis of internal controls for a set of activities affecting a transaction. Various monetary and nonmonetary events can be grouped into similar transactions because they are subjected to similar processes and can be combined into a single transaction review.

The major phases of system flow evaluation include preliminary survey, compliance and substantive testing, other audit and review procedures, closure, housekeeping, and report follow-up. The preliminary survey accomplishes the following:

- Grouping events into similar transactions.
- Obtaining information on all functions affecting each transaction.
- Isolating the control techniques to prevent, detect, and correct irregularities.
- Transcribing this information into flowchart form.
- Testing each information flow line with a minimal number of transactions to ensure accuracy.

Compliance and substantive testing tasks are self-explanatory. Other audit and review procedures include special items that need attention and are not part of the routine audit (e.g., operational audit and special investigations). Closure consists of the steps necessary to prepare the audit report, including the postaudit conference with the auditee.

ORGANIZATIONAL CONSIDERATIONS

Because technical expertise is required to understand business activities, audit departments are often organized around an organization's major business units. IS supports all company activities; therefore, it does not qualify as a separate line of business. The audit organization, however, typically separates the IS audit and financial sections because of the technical expertise required to perform IS audits. The business activity auditors and IS auditors must be aware of the results of both audit efforts.

With integrated audits, IS auditors specialize in environmental and developmental audits. Environmental auditors are technical specialists who concentrate on audits of online systems, systems software, data base administration, and other highly technical areas. They are also best suited to review systems under development. Training costs are minimized because expense technical training is limited to a small group of people.

IMPLEMENTATION

As with any change, the implementation of the integrated approach requires a plan that depends on the existing audit philosophy and approach. To accomplish integration, it is best to use an evolutionary or phased approach.

The first phase is the one-team audit, which merges the audits of IS and non-IS systems into one total review, thereby eliminating the redundancies in completing the preliminary survey, testing, and administrative duties. The objective of one-team staffing is to produce a balance of IS and financial audit expertise that matches the system's sophistication, and to eliminate redundant management, specifically the in-charge, supervisor, and manager levels.

The second phase is total integration in which staff auditors are trained in both disciplines, there is no distinction between IS and financial auditors, and only one audit program is used. Total integration is the next logical step after the successful use of the one-team approach. By either means, the integrated audit approach:

- Produces an opinion of the total control environment.
- Reduces job staffing requirements.
- Reduces the time needed to audit a system.
- Evaluates the manual system flow as it relates to computer processing.
- Reduces scheduling and interface problems of two separate approaches.
- Lowers the recognition and resolution focal point of weaknesses in the total system.
- Simplifies supervision.
- Increases education of the user and programming personnel regarding the total system.
- Improves career path options for auditors.

Either approach requires one manager, one supervisor, and one in-charge auditor. The one-team audit uses an appropriate mix of IS and financial auditors to review a given area. The disadvantage of the one-team audit is IS audit staff supervision and review of IS audit work papers by supervisors and managers with insufficient IS audit experience.

Overnight Change

Implementation of the one-team approach can be accomplished through an evolutionary process or an overnight change (i.e., all audits after today will be accomplished through the one-team approach). The overnight change assumes that:

- Audit management possesses sufficient administrative skills.
- Audit management possesses sufficient IS and IS audit skills.
- The staff is adequately trained.
- An effective standardized planning technique exists.
- Organizational changes are accepted by the staff.

Evolutionary Change

The evolutionary process permits:

- All audit personnel to learn new techniques on the job over a period of time, eliminating intense classroom training in all topics.
- Audit management to learn new administrative and planning techniques through experience instead of in the classroom.
- Implementation of a new planning technique, if needed.
- A series of gradual minor organization changes, if needed, instead of major changes all at once. This gives people time to adjust and increases the chance of staff acceptance. Simultaneous major organizational changes may cause dissension, which could undermine the team spirit needed for this approach.

Phased Implementation

Experience has shown this method to be another effective means of implementation. If the integrated audit approach is to be beneficial to the organization, it should be phased in one audit at a time until all the bugs have been worked out. The phased implementation approach should include the following procedures:

- Selection of a simple automated area that is appropriate for the one-team approach.
- Preparation of a single audit program covering financial and IS functions.
- Selection of a pilot management team and staff to conduct the audit.
- Extensive review of the audit program with the pilot team to ensure it is efficient and effective.
- Training of the pilot team in IS and financial audit disciplines as needed.
- Training of the management team in review techniques for IS audit work papers.
- Conducting the audit and closely monitoring progress of all members of the audit team.
- Documentation of the complete flow of transactions, including the manual and automated interfaces.
- A review of all work papers—including the IS tasks—by the pilot management team. If the IS audit manager and supervisor are not part of the pilot team, one of them should review the IS transactions.
- Preparation and issuance of a single audit report, including comments on IS and the operations area.
- Conducting a postaudit review to isolate problem areas and fine tune the audit program and planning techniques.
- Fixing any problem areas and selecting another area for the pilot team to conduct a one-team audit.
- Repeating the one-team audit pilots until management is confident that the audit process is effective and efficient.

This phased implementation approach is more manageable and less expensive from a training standpoint, because any problems are isolated to one audit instead of several. The usual audit coverage is therefore not disrupted, and the training needs are more readily identifiable.

THE IMPLEMENTATION PLAN—TRANSITION TO TOTAL INTEGRATION

The following implementation plan begins for an audit staff using a separate audit approach and a checklist technique. The point at which a particular audit staff begins in this plan depends on its existing approach. The suggested steps are:

1. Adopt a system flow evaluation technique for appropriate business areas.
2. Adopt a detailed planning technique, including:
   —Task hours budgeting with actual hours tracking.
   —Task start and target dates.
3. Adopt appropriate audit management approval for and a methodology by which to identify and report:
   —Audit objectives.
   —Audit scope exclusions.
   —All transactions that exist and those to be reviewed.
   —Control objectives by transaction.
   —Key controls by transaction.
   —Risks and exposures and their priority by transaction.
   —Budget hours by task for each major phase.
   —Staffing, assignments, and time frame.
4. Execute IS and financial audits of the same area concurrently using standardized communication procedures for the management team, issuing one report if time permits.
5. Assign one team to an audit with dual in-charge auditors, supervisors, and managers when necessary to achieve an appropriate technical and management skill mix.
6. Begin migration to the one-team approach using the phased implementation approach.
7. Adopt the one-team approach with one management team for all audits.
8. Create new job descriptions for all auditor levels and remove the distinction between IS and financial auditors. All auditors have the same authority and responsibility for reviewing the business area activities and application system interface.
9. Create work-paper preparation standards and procedures for total integration, focusing on the fact that one auditor will complete a transaction review.
10. Revise work-paper review standards and procedures, and remove the distinction between IS and financial audit work papers. Focus on work papers that would be prepared under total integration.

11. Select a simple automated area that is appropriate for the integrated approach.
12. Prepare a single audit program covering financial and IS functions considering the fact that one auditor will complete a transaction test.
13. Select a pilot management team and staff to conduct the integrated audit.
14. Extensively review the audit program with the pilot team to ensure it is efficient and effective.
15. Identify training needs (IS and financial audit disciplines as appropriate) for management and staff.
16. Train the pilot team in IS and financial audit disciplines as needed.
17. Train the management team in review techniques for IS areas.
18. Conduct a pilot audit and closely monitor progress of all audit team members.
19. Review all work papers, including the IS tasks, by the pilot management team. An extra review by the IS audit manager and supervisor would help.
20. Prepare and issue a single audit report.
21. Conduct a postaudit review to isolate problem areas and fine tune the audit program and planning techniques.
22. Fix any problem areas and select another area for the pilot team to conduct an integrated audit. Refine audit programs, standards and procedures, and administrative and planning procedures.
23. Repeat the integrated audit pilots until management is confident that the audit process is effective and efficient.
24. Develop a new integrated organization structure, create new roles and responsibilities, and revise job descriptions. Focus on the shift of IS audit specialists to high-tech areas.
25. Obtain audit committee and executive management approvals for the new approach, organization structure, and job descriptions.
26. Implement the integrated audit approach and organization structure.

Staffing

The audit management team must be staffed with appropriately experienced personnel and must be well organized and able to work as a team. The audit manager provides an overview, keeping the audit on track with major objectives and within acceptable time frames. The supervisor concentrates on the details of the survey, testing, and technical advice within the scope of the audit. The auditor-in-charge is responsible for the detailed day-to-day task completion by the staff, isolating problems with the system or the staff, and reporting them to the supervisor for resolution.

The integrated approach is conducive to small audit staffs because they cannot afford to have extensive numbers of specialists for business activities and IS. In addition, new audit standards and regulations, particularly in the banking industry, pressure all audit staffs to conduct more frequent and more comprehensive audits.

Distributed Applications

Information engineering is bringing enterprisewide data bases and coordinated applications into existence. Although these applications are more efficient and flexible, the auditor's job becomes more complex because several business areas may need to be reviewed at the same time. Distributed data bases and applications exist on business area microcomputers, and their effect on the enterprisewide data base needs review. Only total integration can be effective and efficient enough to cope with these challenges.

The implementation of the integrated audit approach cannot happen by itself. Audit management should develop an implementation plan to lead its audit group through a methodical transition. The information supplied herein can help management develop a plan. As the audit staff progresses through the various phases, audit management will discover the information needed to justify the approach, training costs, and salary costs to the audit committee and executive management.

CONCLUSION

Each organization must evaluate the integrated approach to determine whether it is functional and beneficial. The key measurements are reduced costs, increased productivity, and more comprehensive audit coverage. Before implementation, it is necessary to develop techniques that can measure these benefits during a series of pilot audits.

The implementation costs of the integrated approach include training, development of an audit program, management and planning techniques, and possibly salary increases. Maintenance costs include the training of new staff and higher salary levels because of the IS training and experience.

Flexibility and acceptance of change are the trademarks of a good auditor. The changes that are occurring in organizations today exercise the auditor's flexibility. It is the audit manager's decision whether to anticipate and adjust for the change ahead of time or to just wait and react.

XI-2

Developing and Testing Business Continuity Plans

Kenneth A. Smith

COMPREHENSIVE BUSINESS resumption planning is growing beyond the walls of the data center. Business's growing dependence on multiple computing platforms and increasingly sophisticated communications networks is making companies more vulnerable to disaster. Actual disasters highlight the importance and vulnerability of distributed computing systems, even while mainframe recovery is becoming more reliable. Business continuity must address these evolving integrated and networked business environments.

Public awareness of the need for comprehensive business recovery is on the rise as well, probably largely because of the increase in major regional catastrophes during the past few years. The public sector is also getting involved, with increasing federal, state, and local government participation in comprehensive disaster planning.

Companies are reacting to this need by developing enterprisewide disaster recovery plans but are discovering a host of problems associated with comprehensive business recovery planning. These plans require far more participation on the part of management and support organizations than mainframe recovery planning. The scope is no longer limited to recovery; plans must integrate with existing disaster prevention and mitigation programs. These companywide resumption plans are costly to develop and maintain and are frequently prolonged, problematic, and unsuccessful.

Fortunately, there have been successes from which IS and auditing specialists can learn. This chapter presents some of the lessons learned, including some of the tools, techniques, and strategies that have proved effective.

COMPREHENSIVE BUSINESS RECOVERY STRATEGIES

Successful recovery from disaster often depends on workable and timely alternative operating recovery strategies. A well-known set of recovery strategies, including some simple and relatively inexpensive commercial products and services, has made recovery planning feasible for large-scale mainframes and midrange computers. New solutions are becoming increasingly available for small computer configurations and business resumption (e.g., work group) recovery. These evolving solutions are based on experiences gained from a multitude of single-site and regional disasters.

Formal recovery planning and testing is an essential part of the total recovery solution. Companies that develop, maintain, and regularly test their business resumption plans recover far better and faster than those that are not prepared.

Exhibit XI-2-1 illustrates the scope needed for a companywide business continuity program. Business resumption should be thought of as an ongoing program, much like existing avoidance programs (e.g., security) and loss-mitigation programs (e.g., insurance).

Resumption planning is moving into departmental work groups. Executive management and the support organizations are also taking part in business resumption through integrated crisis incident management planning. Numerous planning tools and strategies are available to help companies develop plans. The tools include commercially available software, consulting services, and several public-domain information sources. These tools and services are invaluable in reducing the effort, elapsed time, and cost involved in developing business resumption plans.

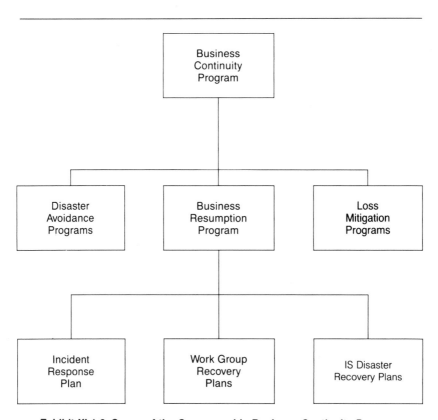

Exhibit XI-1-2. Scope of the Companywide Business Continuity Program

Before discussing how to develop a plan, it would be useful to review the available strategies for both computer and work group recovery. The following sections examine these strategies.

Mainframe Systems

The choice of which mainframe recovery strategy to follow is based primarily on business recovery timing requirements, cost, and reliability. Hot sites are generally the recovery strategy of choice for companies requiring rapid recovery. The commercial hot site is second only to an internally owned redundant site in terms of reliability and timing, and usually at less than 10% to 30% of the annual cost. In some areas (e.g., disaster support and telecommunications infrastructure), hot sites can actually provide a more reliable strategy than an internally owned redundant facility.

The potential strategies for mainframe and midrange computer recovery (discussed in the next section) are listed in Exhibit XI-2-2. Most organiza-

Strategy	Recovery Time Frame	Advantages	Disadvantages
Repair or Rebuild at Time of Disaster	6–12 months	• Least cost	• Time to recover, reliability, and testability
Cold Site (private or commercial)	1–6 weeks	• Cost-effective • Time to recover	• Testability • Detail plans are difficult to maintain • Long-term maintenance costs
Reciprocal Agreement	1–3 days	• Useful for specialized equipment in low-volume applications	• Not legally acceptable in some environments • Testability
Service Bureau	1–3 days	• For contingency planning (e.g. backup microfilm)	• Not available in large CPU environments
Shippable or Transportable Equipment	1–3 days	• Useful for midrange computing	• Logistical difficulties in regional disaster recovery
Commercial Hot Site	Less than 1 day	• Testability • Availability of skilled personnel	• Regional disaster risk
Redundant Facility	Less than 1 day	• Greatest reliability	• Most expensive • Long-term commitment and integrity

Exhibit XI-2-2. Mainframe and Midrange Recovery Strategies

tions use multiple strategies, depending on the severity of the disaster and expected outage duration. During planning, different strategies may be identified for different applications, depending on the potential business consequences.

The recovery time frames in Exhibit XI-2-2 do not imply either minimum or maximum times; these figures represent actual company experiences following disaster. For example, in two recorded examples of a total data center loss, the rebuilding time was 6 months for one company and 12 months for the other. Most recoveries using commercial hot sites have been accomplished within 8 to 24 hours.

When costs for mainframe recovery strategies are analyzed, it is important to realistically estimate personnel and equipment costs. In addition, the strategies should be planned to cover a minimum three-to-five year period to ensure that the cost of maintaining and upgrading equipment is considered. Equipment resources for mainframe strategies should be defined at a fairly detailed level, because the cost of the incidental infrastructure and network can significantly affect actual costs.

Evaluating potential hot-site or cold-site recovery vendors is less clearcut. Quality of service is most important but difficult to evaluate. Decisions are often made on the basis of technical and pricing criteria.

Midrange Systems

Effective business resumption planning requires that midrange systems be evaluated with the same thoroughness used with mainframes. The criticality of the midrange applications is frequently underestimated. For example, an analysis of one financial institution found that all securities investment records had been moved to a midrange system previously limited to word processing. Because it was viewed as office support, this system's data was not protected off site. Its loss would have meant serious if not irreparable damage to this company and its investors.

Midrange systems share the same list of potential recovery strategies as mainframes. In addition, shippable and transportable recovery alternatives may be feasible. Shippable strategies are available for recovery of several specific hardware environments, including DEC/VAX, IBM AS/400, and UNISYS.

Cold-site and repair or replacement recovery timeframes can be much shorter for midrange systems (e.g., days instead of weeks), because many systems do not require extensive facility conditioning. However, care should be taken to ensure that this is true for specific systems. Some systems are documented as not needing significant conditioning but do not perform well in nonconditioned environments.

Special considerations should be given to turnkey systems. Turnkey software vendors often do not package disaster recovery backup and off-site rotation with their systems. On the other hand, other turnkey vendors provide disaster recovery strategies as an auxiliary or additional cost service.

Companies using midrange systems frequently have mixed hardware and network platforms requiring a variety of recovery strategies and vendors.

When recovery strategies are being evaluated, some cost savings can be realized if all of the midrange systems are considered at the same time. Another planning consideration unique to the midrange environment is the limited availability of in-house technical expertise. Recovery at the time of the disaster often requires people with extensive skills in networking, environmental conditioning, and systems support. A single hardware vendor may not be able to supply these skills in the mixed platform environments.

In an evaluation of the recovery timing strategy, special attention should be given to recovery timing issues on midrange systems. Some platforms are notoriously slow in restoring data.

Work Group Systems

The computer recovery strategies can be borrowed and adapted to work group recovery planning. However, the optimum choices frequently differ because of the different technical and logistical issues involved. As a result, numerous commercial products and services are becoming available for work group recovery.

The goal of work group recovery planning is to re-establish essential day-to-day business functions before the consequential effects occur. To accomplish this, most organizations find it necessary to relocate their employees to an alternative location or to relocate the work itself. Exhibit XI-2-3 lists the most common work group strategies.

In addition to these alternative operating strategies, work group planning has some unique computer recovery challenges. Businesses' dependence on desktop computing is growing far faster and with less control than did their dependence on mainframe and midrange systems. Many businesses are absolutely dependent on these systems, but their degree of disaster awareness and preparation is seriously lacking.

Desktop Computers and Local Area Networks

Currently, the most common method of information protection is to back up data at a file server level and accept the business risk of the loss of microcomputer workstation data. In actual disasters, many companies have been found to be inadequately protecting their microcomputer-based information. The ultimate solution for desktop and local area network (LAN) information recovery rests in two major areas: standards and standards enforcement.

Planning for LAN recovery is made more difficult by the absence of standardized backup devices. Unlike mainframes and minicomputers, no backup media (e.g., no equivalent to standard mainframe 9-track tape) has been accepted industrywide. Backup device technology changes frequently and is not always downward compatible. Some companies have found it difficult to acquire older compatible technology at the time of a disaster. Redundant equipment and meticulous testing may be the only feasible solution.

The two most common hardware recovery alternatives for individual workstations are replacement at the time of the disaster and having shippable microcomputers. Ordering, packaging, assembling, and installing worksta-

Strategy	Recovery Time Frame	Advantages	Disadvantages	Comments
Repair or Rebuild at Time of Disaster	1–3 days	• Ongoing cost for office space and equipment	• Availability risk • Limited availability of special equipment and space	Rent space and buy replacement equipment
Shippable or Transportable Equipment	1–3 days	• Ease of use • Reliability	• Ongoing cost	Use commercial products and services
Hot Site or Cold Site	Immediate	• Testability	• Availability in regional disaster	Use commercial backup office space
Reciprocal Agreement	1–3 days	• Useful for specialized equipment in low-volume applications	• Limited application capacity	Arrange office space (internal) and specialized facilities (external)
Service Bureau	1–3 days	• Useful for daily contingency planning	• Not available for large CPU environments	Use commercial services (e.g., print shops and microfilm companies)
Redundant Facility	Immediate	• Greatest reliability	• High cost • Long-term commitment and integrity	Internal use only

Exhibit XI-2-3. Work Group Recovery Strategies

tions is a long and labor-intensive process during recovery. Use of commercial shippable microcomputers is more common because of the prepackaging of these systems. In addition, some disaster recovery vendors are providing LAN capability as part of the shippable offering.

Unfortunately, solutions for file server configurations are less clear-cut. Because these customized machine configurations are frequently not stocked in quantity by local computer suppliers, replacement can be quite difficult. Internal reciprocal and redundant options are being used for the file servers. One network software company and some recovery vendors are also making file servers available as a shippable alternative. This reduces the redundant hardware requirements to a backup device and software.

Technological obsolescence must be considered in any long-term LAN recovery strategy. Equipment purchased and stored off-site (e.g., redundant strategy) rapidly becomes obsolete. Reciprocal agreements require that hardware remain compatible over time, which is often difficult.

An even more difficult planning consideration is network wiring. Companies are wiring their buildings with special network facilities (e.g., IBM Token Ring and EtherNet), making relocation to dissimilar facilities difficult. Companies with multiple facilities (e.g., campus environments) can sometimes use reciprocal arrangements if capacities are sufficient. In the absence of these facilities or in a regional disaster, shippable microcomputers that include preinstalled network capabilities are the safest alternative.

Lack of industry-standard communications hardware is a problem in LAN and wide area network (WAN) recovery, making rapid replacement at the time of the disaster risky. Several shippable products (e.g., shippable bridges and gateways) are commercially available to assist LAN and WAN recovery. When these tools are unavailable, stockpiling of redundant equipment is usually the only recourse.

Wide Area Networks

Disaster recovery planning for WANs is still in its infancy. Even though few companies are addressing recovery of WANs, these networks are often installed to support vital business missions. For example, they are being installed to support mission-critical functions as LAN-resident business applications, electronic data interchange (EDI), and gateways to mainframes.

Recovery of a WAN is primarily a network planning issue. Wide area networks are typically connected using communications lines with massive bandwidth capabilities (e.g., 56K b/s or more). Typically, the same type of network solutions for large mainframe-based networks are available for WAN connections. Unfortunately, that massive bandwidth can also equate to large network expense.

Networking

Business impact studies have shown that voice and data communications networks must be restored in most locations at near-full production capacities, usually in a very short time. Some companies have found that the need for voice and data communications is actually higher than normal during a disaster.

Network recovery strategy decisions are driven by business timing requirements, choice of alternative processing decisions for computer recovery, work group recovery, and cost. The technical strategies and the menu of products and services are far too complicated to discuss here; however, the network strategy planning criteria are quite simple to describe.

Simply stated, network recovery strategies should address all technology and facilities required to reestablish connectivity. This includes person-to-person, person-to-computer, and computer-to-computer connections. All network components should be addressed and appropriate strategies decided on. For most components, the same recovery strategies previously described for computer and work group recovery can be applied. In addition, there are special requirements of work group facilities and communications equipment.

Work Group Facility. Loss of a work group facility requires replacing all equivalent network components. These include telephones, terminals, control units, modems, LAN network wiring, and the PBX. These may be obtained at time of disaster using replacement or shippable strategies. They may already be in place in an existing redundant, reciprocal, or commercial hot-site or cold-site facility. The same set of planning issues and network disaster recovery strategies can be employed.

Access to Communications. A disaster may affect the communications infrastructure outside the work group facility (e.g., loss of phone lines or a central office). In this case, an entirely different set of strategies comes into play. Two possible recovery strategies can be used: relocating to an alternative facility in which the infrastructure is in place or reconnecting to the surviving infrastructure through alternative facilities. Because of timing, these alternative communications facilities are usually redundant and can be quite expensive.

Electronic Vaulting

Electronic vaulting is an emerging disaster recovery strategy. Electronic vaulting allows critical information to be stored off-site through means of a network transfer rather than traditional backup and off-site rotation. Electronic vaulting brings two major benefits: decreased loss of data and shortened recovery windows.

In electronic vaulting, commercial disaster recovery vendors provide both remote transaction journaling and data base shadowing services. Several companies with multiple computer sites are using electronic vaulting internally on a variety of computer platforms. Electronic archiving is becoming fairly common in the microcomputer arena. Although use has been limited because of significant hardware and communications costs, these costs are expected to decline, making electronic vaulting more attractive in the future.

Until the costs become more reasonable and standardized technology is in place, however, electronic vaulting will be limited to selected applications needing its unique benefits. The business impact analysis process helps determine when this strategy is justified.

DEVELOPMENT APPROACH

Exhibit XI-2-4 is a graphical representation of a simple but effective three-phase approach for developing a business resumption plan. The foundation phase of the development methodology is identification of disaster recovery business requirements. Once these requirements are fully understood, appropriate recovery strategy planning can be conducted. Finally, detailed resumption plans, or action plans, may be developed and documented. All three of these recovery phases involve the surrounding elements of personnel, recovery, resources, and planned recovery action.

Project Planning and Management

Two of the first crucial activities within project planning are clearly defining the scope of the project and enlisting management support. In larger companies (e.g., those with more than 500 to 1,000 employees), the sheer magnitude of the task may justify staging work group recovery planning. Usually computer disaster recovery planning should be done before or at the same time as work group recovery planning. The business requirements phase helps identify the areas that need to be planned first as determined by the consequences of losing those organizations.

Important business decisions must be made during the planning process regarding preparedness and eventual recovery issues. Active management

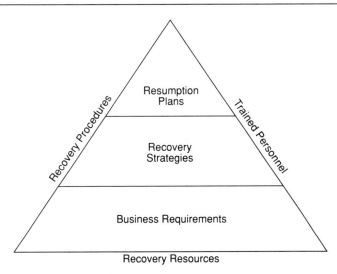

Exhibit XI-2-4. Recovery Planning Phases

support throughout the planning process is essential if the planning project is to be successful.

The success of the project is affected by selection of the development project team and distribution of planning responsibilities. Care should be taken to select a qualified project leader. The skills needed for an effective project manager or business resumption planner include:

- Extensive large project management skills.
- A thorough understanding of records and data protection concepts.
- A basic understanding of network concepts and recovery capabilities.
- Outstanding communication skills, both written and verbal.
- Knowledge of business resumption concepts.

Delegating responsibility for planning to individual work groups usually is not practical. Because of the learning curve and documentation skills required, it is more cost-effective to lend a specific work group these skills in the form of a qualified project manager. In addition, many recovery planning decisions involve centralized strategy planning (e.g., determining how the voice network will be recovered or how office equipment and departmental computers will be replaced). These activities would be better managed by a centralized project team.

On the other hand, some planning activities are more effectively conducted at the individual work group level. For example, inventorying of equipment resources, identifying minimum acceptable configurations, and identifying specific implementation requirements are all handled best by departmental management. Responsibility for maintaining the recovery capability must remain the individual work group's responsibility because it must use the plan when a disaster occurs.

Defining the Business Requirements

Once the project plan has been developed, actual business resumption planning can begin. The first and most essential step in this process is to gain an understanding of the business recovery requirements—that is, determining which functions must be recovered and when.

The business impact is often intuitively obvious without a formal analysis. For example, loss of a reservation system is a catastrophic event to an airline company. Other businesses and functions may need to conduct a formal business impact analysis to quantify the potential impact and timing requirements. In either case, it is necessary to understand the consequences and timing of the negative business impact of a disaster to each work group. Most of the negative effects on the business develop in spurts over time. For example, an outage of a few hours may be acceptable, but cessation of business operations for a few days may be intolerable.

The business impact may be quantified in tangible values, such as revenue (e.g., income), loss of assets (e.g., warehouse shrinkage), or lost sales (e.g, underwriting support). The impact may also be intangible, affecting such areas as company reputation, client satisfaction, and employee morale.

Gathering and analyzing business impact information and the current level of preparedness is best done by the project management team working with work group management. Care should be exercised to identify the appropriate level of management; the size of the organization often dictates the level of analysis. Questionnaires should be used sparingly; besides the obvious difficulty in getting responses, questionnaire responses almost always miss unique characteristics and effects on some work groups.

Selecting Appropriate Recovery Strategies

Once the business recovery timing requirements are understood, the choice of an appropriate recovery strategy becomes a business risk issue rather than an emotional issue. Recovery strategies vary by cost and the speed at which business operations can be resumed. Recovery strategies providing very fast recovery (e.g., redundant facilities) are usually expensive. At the other end of the scale, strategies for replacement at the time of the disaster may lower ongoing costs but can take considerably longer. The choice of recovery strategies must weigh the potential impact from loss of the business functions, relative timing of the impact, and the cost of protection compared to the business risk.

Once the business recovery timing requirements are understood, a company can immediately eliminate those strategies that do not meet the business needs. The remaining strategies can then be analyzed on the basis of their relative merits and costs, resulting in an informed business decision.

It is important to determine all strategies, not just the alternative computer processing strategy. For example, recovery of the voice network, the level of detailed planning, and the degree of training are all strategy issues that must be considered. As these recovery strategy decisions are weighed and decisions made (either explicitly or implicitly), these decisions should be documented along with the reasons for reaching the decision. Any resulting exposures should be documented.

Developing Detailed Resumption Plans

The final phase of business resumption planning is the detailed resumption planning. Planning must address all three recovery elements:

- Personnel.
- Recovery resources.
- Recovery actions.

A common mistake is to focus on personnel and recovery resource planning and to overlook planning and documenting the actual business resumption activities needed to resume operations.

Planning is best done in a series of working sessions conducted jointly by the project team and work group management. Testing is an integral part of the development process. Each of the following steps represents a work group planning session:

- Step 1: Formulating the strategy.
- Step 2: Analyzing the implementation.

- Step 3: Validating the implementation.
- Step 4: Approving the recovery plans.

The project team may assist the work groups in carrying out these steps. In addition, the project team is responsible for much of the preparatory work for these steps, because these team members have more knowledge of disaster recovery and more experience in writing plans. The work groups bring special knowledge of their particular areas to the planning process.

Formulating the Strategy. The work group must review the business requirements and high-level recovery strategies and then formulate implementation plans and strategies. As a result of this planning session, recovery management and logistical issues will be defined and documented.

Analyzing the Implementation. A work-flow analysis is a useful tool with which to conduct this planning. By reviewing how work is processed on a daily basis, the work group can identify which recovery actions would be required to recreate this environment in an alternative operating location.

Detailed planning should identify those individuals responsible for managing the recovery process. In addition, any key technical resources (internal or external) necessary for effecting recovery should be identified and documented within the recovery plan.

Logistical arrangements and administrative activities must be clearly documented in a plan. A frequent complaint of companies recovering from a disaster is that the logistical and administrative activities, particularly in regard to personnel, are inadequately planned.

Testing should be considered in planning the recovery activities. Resources should be documented in such a way that their presence may be validated during exercises. Information resources (e.g., vendor contacts and emergency phone numbers) should be usable during exercises.

Validating the Implementation. Once plans have been defined and documented, they should be validated through testing. This can be done in a manual exercise of the plan, comparing the plan's recovery actions against a hypothetical disaster scenario. Following this validation, iterative implementation planning sessions may be required.

Approving the Recovery Plans. In each step, recovery strategies, actions, and resources are documented. As a final step, the plans should be formally reviewed, accepted, and turned over from the project team to the respective work groups.

TESTING THE PLAN

There is no surer way to turn a disaster recovery manual into waste paper than to fail to frequently and periodically test the plan. Testing is critical in the development and ongoing maintenance of business resumption plans.

There are five important reasons why business resumption plans should be tested periodically. These reasons apply equally to traditional mainframe and midrange planning and work group recovery planning. The reasons are:

- Testing proves whether the recovery plan works and whether it can meet the business's recovery requirements.
- Testing the plan identifies the weak links in the plan, allowing them to be corrected before the plan is actually needed.
- Testing the plan is the primary employee training tool. Frequent testing of the plan enhances employees' familiarity with the strategies and implementation process and also raises general awareness levels.
- Periodic testing is necessary to comply with legal and regulatory requirements for many organizations. Although this is especially relevant in the banking industry and some insurance companies, it is fast becoming a de facto regulatory requirement for all industries.
- Testing is a prudent business practice. The testing program protects the initial development investment, reduces ongoing maintenance costs, and protects the company by ensuring that the plan will work when a disaster occurs.

Testing is a universal term used in the disaster recovery industry. Unfortunately, testing has a negative pass/fail connotation carried over from school days. The term *testing* would be better replaced by such terms as *exercising* or *rehearsing*. Finding problems during a test should not be viewed as failure when it is really the basic reason for conducting the exercise. Attention should be focused on the positive, not the punitive. For the testing program to be successful, this attitude should be carefully communicated to employees.

Testing Approaches

An effective testing program requires different types of tests to cost-effectively examine all components of the plan. For the purposes of this discussion, testing can be categorized into four types.

Desk Checking or Auditing. The availability of required recovery resources can be validated through an audit or desk check approach. This type of test should be used periodically to verify stored, off-site resources and the availability of planned time-of-disaster acquisitions. Desk checking or auditing is limited to validating the existence of resources and may not adequately identify whether other resources are required.

Simulations by Walkthroughs. Personnel training and resource validation can be performed by bringing recovery participants together and conducting a simulated exercise or plan. A hypothetical scenario is presented, and the participants jointly review the recovery procedures but do not actually invoke recovery plans. This type of exercise is easy to conduct, inexpensive, and effective in verifying that the correct resources are identified. More important, this testing approach helps train recovery personnel and validate the recovery actions through peer appraisal.

Real-Time Testing. Real-time testing is frequently done on the mainframe or hot-site backup plan and is gaining popularity in work group recovery planning. Real-time testing provides the greatest degree of assurance but is the most time-consuming and expensive approach. If only limited real-time testing is planned, priority should be given to high-risk areas.

Mock Surprise Testing. Surprise tests are a variation of the other three approaches but with the added dimension of being unanticipated. This type of test is frequently discussed but rarely used. The inconvenience for personnel and the negative feelings it generates tend to outweigh its advantages. The benefits derived from a mock surprise disaster can be achieved by careful attention and implementation of controls to avoid the possibility of cheating during planned exercises.

These four testing approaches can be combined into an unlimited variety of tests. For example, walkthroughs can be extended by actually performing some recovery activities (e.g., notifying vendors). Training facility equipment can be used to test replace-at-time-of-disaster strategies, alleviating the need to actually purchase replacement computers, desks, tables, and chairs.

Test Planning Matrix

Orderly and organized testing is necessary to ensure that all recovery strategies and components are being adequately validated. A matrix approach may be used to ensure that all plan components were adequately considered, as determined by their level of importance (e.g., business impact) and risk (e.g., reliability and complexity of recovery strategy). The matrix presented in Exhibit XI-2-5 illustrates this concept.

PLAN RECOVERY COMPONENTS / TEST PLAN	Type of Test	Frequency of Testing	Comments
Crisis Management Plans			
Data Center • Phase 1			
• Phase 2			
• Phase 3			
Work Group 1			
Work Group 2			
⋮ Work Group *n*			

Exhibit XI-2-5. Test Planning Matrix

In this approach, one or more tests are identified for each component of the plan. The organization can develop a long-range (e.g., two-year) test program during which each element and component of the plan is verified or validated. The test program can then be reviewed and revised periodically (e.g., annually) on the basis of testing results, identified exposures, and training requirements.

Work groups testing approaches and frequency depend on the complexity of the organization. For ease of testing and awareness purposes, some plans may be separated and tested by phase (e.g., test alert notification and alternative-site restoration). In general, technical resources (e.g., computer systems or network recovery) require frequent real-time testing. Work group computing needs occasional real-time testing to ensure that the recovery strategies work when they are needed.

Some departments (e.g., outside sales and long-term strategic planning) have fairly low risk in recovery, allowing less rigorous testing to be done. Process-oriented departments, such as order processing, credit and collections, and plant scheduling, have greater risk and recovery complexities, justifying more frequent personnel training and recovery testing.

CONDUCTING THE TEST: GUIDELINES AND TECHNIQUES

There are several important ground rules that must be followed in developing a testing program.

Limit Test Preparation. Test preparation should be limited to developing a test disaster scenario, scheduling test dates and times, and defining any exceptions to the plan. Exceptions should be limited to defining the test scope (e.g., testing only the notification component) or resource acquisition (e.g., substituting a training center for rented office space). Actual testing should follow the documented recovery procedures.

Avoid Cheating. An independent observer should be identified for each recovery test. Controls should be put in place to ensure that only resources identified in the recovery plans are used for the recovery effort. Exceptions to the recovery plan should be noted for subsequent follow-up. The object of limiting cheating is not to be punitive but to ensure that all activities and essential resources have been identified and will be available at time of disaster.

Document and Communicate Test Results. The results of the recovery test should always be documented, including follow-up activities, when possible. Corrective actions should be identified, responsibilities defined, and dates set. Test results should be communicated to the participants and management in a positive manner. Successes should be clearly documented and recognition given to those contributing to the success. Likewise, identified problems should be stated in a positive manner with emphasis on the corrective actions.

Test Information Reconstruction. Difficulties in data restoration and recreation are usually discovered only through real-time testing. The off-site storage facility should be periodically audited to ensure that backups are present and safely stored. The ability to restore should be tested using the actual off-site backup media. When information recreation depends on other facilities (e.g., paper in branch offices or microfilm at the off-site vault), the ability to access this information should be verified. Sufficient volume should be tested to ensure that recovery actions are effective at production volumes.

CONCLUSION

To develop an effective and comprehensive business resumption plan, companies can take advantage of the lessons learned from other companies and approach disaster planning from a business perspective as well as a technical perspective. The course of action depends on the status of the organization's current disaster recovery plans and business priorities. A company can expand its current plans into a comprehensive business resumption plan by:

- Conducting realistic and critical evaluation of the current recovery program. This evaluation should clearly define the status of the entire business resumption plan scope, including incident crisis management, computer disaster recovery, and work group business resumption.
- Developing a project plan to expand the current program, using the development guidelines presented in this chapter. This planning involves:
  —Analyzing the business's recovery requirements.
  —Adopting appropriate recovery strategies to meet the recovery requirements.
  —Developing detailed recovery action plans necessary to implement the proposed recovery strategies.
- Developing an ongoing testing, training, and maintenance program for the business resumption plan.

Section XII
Quality

THE CHAPTERS in this section deal with quality—or, more specifically, techniques for improving the quality of the service that IS departments provide. Chapter XII-1, "Improving Service Quality," discusses one of the truly important success factors for IS: customer service quality.

Improving the quality of customer service is a key way for an organization to gain advantage over competitors who sell similar products or offer similar services. Customers recognize and appreciate quality in such areas as courtesy, responsiveness to special needs, and communication just as much as, if not more than, they appreciate the technical specifications of a product. As a service function within an organization, the IS department can measure its success only by how well it serves its customers—the end users. IS departments that market their services to in-house customers may want to follow the lead of forward-thinking companies by implementing a service strategy for themselves.

Another way to improve quality is to improve the way IS develops systems. We know that the key to better systems is to find systems errors as early in the development process as possible. High-quality analysis is the key to improved systems. To ensure this quality, testing and validation of data and process models must be performed. In addition, customer requirements and business objectives must be reflected in the models used in analysis. Chapter XII-2, "Quality Testing the Products of Analysis," presents steps for ensuring higher-quality systems analysis.

XII-1

Improving Service Quality

Jeffrey M. Ferguson
Robert A. Zawacki

PROVIDING QUALITY SERVICE to customers is now recognized as a key competitive strategy in many organizations. Companies that have shifted their focus to improving the quality of services they provide are achieving improved business success in terms of growth, profit, customer retention, and customer acquisition. The growing interest in service is to a large extent a reaction to the demands of customers who have not only lost their tolerance for inadequate service but who—for the most part—enjoy the benefits of a buyer's market and can purchase similar products from any one of a number of competitors.

Information systems organizations within these and other companies have begun to realize the importance of quality in the services they provide. Just as the company's external customers are becoming more demanding, so are the IS departments' internal customers. The trend toward outsourcing IS services represents these internal customers' ability to find similar support elsewhere. Therefore, to retain the substantial impact they currently have on the business and to continue to provide a valuable contribution to the business units of the company, IS organizations must examine their own ability to provide quality services and to meet the IS needs of the company.

COMMON COMPETITIVE STRATEGIES

To gain a better understanding of a quality service strategy, IS managers must first understand the basic strategies organizations use to differentiate themselves from the competition. Exhibit XII-1-1 lists the strengths and weaknesses of some commonly used competitive strategies.

Technical Quality Strategy

One of the most widely used strategies, especially for producers of industrial goods and services, is the technical quality strategy. This approach is based on developing and maintaining superior technical quality in goods and services. Although a product will definitely not be successful if its technical capabilities are not up to par, the technical dimensions of a product do not

Service Strategy

Strengths

Enhances customer relations

Source of long-term differential advantage

Creates value for customers

Effective in mature markets

Weaknesses

Organization must be oriented toward service

May be susceptible to price competition in the short run

Technical Quality Strategy

Strengths

Technical excellence is of critical value

Commonly used for industrial goods and services

A necessary component of quality

Effective in new markets

Weaknesses

Value diminishes as competitors acquire technical skill

Differential advantage may not be possible

Price Strategy

Strengths

Attractive benefit for many customers

Effective approach for attracting business

Differential advantage in the short run

Quantitative and easy to communicate

Weaknesses

Difficult to maintain in the long run

Does not build lasting relationship with customers

Trains customers to shop for best price

May not generate the funds necessary to maintain service quality

Image Strategy

Strengths

Source of differentiation

Set value by managing expectations

Weaknesses

Does not provide technical quality

Exhibit XII-1-1. Commonly Used Competitive Strategies

represent the whole story for most customers. This strategy may therefore work well when technical excellence is of critical value to the customer; however, in the competitive environment facing many organizations, it may be difficult to demonstrate technical superiority. For many organizations, it may be too expensive or impossible to create a differential based solely on technical quality. The technical strategy therefore provides necessary but insufficient benefits to customers.

Price Strategy

Another common approach is the price strategy. This strategy has a strong intuitive appeal because of the powerful motivator low cost can be. In addition, price is a quantitative dimension that can be easily communicated to the customer.

The biggest drawbacks to this approach are the difficulty of maintaining an advantage over the long run and the subtle message it relays to customers to shop around for the best price. It is difficult to develop a lasting relationship with customers who have become preoccupied with finding the lowest price. The drive for the lowest operating costs may also suppress efforts to deliver a quality product or service. The organization that skimps on technical quality to lower prices may be unlucky enough to find that its customers are willing to pay more for a better-quality product from a different company.

Image Strategy

The image strategy focuses on creating an environment or aura around the service or product through marketing efforts. For example, clothing and cosmetics are traditionally marketed through image appeals. Services such as American Express and IBM computer leasing use a strong element of image marketing to make customers feel confident and even proud of the service vendor they are using.

This approach can be successful at setting customer expectations and reinforcing value if the services that are promised are actually delivered. The tendency to concentrate more on talking about the service than on delivering it should be avoided at all cost.

Service Strategy

The service strategy creates a differential advantage by developing a range of services that add value for the customers and build strong relationships with them. It does not mean giving less attention to technical quality. The emphasis is on delivering a broader component of quality that includes both functional and technical quality.

The goal of this strategy is to cement relationships with customers so that the organization is less susceptible to outside competition. IBM Corp. provides a classic example of this strategy. Not known for low price or state-of-the-art technology, IBM became the market leader by providing customers with superior service.

To be successful with its internal customers, an IS organization should combine various elements of these strategies. However, the service strategy represents the best approach for IS organizations, and they should consider it to be their driving philosophy.

THE CHALLENGES OF SERVICE QUALITY

Before attempting to improve the service quality they offer, IS executives must understand the basic complications inherent in improving service quality or implementing a service strategy. Because of the overwhelming problems that can arise if the IS organization overpromises the level of services it offers, these principles must be taken into consideration as part of a program to improve the quality of IS services:

- *Service depends on the performance of employees.* Because quality service occurs during delivery, it is subject to the vagaries of the human disposition. In addition, services are performances rather than objects, which makes precise specifications difficult to establish and enforce.
- *Service quality is defined by the customers.* Because service quality cannot be objectively measured by weight, size, or durability, organizations must rely on customers' perceptions of service quality. Service delivery personnel must view service from the perspective of their customers. The IS organization must therefore collect input about service quality from the customers and base its definition of quality on that input.
- *Services are evaluated not only by what is done but by how it is done.* Technical quality relates to what service is delivered; functional quality relates to how the service is delivered. For an IS organization, technical quality might pertain to the accuracy, timeliness, and relevance of a particular application. Functional quality, on the other hand, would be represented by courtesy, responsiveness to any special needs of the end user, recovery from errors, and a smooth change from a previous application.

The IS organization is not a collection of material assets; it depends on the quality of the contacts between IS systems and operations people and their clients. It is during each of these contacts that the IS department has the opportunity to prove to its customers that it is a quality provider of the services they need.

ADVANTAGES OF A SERVICE STRATEGY

The service strategy has two primary advantages for IS organizations. First, it views total service quality as a function of both technical quality and functional quality. This balanced view is more in keeping with customer (i.e., end user) demands. When functional quality is neglected, total service quality suffers. Technical dimensions remain important in the service strategy but are not considered the main points of differentiation. They are a necessary but not a sufficient condition for delivering total service quality.

Organizations focus on technical quality when their highest priority is developing state-of-the-art technology. Organizations driven by research and development would probably view their priorities this way because research requires this type of focus. Service customers, on the other hand, have a different set of needs representing more of a balance between technical and functional quality. They are not as concerned about the technology being used as they are about the benefits they receive. The strengths of the IS organization using the technical quality strategy do not match the needs of its clients, leaving the organization susceptible to competitors. The service strategy, on the other hand, provides the balance required by most customers.

The second strength of the service strategy is that the organization's strategic focus becomes customer relationships. Because competitors often can duplicate the technical aspects of services, the customer service strategy provides a greater opportunity for maintaining a differential advantage. The customers who experience only the outcome of a service may not even be aware of the technical aspects of service quality. Interactions with the service personnel (i.e., functional quality), on the other hand, are highly visible, and as a result customers evaluate these activities in detail. IS organizations should therefore focus more on these relationships with customers—relationships they may have been ignoring in favor of internal process improvement.

Because most IS people's motivation, training, and experience are concentrated on seeking technological solutions to problems, refocusing the IS organization is not a simple task. To encourage this new focus, IS managers should look for such service skills as implementing effective change with the customer, negotiation and conflict resolution, and group dynamics when hiring new employees. In addition, training in these skills should be provided for current employees.

IMPLEMENTING A SERVICE STRATEGY

There are five basic steps to be considered when implementing a service strategy in the IS organization:

- Identifying customers' definition of service quality.
- Developing a customer orientation.
- Training employees in both technical and functional quality skills.
- Providing excellent internal service.
- Making the most out of your moments of truth.

Customer Assessment

Customer assessment is the cornerstone of the service strategy for two important reasons. First, without an understanding of how customers define quality service, any actions taken are merely guesses about what benefits customers truly are seeking. Second, quality will not be improved unless it is measured, and the only way to measure it is by having a definition to compare results to.

The assessment of customers' service expectations should include both functional and technical dimensions of service quality, including:

- Reliability.
- Responsiveness.
- Competence.
- Access.
- Courtesy.
- Communication.
- Credibility.
- Security.
- Understanding the customer.
- Tangibles.

Reliability and competence relate to technical quality, but all the rest are elements of functional quality.

Customer Orientation

For IS organizations, adopting a service strategy means shifting from a technical orientation to a customer orientation. Technically oriented organizations focus on internal procedures. Their objective is to develop systems that allow for efficient work flow. A production-dominated system is designed and evaluated in terms of readily measurable criteria, such as uptime, or the number of jobs completed, as opposed to the extent to which customers' needs are being met. The focus is typically on tasks rather than on people. Production-oriented organizations embrace the bureaucratic model, value efficiency, and specialize in the unwavering and timely performance of routine tasks.

Fundamentally and strategically, a customer-oriented organization focuses on ways of meeting customers' needs rather than the systems' needs. It takes a proactive approach to developing and delivering benefits for those it serves. This is a key difference from a production-oriented organization.

Because service quality is defined by the customers, a strong customer orientation is a requisite for the service strategy. It means giving priority to customer needs over systems needs and delivering functional as well as technical quality. In sum, the service strategy delivers a more complete package of quality to the customer.

Because of technical training and the current corporate culture, it is likely that change will be difficult. Research indicates that the probability of implementing effective change within and outside of IS can be increased by:

- The extent of information affected employees have.
- The extent of their participation in the planning and design process.
- The participants' trust in the IS management team.
- The participants' past experience with IS and how change was implemented in the past.

The quick-fixes of technical systems do not work on the human issues. As a result, the customer behavioral response to technologically driven change must be a primary concern of the IS management team.

Training Employees

Technically oriented organizations with highly skilled professionals run the risk of defining quality too narrowly. Many of these organizations require that their employees receive substantial training in the technical aspects of the business but neglect customer interaction skills and procedures. Service delivery personnel must be versed in both technical and functional aspects of quality.

Internal Marketing

Excellent service to internal customers is a necessary prerequisite for delivering quality service to external customers. Internal marketing involves applying the philosophy and practices of marketing to employees. Its main objectives are to employ and keep the best people and to motivate them to high levels of performance.

In effect, internal marketing sells the employees of the organization on the organization and its products or services and encourages them to communicate their commitment to service to outside clients. This works within the IS organization as well. In essence, the way that IS employees are treated is reflected in the way they treat their internal clients. As a result, any service quality program must begin with service to employees before service for customers can be expected.

GUIDELINES FOR SERVICE QUALITY IMPROVEMENT

Implementing an effective service quality program is a major cultural shift for an IS organization. These cultural changes usually take between two and three years to implement; they are evolutionary, not revolutionary. The following guidelines and the checklist shown in Exhibit XII-1-2 should assist the IS director in successful implementation:

- *Implement a service quality improvement program only after a careful diagnosis of the organization's readiness for change.* Do not start a change program if the IS organization is going through extreme stress (e.g., a movement of systems people to the end-user community or a reduction in workforce).
- *Plan for institutionalization of the change program.* Many change programs in IS do not last because more effort goes into planning and implementing the change program than into maintaining it. Establish a steering committee that reports directly to the top IS person. In addition to managers, have three or four individual contributors serve on this committee. It will increase the quality of the decisions and provide links to the other individual contributors.
- *The senior IS leader must constantly reinforce the quality program.* For example, if the senior IS person is making a presentation to other IS people, make certain that quality is mentioned at least three times.
- *Ensure that change efforts are compatible with organizational values.* For example, the senior IS manager may express the need for open

Activity	Before Design and Implementation	3 mo.	6 mo.	9 mo.	12 mo.	18 mo.	24 mo.
1. Steering Committee Meets	X	X	X	X	X	X	X
2. Provide Leadership	X	X	X	X	X	X	X
3. Establish Goals	X				X	X	X
4. Define Assumptions	X						
5. Provide Training in:							
• Quality	X						
• Presentation Skills			X				
• Change Skills				X			
6. Measure Performance							
• Internal	X				X		X
• Customers (value added)	X				X		X
7. Establish Links							
• Meeting Report	X						
• Cost Benefit			(every meeting)				
• Presentation to Senior Management			(every meeting)				
• Posting Results	X		X	X	X		X
8. Reward Success							
• Team Members			X				
• Leaders			X				
9. Operating Hints							
• Be Patient							
• Encourage a Cultural Shift							
• Think Beyond Cutting Costs							
• Take Risks							
• Give the Team Credit							
• Change the Reward Structure and Give Feedback							

Exhibit XII-1-2. Checklist for Implementing a Service Quality Program

communication; however, when a quality group makes a recommendation that challenges senior management, does senior management send a signal that it devalues openness?

- *Establish measures of customer service before the quality training begins and track progress.* In the future, the senior IS director will need to demonstrate value added to the CEO.
- *Review the reward structure.* Link rewards (e.g., bonuses) to desired new behavior. Can the steering committee or key contributors receive a reward? The behaviors that are rewarded are repeated in IS organizations.
- *Stay the course and establish adequate links both across functional areas and from top to bottom.* Prepare a simple one-page report that describes what happened at the quality meeting and then have that report sent to other quality teams and IS managers. Some IS organizations have an online data base that anyone can access to review what other quality teams are doing.

CONCLUSION

High-performance IS organizations of the future will need leaders who recognize that service quality and successful implementation of the quality program are critical success factors. Furthermore, service quality will be measured not only by the contacts between IS and the user or customer but by how IS leaders respond to the needs of their individual contributors within IS. The effective IS manager must value employees and develop a service quality orientation within them that provides exceptional service to the customers.

XII-2

Quality Testing the Products of Analysis

Lou Russell

FOR THE LAST 15 YEARS, IS professionals have been encouraging project teams to spend more time on analysis to increase the quality of systems. However, the problem remains that those outside the development organization believe that the project team is not doing anything productive when team members are gathering the requirements. CASE tools have given developers the ability to look busy, but this ability has not solved the original problem: how to raise the level of systems development quality. A better solution is to involve the clients in the validation of requirements so that they see the deliverables and see their value.

This chapter discusses steps for quality testing the products of analysis as well as the way CASE tools can assist teams in this effort. Because different techniques are used for different methodologies, the testing criteria for different popular alternatives are examined here.

COMPLETENESS OF MODELS

Before quality testing can begin, it is important that the analysis work be "good enough." Analysis reaches this point when the process of finding additional—and usually obscure—requirements costs more than the additional analysis is worth. It is difficult for a project team to know when it has reached this point in analysis; experience from previous projects usually is the most effective guide for judging whether this point has been reached. There is, however, a rule of thumb that is based on practical experience. It is the 80% rule: analysis is "good enough" when 80% of the needs have been captured.

For process-based requirements analysis, a data flow diagram may be used to document the requirements. Before quality testing can begin, the data flow diagram must be checked for completeness. The most efficient way to do this is to determine whether it is balanced. A balanced diagram ensures that what goes in also goes out.

Every data store on a data flow diagram must be looked at to ensure that the data elements in each data store are exactly the same as all the data

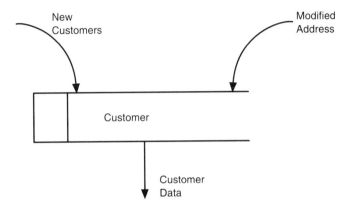

Exhibit XII-2-1. Balancing of Data Store Elements

elements that are coming in and going out on data flows. Exhibit XII-2-1 presents a diagram that illustrates this technique.

Processes on a data flow diagram must also be balanced. In this case, the number of inputs must equal the number of outputs too, but it is possible that a process may legitimately be out of balance. Because processes can create new data elements through calculations, the number of data elements leaving a process may not equal the number of data elements entering the process (see Exhibit XII-2-2). Analysts must be able to determine whether it is acceptable for a process to be out of balance.

An alternative technique for process analysis uses the functional decomposition diagram. In this technique, the bottom row of each branch on the diagram must be composed of elementary processes. Simply stated, an elementary process is the smallest unit of activity that is important to an organization. It is a challenge, however, for an analyst to know when a process has been broken down into elementary processes.

There are two approaches to determining whether enough or too much work has been done on the functional decomposition diagram: the rule-based approach and the picture-based approach.

Rules for determining whether a process is elementary answer the following questions:

- Does the process perform one and only one action of interest to the business?
- Is there at least one piece of input and preferably one piece of output?
- Is the input transformed by the process?
- Is the process somewhat autonomous, or does it depend on other activities to have meaning?

The picture-based approach is basically the same with the addition of a visual element. Exhibit XII-2-3 presents a drawing using data flow diagram symbols of a process with its input and output shown. If a process has many

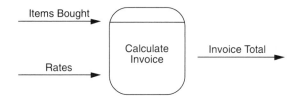

Exhibit XII-2-2. Process Creating Data Elements

varied pieces of input and output, the process is probably carrying out more than one activity. The subprocesses can be easily separated according to the different types of output.

On the data side of analysis, the entity-relationship model must be checked for completeness. There are two steps in completing data analysis: normalization and refinement.

Normalization looks at each data entity to determine whether it should be decomposed to reduce redundant attributes. A series of steps (i.e., forms) ensures that a model is decomposed completely. Most businesses require that data models be in third normal form, but fifth normal form is more exact.

Refinement is a three-step process to prepare the data model for design, which is the next phase in the development process. Although these steps are usually performed throughout the entire analysis phase, they should be

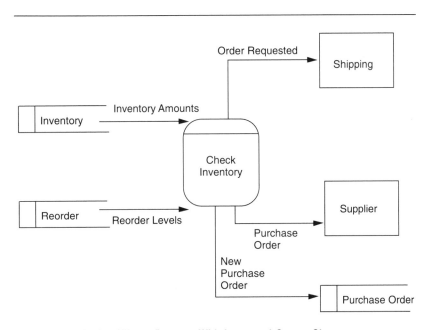

Exhibit XII-2-3. Process With Input and Output Shown

completed before it ends. They are:

- Reduction of one-to-one relationships.
- Reduction of many-to-many relationships.
- Elimination of redundant relationships.

QUALITY TESTING

Once the models have been checked for completeness, the analyst can use the process-side products to validate the data-side ones and vice versa. Many techniques can be used in combination or alone for this validation.

The first technique is to match exactly the data elements in data entities on the data model to the attributes stored in data stores on the data flow diagrams. If process dependency diagrams are used instead of data flow diagrams, this same validation can be performed through the creation of an attribute-to-process CRUD matrix, which is discussed further in the following section. For the successful implementation of requirements, the data being stored in the data bases must be the data that the programs are expecting.

Another technique, the entity life cycle history, validates that all the required processes have been identified, by examining the data entities from a different perspective. For each data entity, the project team brainstorms about all that might happen during the life of that entity. For example, a customer data entity might be added, changed, archived, invoiced, marked overdue, moved, or removed. This list of activities is compared to the processes on either the data flow or the process dependency diagram to ensure that there is processing to cover the entire list of activities.

Matrix Validation

Matrices are used in another popular and rigorous validation technique. Two-way tables can be set up to compare almost any objects that were documented during the requirements phase. The most popular matrix is the create-read-update-delete (CRUD) matrix. This matrix compares the data entities to the elementary or data flow diagram processes. For each data entity, the matrix shows which processes create, read, update, and delete it.

This information can be used many ways. Analysts should ensure that there is creating, reading, updating, and deleting for all data entities. By using the CRUD matrix, analysts usually discover that one of these activity types has been missed.

Another benefit of the CRUD matrix is that it identifies places in which more than one process performs the same action (e.g., multiple processes update the same data entity). Thus, lists can be created that help designers identify systems components that can be reused or reengineered to clean up the proposed requirements.

Matrices can also be used to ensure that the original problems and opportunities identified by the customer remain part of the requirements specification and that the scope of the analysis has not strayed. Business-rules-to-relationships matrices can be used to ensure that all the original business rules have been incorporated into the data model. Current-processes-to-proposed-processes matrices can be used to check that no processes included in the current system will be dropped in future development.

The final step in this quality analysis is to track the intent of the project through the entire analysis phase. At the beginning of a project, the project team creates a list of business and system objectives that contribute to meeting the specified business goals. The team should also have a list of problems and opportunities for that project to address. When building detailed analysis models, a project team can easily lose perspective, so it is critical that this perspective be validated before going on to design.

Business Objectives

Business objectives (i.e., the goals of increasing revenue, avoiding costs, or improving the service level of the organization) should map to system objectives. Every activity that a system performs should contribute to achieving a business goal. Likewise, every problem to be solved or opportunity to be met should map to a system objective. The system objectives in turn should map directly to one or more processes.

Use of CASE

CASE provides the record-keeping capability to facilitate many of these validation steps. Organizations should develop procedures or customized CASE reports that help them with as much of this validation as possible.

Balancing data flow diagrams is most effectively done with a CASE tool. The data flow diagram cannot be balanced until it is has been completely documented in the CASE repository. It should not be a difficult process to have the CASE tool print exception reports showing where the data stores or processes are out of balance.

The CASE repository shared by the data model and process model can be used to rigorously check whether the data elements on the data flow diagram are the same as the attributes on the data model. For this to be done, the models must share one repository. CASE reports, again, can be used to show exceptions.

CASE is not a useful tool for entity life history analysis. This is a brainstorming activity that is best done on a big piece of paper. The CASE repository, however, should provide the final say on whether or not processing is included in the model. Every process on a functional decomposition diagram, data flow diagram, or process dependency diagram should be fully documented in the repository before analysis validation can begin.

Matrices are most easily implemented with a CASE tool. If the models are complete, matrices can be generated easily by the CASE tool and filled in by the analyst. Troubleshooting remains a mental exercise, of course.

Some CASE vendors claim that their tools normalize data entities, but buyers should be wary of such claims. Normalization is more of a subjective activity than it seems; only detailed understanding of the relationships between elements in the data base model guarantees correct normalization. The CASE tool has to be given this information by the user; the tool cannot get it automatically.

CONCLUSION

The fairy tale view of the future shows systems developers maintaining requirements and generating systems from these requirements through software. To move toward this goal, the analysis paradigm must change—the deliverables of analysis are the deliverables of the system. This chapter explains the importance of these deliverables and gives concrete steps for ensuring their quality. These steps include:

- Verifying the completeness of data and process models:
  —Balancing data flow diagrams.
  —Creating functional decomposition diagrams.
  —Normalizing and refining entity-relationship models.
- Mapping data elements in the data model to data store attributes in the data flow diagram.
- Validating the models with the entity life cycle history technique.
- Ensuring proper processing activities through use of CRUD matrices.
- Ensuring that customer requirements are met through use of business-rules-to-relationships and current-processes-to-proposed-processes matrices.
- Tracking the intent of the project during the analysis phase.
- Mapping business objectives to systems objectives.

CASE tools can be used to perform some of these steps with the rigor that quality testing the products of analysis requires.

Section XIII
Productivity

PRODUCTIVITY IMPROVEMENT is a topic of such importance that many IS managers have begun a formal productivity improvement program. This section contains two chapters relating to productivity: one on reengineering and one on better project management.

In Chapter XIII-1, "Productive Systems Maintenance" is part of the reengineering effort that relates to improving the performance of existing application systems. Effective systems development techniques attract a lot of attention, but relatively little has been done to improve systems maintenance. This is true despite the fact that most institutions spend at least half of their systems development dollars on maintenance. Chapter XIII-1 describes an effective, proven approach to resurrecting existing systems and increasing their useful life. The approach employs both software tools and a rigorous methodology.

The problems of managing large IS projects have been with us for 30 years. Systems development has always depended on effective project management for its success, and that means competent project managers.

The effective planning and control of three variables—work, resources, and time—is what ensures project success. Chapter XIII-2, "Productivity Through Project Management," points out both the problems and opportunities associated with project control. By understanding the dynamics and the relationships of these variables, the IS manager can better manage resources, balance the use of time and people, and keep projects on track and performing productively.

XIII-1

Productive Systems Maintenance

Philip Friedlander
William E. Toothman

CURRENTLY, LESS THAN 10% of any IS budget is being directed at competitive advantage. Why are so few corporate resources being directed where investment clearly can be most effective? The reason is that the demand for system maintenance is consuming more than 50% of the professional resource time in most IS organizations. All the progress toward making the systems development process more efficient and effective has done little to stem the growing maintenance backlog.

Adding to the problem is the fact that today's IS graduates may be well trained in developing new information systems but poorly trained to address the maintenance of existing systems. Consequently, managers face a growing maintenance backlog and a shrinking population of professionals equipped to handle it. Traditional conventions of assessing the IS portfolio suggest that any application system that has either low functionality or low maintainability should be considered a candidate for redevelopment.

INFORMATION SYSTEMS AS INVESTMENTS

One of the problems is that information systems are treated too much like expenses and not enough like investments. Generally accepted accounting principles (GAAP) encourage the expensing, instead of the capitalization, of systems. However, some of the blame deserves to be spread to IS management. IS management is often too willing to take one of two extremes concerning existing information systems—patch or scrap—even though an intermediate solution may be the most cost-effective.

When an organization buys a truck, it periodically performs preventive maintenance on it so that the vehicle continues to perform well. Even with preventive maintenance, the truck will eventually wear down to the point that maintenance costs exceed the amount that it would take to justify the purchase of a new truck. However, there is often an intermediate alternative before the scrapping the vehicle. Sometimes that same truck can get a major overhaul—rebuilding the engine, for example—to extend its useful life at a cost significantly less than the purchase of a new truck. The same opportunities exist with information systems if effective overhaul techniques are used.

Some would say that information systems do not wear out the same way that equipment does. However, systems frequently evolve away from their original design and away from the current needs of the business. Michael Hammer suggests, for example, that the answer is not to reautomate but to obliterate the system and reengineer the business. This often is neither practical nor economical with the increased demand in both maintenance and new systems development, as well as strategic system implementation.

The resource economy and time-line compression achieved with the program overhaul or resuscitation approach is illustrated in Exhibit XIII-1-1, in contrast to the popular process innovation and process redesign schools of thought. The length of the various lines from existing system to new system is a relative measure of both time and cost.

For the most part, the existing programs still effectively address the basic business processes. The only problem is that even if they were originally developed well, through careless maintenance they have evolved into maintenance problems. The old saying "If it ain't broke don't fix it" only par-

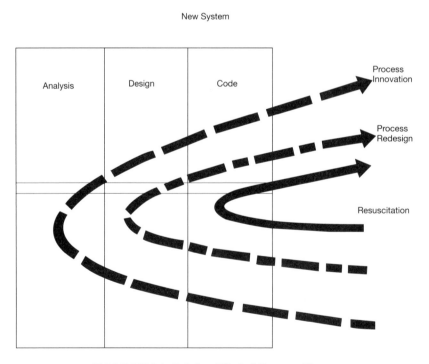

New System

Analysis   Design   Code

Process Innovation

Process Redesign

Resuscitation

Exhibit XIII-1-1. Relative Effort of Process Change

tially applies here. While the programs may not be on death's doorstep, they certainly are ill and need resuscitation.

COMPONENTS OF MAINTAINABILITY

Several qualities make systems and programs more maintainable. Four of them are documentation, readability, data definition, and complexity of data and process manipulation.

Documentation. The availability, quality, and accuracy of system (as well as program) documentation adds to the maintainability of systems. The more understanding the programmer can gain without having to sequentially browse through the source code, the more effective the maintenance effort. Program documentation alone does not significantly enhance maintainability.

Readability. The readability of the program greatly affects the cost of maintenance. Each change to a program requires a certain degree of replication of the learning effort. The faster a programmer can gain an understanding of what the program does and how it does it, the more expeditious maintenance becomes. Readability comprises the overall structuring of the program as well as the structure of the source code. This includes the indentation of the verbs subordinate to IF statements and the overall white space in the program. Readability can also be enhanced if the program follows either of the two classic maintainable program structures: transform or transaction-centered hierarchies.

Data Definition. Data definition deals with the meaningfulness and understandability of the data and procedure names in the program. It also includes the consistency of data naming across multiple programs. This consistency allows the programmer to reuse knowledge gained in the maintenance of one program and apply it to the maintenance of another program.

Complexity of Data and Process Manipulation. Maintainability is reduced by increasing numbers and complexity of verbs within the program. Statements nested too deeply deter the reader from gaining an understanding of the procedural logic. Alters and transforms are particularly troublesome to the maintenance process.

AN EFFECTIVE APPROACH

The Toolset: Automating the Tedious

The first prerequisite in increasing the effectiveness of any given process is to understand the metrics of the problem. The metrics of program complexity, such as the four components of maintainability just discussed, have traditionally been difficult and tedious to capture manually. Years ago we estimated reengineering work solely by manually reviewing the source code, documentation, and JCL using loose judgment and no hard metrics. Today, because most of the measures of maintainability are rigorous, requiring little human judgment, they are suitable candidates for automation. The program survey and grading can now be totally automated.

All exhibits for this chapter were generated using the Resuscitator Analyzer (COBOL), which is referred to as the survey toolset. Exhibit XIII-1-2 shows an example of the types of metrics analysis reports produced. PARAGRAPHS are ranked in descending order by the number of logic nodes within the COBOL paragraph or section. Listed is the PARAGRAPH NAME, the METRIC count (a simplified combination of the Halstead and McCabe metrics), the executable lines of code (ELOC) contained within the paragraph as defined previously, and the DENSITY, expressed as the percentage of METRIC to ELOC. As a general rule, any paragraph with a METRIC greater than 9 and whose DENSITY is greater than 50% will be difficult to maintain.

Exhibit XIII-1-3 shows verbs that are questionable. The survey toolset takes into account the use and complexity of copybooks. These verbs are questionable as defined within the context of the computing environment in which they exist. This is the most flexible and tailored portion of the survey toolset in that any keyword desired can be added to the survey control file, and the parser portion of the complexity analyzer can be used to scan and locate that keyword's occurrences.

The user has the ability to determine what verbs appear on this report. Examples such as data dependent branch logic and file I/O consolidation should be considered for specific isolation. If the occurrences are not contained within the native (i.e., noncopied) code, the designation COPY will be placed in the address location. In the exhibit, OPENs and READs are also listed. In addition, the survey toolset reports specific problem areas and expectations of a given program and summarizes the information by subsystem (Exhibit XIII-1-4).

In Exhibit XIII-1-4, EXEC CODE is executable lines of code. It is a count of native lines of Procedure Division statements, excluding copied (copybooks/includes) logic, notes, comments, blank lines, and printer control statements such as EJECT and SKIPX. This is a measurement of the actual size of the logical executable module.

DOCUMEN/COMMENTS is a count of COBOL documentation and comment lines. This is a measurement of inline comments and documentation contained within the logical executable module.

NBR OF FILES is a count of all COBOL SELECT statements. An indication of external files referenced by the logical executable module is necessary if function points are to be used and as an indicator of I/O operations and external file processing. It is a contributing factor to program complexity.

TRANSFER COUNT is transfers of control counts. It is a measurement of the structure of the logical executable module. Generally, the higher the ratio of transfers of control to ELOC, the less structured the code contained within the logical executable module.

SAI0140
21:23:11

SOFTWARE ANALYSYS INC.
SYSTEM: DIVIDENDS — INSURANCE

CLIENT: APEX INDUSTRIAL INC.
SUBSYSTEM: DIVIDENDS

PROGRAM: DIVMAC00

PARAGRAPH NAME	METRIC	ELOC	DENSITY
DIVIDEND-DO-SCRN200	34	140	24.29%
DIVIDEND-CONVRT-211	18	149	12.08%
DIVIDEND-EDIT	16	67	23.88%
DIVIDEND-EDIT-HEADER	15	62	24.19%
DIVIDEND-CALC-211	15	145	10.34%
DIVIDEND-CROSS-EDIT	14	30	46.67%
DIVIDEND-BUILD-FIR	14	62	22.58%
DIVIDEND-STORE-CUR-END-F	14	73	19.18%
DIVIDEND-DISP-C-INX	14	36	38.89%
DIVIDEND-CALC-220	12	64	18.75%
DIVIDEND-CONVRT-210	12	86	13.95%
DIVIDEND-DO-SCRN240	11	53	20.75%
DIVIDEND-EDIT-DATA	11	76	14.47%
DIVIDEND-DISP-RATE	11	37	29.73%
DIVIDEND-PF10-KEY	11	69	15.94%
DIVIDEND-CALC-F-INX	11	40	27.50%
DIVIDEND-STORE-NEXT-F	11	66	16.67%
DIVIDEND-CROSS-EDIT1	10	22	45.45%
DIVIDEND-MV-FIR-UP	9	28	32.14%
DIVIDEND-FRMT-230	9	63	14.29%
DIVIDEND-STORE	9	63	14.29%
DIVIDEND-INIT-CHK-KEYS	8	21	38.10%
DIVIDEND-BUILD-MENU	8	45	17.78%
DIVIDEND-GET-INX-VLS	8	48	16.67%
DIVIDEND-PF08-240	7	42	16.67%
DIVIDEND-NEXT240-RPT	7	28	25.00%
DIVIDEND-ADD-RATE	7	30	23.33%
DIVIDEND-GET-ISA	7	29	24.14%
DIVIDEND-GET-IPR	7	36	19.44%
DIVIDEND-STORE-FIX-CURR	7	34	20.59%
DIVIDEND-GET-VLN-DTS	7	62	11.29%
DIVIDEND-CHANGE-RATE	6	25	24.00%
DIVIDEND-GETNEXT-FIR	6	44	13.64%
DIVIDEND-BLD230-INX	6	54	11.11%
DIVIDEND-BUILD-240	6	14	42.86%
DIVIDEND-GET-INX	6	30	20.00%
DIVIDEND-GET-IHR	6	30	20.00%
DIVIDEND-UPDT-IHR	6	30	20.00%
DIVIDEND-UPDT-INX	6	30	20.00%
DIVIDEND-UPDT-IPR	6	30	20.00%
DIVIDEND-SCREEN-IO	5	12	41.67%
DIVIDEND-SET-UP-240`	5	41	12.20%
DIVIDEND-PUTNEXT-240	5	35	14.29%
DIVIDEND-FIND-EOT	5	33	15.15%
DIVIDEND-MOVE-S240	5	34	14.71%
DIVIDEND-CHK-PF4	5	16	31.25%
DIVIDEND-FRMT-211	5	99	5.05%
DIVIDEND-LAST-MENU	5	44	11.36%

Exhibit XIII-1-2. Program Metrics Analysis

SAIO140
21:23:11

PAGE 30
8/15/94

SOFTWARE ANALYSYS INC.

CLIENT: APEX INDUSTRIAL INC.

SYSTEM: DIVIDENDS — INSURANCE

SUBSYSTEM: DIVIDENDS

PROGRAM: DIVMCT00

VERB	PROGRAM LINE NUMBER					
ALTER	000140	000145				
DISPLAY	000830 001270	000930 001290	001040 001520	001090	001110	001220
ENTRY	COPY					
GO	001150 001530	001180	001280	001300	001340	001480
CLOSE	001020					
OPEN	000890					
READ	001000					
STOP	000940	001120				

Exhibit XIII-1-3. Questionable Verbs

SAI0140
21:23:11

SOFTWARE ANALYSYS INC.

SYSTEM: DIVIDENDS — INSURANCE

CLIENT: APEX INDUSTRIAL INC.

SUBSYSTEM: DIVIDENDS

PROGRAM	TOTAL LINES	EXEC CODE	DOCUMEN/ COMMENTS	NBR OF FILES	TRANSFER COUNT	LOGIC NODES	NBR OF VERBS	DOC/COMM INDEX %
DIVMAA00	2,534	581	288	0	90	134	218	33.14
DIVMAB00	18,767	4,842	2,068	0	775	865	1,302	29.93
DIVMAB80	9,357	701	114	0	36	133	215	13.99
DIVMAC00	7,639	3,718	889	0	438	723	1,408	19.30
DIVMAD00	2,778	568	370	0	69	116	241	39.45
DIVMAD01	2,636	418	315	0	48	82	180	42.97
DIVMAE00	4,130	1,322	517	0	229	254	404	28.11
DIVMAF00	9,555	2,827	714	0	412	817	668	20.16
DIVMAF10	6,599	1,540	537	0	237	395	332	25.85
DIVMAF11	4,878	718	216	0	32	139	261	23.13
DIVMAF20	7,549	2,028	731	0	282	511	485	26.50
DIVMAF21	7,979	3,022	490	0	119	596	1,460	13.95
DIVMAG00	4,487	1,177	336	0	188	275	388	22.21
DIVMCALC	4,058	425	53	1	42	92	125	11.09
DIVMCT00	611	95	56	0	15	14	49	37.09
DIVMCT01	5,420	302	82	0	58	90	56	21.35
DIVMCT04	3,229	436	152	0	33	29	224	25.85
DIVMCT05	3,456	459	158	0	34	34	232	25.61
DIVMCT06	2,648	279	43	0	23	28	134	13.35
DIVMCT07	2,358	186	21	0	36	37	50	10.14
DIVMCT09	3,210	434	152	0	33	28	223	25.94
DIVMER00	10,172	369	245	0	7	113	128	39.90
DIVMFR90	748	123	38	0	11	30	39	23.60
DIVMSC00	420	34	115	0	8	9	0	77.18
DIVMSC01	441	72	99	0	15	20	6	57.89
** SUBSYSTEM TOTALS**	125,659	26,676	8,799	1	3,270	5,564	8,828	25.00

Exhibit XIII-1-4. Program Analysis

PRODUCTIVITY

SOFTWARE ANALYSYS INC.   CLIENT: APEX INDUSTRIAL INC.

SYSTEM: DIVIDENDS — INSURANCE

AUTHOR	PROGRAM	DATE WRITTEN
NO AUTHOR NAME FOUND	AJBCGA06	03/01/76
A K TOPPER	AJBCSA06	01/31/70
	AJBCSB06	03/09/70
	AJBCS106	03/12/70
B SMITH	AJISCB10	NO WRITTEN DATE FOUND
BLACK WIDOW	AJBPYC01	12/13/88
	AJBPYD01	01/13/89
B COOK	AJBC5106	04/01/77
B WHITE	AJISCE06	10/25/73
C HOUSE	AJBC3Y26	03/29/71
	AJBC3806	04/07/71
	AJBC3706	05/11/71
E C PULLOUT	AJBCXB06	06/01/78
H HOLTZ	AJMCDI06	11/01/72
	AJMCDQ06	11/01/77
J CARR	AJBCMD06	02/18/70
	AJBCMA06	02/25/70
	AJBCMB06	04/07/70
J E BURNMAN	ANCSNSP	05/25/70
K NEWMAN	AJBCUM06	01/21/83
K NEWHOUSE	AJBCEO06	11/06/92
R NEWMAN	AJBPYA02	01/27/87
	AJBPYB02	02/17/87
R BROWN	AJBCMG06	02/01/70
	AJBCKE06	03/01/70
	ANCS405	04/01/70
	ANCS407	04/01/70
SAI CORPORATION	DVDMAA00	05/24/83
	DVDMAB00	09/28/83

Exhibit XIII-1-5. Programs by Author-Date-Program

LOGIC NODES are discrete (i.e., noncompounded) logic nodes within the network of the logical executable module. They are a measurement of program complexity. Generally, the higher the ratio of LOGIC NODES to ELOC, the greater the complexity of the logical executable module.

NBR OF VERBS refers to data manipulation verbs counted within the logical executable module. It is a measurement of internal program activity. Generally, the higher the ratio of data manipulation verbs to ELOC, the greater the modification level of data accepted into and sent from a logical executable module.

DOC/COMM INDEX is documentation/comment lines expressed as a percentage. It is the ratio of documentation/comment lines to total Procedure Division lines (ELOC plus comment lines). This is an index of the inline documentation/comment level of the logical executable module. A comparison of indexes of programs is useful in determining the understandability of code due to the level of inline documentation.

SAI0150   PAGE 1
17:07:59   8/11/94
SOFTWARE ANALYSYS INC.   CLIENT: APEX INDUSTRIAL INC.
SYSTEM: DIVIDENDS — INSURANCE   SUBSYSTEM: DIVIDENDS

PROGRAM	ALTER CNT	GOTO CNT	PERFORM THRU CNT
DIVMAA00	0	20	5
DIVMAB00	0	175	10
DIVMAB80	0	7	0
DIVMAC00	0	96	0
DIVMAD00	0	20	0
DIVMAD01	0	12	22
DIVMAE00	0	32	0
DIVMAF00	3	96	0
DIVMAF10	3	30	0
DIVMAF11	3	8	0
DIVMAF20	0	44	0
DIVMAF21	0	31	0
DIVMAG00	0	34	0
DIVMCALC	0	7	12
DIVMCT00	2	7	0
DIVMCT01	0	9	0
DIVMCT05	5	0	0
DIVMER00	2	0	0
DIVMFR90	0	1	0
DIVMSC00	2	2	0
DIVMSC01	0	2	0
TOTALS	20	633	49

Exhibit XIII-1-6. Alter-GOTO-Perform Thru

The toolset also gathers longitudinal information. For example, not only are the tools able to evaluate the complexity of programs using the metrics described, but a report is generated that lists AUTHOR by DATE by PROGRAM (Exhibit XIII-1-5). By reviewing this report and then manually reviewing more current programs that an author has created, the manager can determine whether an author has improved over time.

The toolset also identifies land mines in the system, such as Alters (Exhibit XIII-1-6) and other problematic verbs (Exhibit XIII-1-7). OPEN and READ are not problematic, but multiple recurrences require a considerable amount of overhead through memory paging and could affect execution time. In addition, from a maintenance standpoint, multiple input-output verbs for the same file could indicate a lack of functional cohesion in the program. For these reasons, these verbs should be reviewed.

The second set of tools is part of the Resuscitator Reengineering Methodology (COBOL). These will be referred to as the reengineering toolset. The reengineering toolset can solve many of the inherent maintenance problems. Issues such as readability are addressed by having the software reformat the COBOL source code using proper spacing, identification, and alignment conventions. The toolset ensures proper sequencing and initialization of data division components. It fixes most missing period problems and standardizes all picture clauses. Cross-program data definition problems are addressed by having the toolset globally replacing local, nonstandard data

SAIO160
14:39:35

CLIENT: APEX INDUSTRIAL INC.

PAGE 1
8/11/94

SOFTWARE ANALYSYS INC.

SYSTEM: DIVIDENDS — INSURANCE

SUBSYSTEM: DIVIDENDS

VERB	PROGRAM	COUNT	PROGRAM	COUNT	PROGRAM	COUNT
ACCEPT	DIVMAA00	1	DIVMAB80	3		
ALTER	DIVMAF00	3	DIVMAF10	3	DIVMAF11	3
	DIVMCT00	2	DIVMCT05	5	DIVMER00	2
	DIVMSC00	2				
CANCEL	DIVMAA00	1	DIVMAB00	1		
CLOSE	DIVMCT00	1				
DISPLAY	DIVMAB80	10	DIVMCT00	9	DIVMCT01	6
ENTRY	DIVMAA00	1	DIVMCT00	1		
GO	DIVMAA00	20	DIVMAB00	175	DIVMAB80	7
	DIVMAC00	202	DIVMAD00	20	DIVMAD01	12
	DIVMAE00	32	DIVMAF00	202	DIVMAF10	30
	DIVMAF11	8	DIVMAF20	44	DIVMAF21	31
	DIVMAG00	34	DIVMCALC	7	DIVMCT00	7
	DIVMCT01	9	DIVMFR90	1	DIVMSC00	2
	DIVMSC01	2				
GOBACK	DIVMCT01	2				
OPEN	DIVMCT00	1				
READ	DIVMCT00	1				
STOP	DIVMCT00	2	DIVMCT01	1		
TRANSFORM	DIVMAA00	1	DIVMAB00	12	DIVMAC00	12
	DIVMAE00	1	DIVMAF20	1	DIVMER00	1

Exhibit XIII-1-7. Verb Counts

names with the cross-program standard names. Procedural alignment and process flow optimization are also addressed.

TOOLSET IS NOT THE TOTAL ANSWER

It would be foolish to believe that the entire reengineering process can be performed automatically by a software tool. Many vendors claim their tools do just that; however, what they do is make artificial improvements to the logic of the program.

For example, many software packages will take an IF statement more than three levels deep in nesting and break out a portion of the nested logic into its own paragraph. This adds neither better structure nor readability to the program because it has not improved the logic. In addition, these arbitrary changes may adversely affect the maintainability of the program because the factored-out logic was put way down in the program, taking away the reader's ability to customize and understand the business rules embedded in the program.

The more realistic approach is to have a powerful set of software tools that support an effective, rigorous engineering methodology. Once the reengineering toolset has completed the mechanical improvements to the programs, a manual methodology is needed. Using the toolset's reports and guidance on problem programs and problem areas within programs, the systems professional is ready to take a systematic approach to resurrecting the program.

There is the principle of the 80-20 rule: 80% of the maintenance problems are found in 20% of the programs. The reengineering toolset and its supporting methodology focus resources on the programs identified by the survey toolset as difficult—in other words, the 20% or so of programs that present the greatest obstacles to effective maintenance.

The reengineering process includes procedures to remove nested IFs, not in a mechanical way but by using a well-thought-out, rule-based approach. You do not have to rethink all programs, only the truly problematic ones. GOTOs other than to an EXIT are removed and individual math verbs (ADD, SUBTRACT, MULTIPLY, and DIVIDE) are replaced with COMPUTE statements. All literals used in the procedure division are converted into meaningful data names and defined in working storage. Duplicate code is identified and converted to fan-in reusable code where possible.

A fundamental principle of the reengineering toolset and methodology is incremental change; doing one defined step at a time and then immediately testing the program. A rule of thumb to enforce incremental change is to never go more than two hours between tests. (This principle was discussed in Glen Meyer's book *The Art of Software Testing*.) Many reengineering projects fail because individuals have a natural tendency to do all the coding work first before testing the entire program. When the test fails, the professional is faced with trying to figure out which step introduced the error. By testing after each defined step and never going more than two hours between tests, the professional knows exactly what introduced the defect. As a result, professional time for defect elimination is reduced. This process of stepwise incremental changes produces an assembly-line environment in the reengineering team.

Not a One-Time Effort. In addition, the toolset and methodology are not just a one-time benefit. They can be used as ongoing maintenance aids to measure the effectiveness of the maintenance process. For example, the before-and-after image of a changed program can be run through the survey toolset to see whether the change had a detrimental effect on the maintainability of the program.

CONCLUSION

Unlike other software products, the survey and reengineering toolsets and methodology described here do not rely on mechanical fixes to programs. They include a rigorously applied methodological approach with proven metrics and incremental testing of manual steps. The toolset and approach described constitute a proven, working methodology. Although the methodology's main objective is to revitalize legacy systems and improve their maintainability, some companies have realized a 2% to 22% improvement in execution time as a result of implementing the methodology.

Many existing systems rely on six-digit date fields in year/month/day or month/day/year format. Many of these systems include relative date testing—that is, one date being greater than another. Because the year is stored with only its last two digits, when the year 2000 arrives, all of these comparative date checks will begin to fail because the year 2000 (stored as 00) is not greater than the year 1999 (stored as 99). An important byproduct of this methodology is that companies have gained, without additional effort, the conversion of century-date problems that are about to plague our industry.

XIII-2

Productivity Through Project Management

James A. Ward

A SURVEY BY A LARGE consulting firm found that 25% of large systems development projects were canceled, 60% experienced significant cost overruns, 75% had quality problems, and less than 1% of all systems development projects were delivered on schedule and met requirements. This represents an awesome waste of an organization's resources.

When faced with a potential systems development disaster, can the IS manager turn a project around and achieve success? Better still, can the manager institute measures that prevent projects from failing in the first place, thereby ensuring productive use of systems development resources?

The answer is yes. This chapter offers a prescriptive approach to project control that has been consistently successful in achieving on-time delivery of systems that meet requirements.

KEYS TO GETTING STARTED

The key activities that occupy the project manager at the start of the project are planning and scheduling. These activities must also be repeated when attempting to salvage a project that is heading for disaster.

Project Definition

Projects can and do fail if requirements are known, but there has never been a complete disaster when all requirements were fully defined, documented, understood, and agreed on by all involved parties. Many projects fail when resources are devoted to doing the wrong things.

System scope, objectives, and requirements must be completely defined, documented, reviewed, and approved. This definition must take place before the initiation of a project or as the first activity undertaken during project execution. When a project is in trouble, requirements must be revisited, restated, and reapproved.

In addition to defining the scope and objectives of the system to be developed, the project manager must also define the project in detail. This definition addresses the work to be done, the resources devoted to that work, and the time that the effort will take. Management must review and approve this project definition to ensure that resources are being applied productively. Systems development productivity results from the ability of the project manager to produce the greatest amount of work with the least resources in the shortest possible time.

Work. The work to be performed should be defined in such a way that when it is accomplished, the project will be successfully completed. Although it may sound elemental, this is not always the case. Given the current state of the art of systems development, it is unlikely that any two project teams, attempting to develop the same system within the same organization, would perform an identical set of tasks or activities in the same manner or sequence. It is also unlikely that they would produce the same results. No two systems are exactly alike. Each project defines its own work.

Standardized work processes are essential to systems development success. Stable and repeatable systems development procedures are required if IS managers are to effectively plan, schedule, and control work.

Resources. Resources consumed are primarily the efforts of the personnel assigned to the project, but they also include dollars, computer time, purchased software, supplies, and management and support time. Resources may also be defined to include the tools and methodologies used.

Time. Time is defined as the elapsed calendar time from the inception of the project to its successful completion.

PROJECT PLAN AND SCHEDULE

Once the work to be done is defined, the manager can apply resources over time to accomplish that work. Intuition tells us that if one variable is held constant—in this case, the work to be done—then the other two variables can be adjusted in opposite directions. More resources to do the same work ought to take less time.

Intuition is correct, but only within certain limits. Unless project managers understand the dynamic interaction of the three variables of work, time, and resources, the negative effects of these dynamics during project execution will drive the project to disaster.

Resources Versus Time

Resources assigned past a certain level will not shorten project time. Beyond a point, more resources will actually lengthen the time it takes to develop a system. Brooks' Law states that adding resources to a late software development project makes that project later. Even at project inception, this holds true.

Usually, the formula is that no more people can be productively used on a project than the square root of the total amount of estimated worker months needed. If a project is estimated to take 100 worker months (8½ years) of effort, then more than 10 people assigned to the project will not shorten the calendar time it takes to complete the project. Excess resources become wasted or counterproductive.

This dynamic holds true because of the nature of systems development project work. Certain tasks require the output of other tasks. Tasks must be performed in a specified sequence. There is a limit to the number of concurrent tasks that can be performed effectively. After a certain point, tasks cannot be effectively broken down and assigned to more than one person. In addition, the more people assigned to a project, the more overhead is incurred in communications, management, and coordination of activities. If one person had all the requisite skills to complete a 100-worker-month project, that person could probably do so more efficiently and use less resources than a larger project team. However, you don't want to wait 8½ years to find out.

The Law of Marginal Utility

The law of marginal utility operates in systems development projects. Accordingly, the second person assigned to a project will contribute less than the first; the third less than the second, and so on. Although each new person makes a positive contribution and thereby reduces the overall calendar time it takes to complete the project, at some point the marginal utility curve turns on us, and the next person's contribution becomes negative.

The actual contribution of the eleventh person in this example will probably not be negative, but you begin to see rapidly declining marginal contribution at about that point. Therefore, a 100-worker-month project should take at least 10 calendar months to complete no matter how many resources are assigned to it.

Because the productivity of each additional person added to the project will be less than the preceding person's, the average productivity of the entire project team is reduced. In allocating resources, management must achieve the optimal size of the project team that balances resources against time to achieve the most productive mix.

Overall Elapsed Time

If after estimating the total elapsed time for the project you find that the project will take more than one calendar year to complete, you should seriously think about redefining the project. You can break the project into phases or define multiple projects. A 144-worker-month (12 year) project is about the largest discrete systems development project you should contemplate tackling.

There are some compelling reasons not to undertake very large systems projects. First, an organization loses its attention span at some point. Other priorities intervene. Resources tend to disappear, through either attrition or reassignment.

Second, business conditions change. If a project cannot be completed within one calendar year of its inception, this project risks the delivery of an obsolete system from a business standpoint. Competition is moving more rapidly all the time. The government regulatory climate may change (this applies to virtually any industry). Reduced cycle time is a concept being preached for all products and services. It has always been true for effective information systems.

Third, the larger the project the greater the risk of failure. Even the best project managers and the best project management methodologies and tools become strained when attempting to control projects that are too large. Degrees of error in planning or estimating that would be easily correctable on small projects can be overwhelming on large ones. A 50% overrun on a project of one worker year can be handled. The same 50% overrun could prove fatal to a 20-worker-year project. Management must have the visibility and the ability to control overruns and cut losses, and this is much more likely on smaller projects.

Many organizations have obviously undertaken very large projects. Chances of success are significantly enhanced when a project is carved up so that a major implementation occurs at least once a year. This method also provides ongoing visibility and organizational commitment to the project.

Estimates

Every organization has a way of estimating systems development projects. Whether this involves drawing lines on a Gantt chart, applying sophisticated estimating algorithms, or just stating what the dates must be, the project manager either develops or is given an estimate of how long a project should take.

Estimates that are based on fact and are accurate can be a tremendous advantage in project control. Estimates that are no more than a guess or someone's wish can be extremely detrimental. Unless estimates have a real basis in fact and are developed by the individuals actually assigned to do the work, they are best ignored except when reporting progress to management.

The value of estimates is in productively allocating resources and in coordination of task interdependencies. Estimates should not be used as evaluation tools. The project manager must be free to adjust plans and estimates on the basis of actual project feedback without having to explain why initial estimates were not totally accurate.

Remember, plans are guides. Estimates are just that—the best and most educated guess about what should happen. The reality is the actual project work that is being performed. If the reality does not always conform to the plan, it is likely that the plan may need some modifications.

FACTORS THAT DISRUPT THE BALANCE

Systems development projects that cannot be completed in one calendar year should be restructured as multiple or phased projects. More than a certain amount of resources assigned to a project will not be productive.

In many organizations, there are other factors that further reduce the manager's ability to productively plan and schedule resources over time to work on systems development projects. These factors work against the ideal relationships between work, resources, and time.

Systems Development Methodology

A systems development methodology consists of two components: a systems development life cycle and a project management methodology. The systems development life cycle (SDLC) is the guide that the project team follows; it defines the tasks that must be performed during the systems development process. Furthermore, it provides for correct ordering and interrelationships between these tasks. An SDLC should provide the stable and repeatable work processes that are essential to productive systems development planning and control. Without this definition, large projects are simply too complex to successfully plan and control.

Project management is not software. An automated project management system will not manage projects. Software is merely a tool to automate some of the functions of project scheduling and status reporting. In the hands of an effective project manager using a proven methodology, software may provide some benefits. However, the chief benefactors of these tools are higher-level management who want to know where resources have been expended.

Without a proven systems development methodology, organizations cannot hope to successfully accomplish projects requiring the effort of more than one or two persons. They can muddle through on smaller projects but are in trouble when they try to tackle anything larger.

Systems Development Standards

A second factor that limits an organization's ability to productively use optimum levels of project resources over time is a lack of standards. People are limited in their ability to work independently on concurrent tasks because no one knows what will be produced by a task until that task has been completed. The quality of the work becomes purely subjective.

Where standards do not exist, management's span of control is reduced. Project managers must directly supervise personnel at a much closer level of detail. A manager may be able to supervise the work of 10 to 12 people on a project for which standards are in force. Without standards, that same manager may only be able to coordinate the efforts of three or four people. For the organization, this has the further negative effect of reducing the contribution of the best people, because they must closely monitor the work of others. Lack of standards usually lowers overall organizational productivity.

Task Splitting

A third factor that reduces an organization's ability to use resources productively is task splitting. By assigning personnel to more than one project, management may think that more things are being accomplished or that resources are being used more productively. In fact, the opposite is true. Task splitting has a negative effect on productivity and efficiency, and this reality should not be ignored.

A person can devote 100% of his or her time to one project. That same individual will be productive only 40% of the time on each of two projects, 20% on each of three projects, and so forth. Deciding among tasks adds coordination and decision time. Time is lost in switching from one task to another. Task splitting is a notorious resource stealer. Dedicated resources are always the most productive.

PROJECT STATUS REPORTING: MONITORING PROGRESS AGAINST THE PLAN

For the project manager, project execution involves monitoring progress against the plan and schedule on a regular basis, recognizing deviations, and taking appropriate corrective action. The project manager is chiefly responsible for ensuring that the work meets all quality standards and that it conforms to requirements and specifications. Providing high project visibility to users and management is also a primary project management task.

Work Completed, Resources Expended, Time Used

The project manager must invoke regular and formal status reporting. All project team members should report progress against the plan and schedule weekly. This reporting should be done at the lowest task level.

Each week, the project team members should answer the following questions about their assigned tasks:

- Is it done?
- If it isn't done, when will it be done?
- If it is behind schedule, what are the reasons?

The intent of status reporting is to chart real progress and at the same time to verify the efficacy of the project plan, schedule, and estimates. Avoid any reporting of percentage of completion on any task, however, because this reporting is invariably overly optimistic and conveys no real information that the project manager can use. In any event, the tendency to report percentage of completion usually indicates that tasks are too large to be accomplished in a time period in which they can be effectively controlled.

Providing High Visibility

When project managers report status to management and users, they should emphasize deliverable products. Managers should report progress against major milestones and major deliverable products as defined in the project plan.

A project cannot be too visible. High visibility ensures management support. Management meddles in projects when it doesn't know what is going on. When and if the project hits rough sledding, the project manager will need the support of management to take action. This support must be nurtured through the confidence that comes from keeping management informed.

Frequency of Status Reporting

Each member of the project team should have at least one task due for completion each week and on which to report. Under no circumstances should a team member ever have more than two weeks between task completion dates. If this is the case, go back to the plan and break the tasks down further.

Management is not interested in weekly task-level reporting, however. Status reporting that is too detailed (or too frequent) usually obfuscates rather than clarifies project status.

A major milestone or deliverable product should be scheduled each month. Never let a project go more than two months without planning some significant event. The completion of a project phase with a formal report, including submission of the plan for the next phase, dramatizes progress most forcefully. The submission of a major deliverable product that requires management and user review and approval is also a critical event. If at least one of these events does not happen in more than two months, the project should be restructured and replanned.

Recognizing Deviations Early

Equipped with accurate project status information, the project manager can assess progress and detect any deviations or problems at the earliest possible point. An axiom of effective project management is "act early, act small." Corrective action can be instituted in small doses and in ways that will not be disruptive.

Upon receiving weekly project team status reports, the project manager must post actual progress against the plan and note any deviations. If the project or some members of the project team are consistently ahead or behind the estimates, think about adjusting estimates accordingly. Minor adjustments in estimates, scheduled task completion dates, and task assignments should be done weekly as the project progresses. These minor adjustments need not be communicated beyond the project team as long as they do not affect the scheduled dates for major milestones or deliverable products.

Identifying Causes of Deviations

In even the best planned projects, deviations will occur. The first place to look for corrective action is in the plan itself.

There will be times in the course of any project when monitoring progress and making minor adjustments to the plan will not be sufficient to keep the project on schedule. This may happen for any number of reasons, and the reasons will undoubtedly influence the actions the project manager may take.

The work may change because of changes in project scope. Resources may be lost to the project. Technology may be poorly understood. The project team may have problems interacting effectively. Computer time may be unavailable. When projects deviate significantly from plan and schedule, the dynamics of the key variables of work, resources, and time will determine the likelihood of success of any action that is taken to get the project back on schedule.

Leaving aside those occurrences that significantly alter the work to be done (such as changes in scope or incorrect requirements definition), the most frequently encountered problem is severe or persistent schedule slippage. The easiest course of action is to admit that estimates were overly optimistic and that the project will simply take more time to complete. However, persistent schedule slippage is more likely to be a symptom of underlying problems than the cause of the problem. Extending project time will not cure these problems and may only allow the project team to dig a deeper hole for itself. It is lack of time that forces most project teams to face the reality of failure.

Instituting Corrective Measures

If the project manager is thoroughly convinced that the problem is simply caused by overly ambitious estimates and schedules, then the schedule should be altered. Otherwise, under no circumstances will increasing resources against the same overall schedule be successful in and of itself.

The project manager must subject a troubled project to detailed analysis, usually with the help of an independent party. Unless the underlying causes of problems are eliminated, the project will only experience greater problems as the project manager (and others) attempt to apply corrective action. Management must be supportive of this process.

Once appropriate corrective action has been initiated, the project manager must then go back to square one and prepare a formal project status report. Bearing in mind that the dynamics of work, resources, and time will be much different from what they were when the project was initially planned, the manager can then develop a new project plan and schedule.

CONCLUSION

A predictable pattern results when project managers fail to understand the dynamics of work, resources, and time. First, schedules are extended, usually more than once. When this does not work, resources are added, making problems that much worse. Finally, in an attempt to bring the project to a conclusion, the work effort is cut back, often to the point at which the resulting system no longer meets the requirements it was originally meant to address.

Heroic efforts to meet the original schedule by working large amounts of overtime for extended periods will not work. Error rates will soar, project communication will become increasingly difficult, and teamwork will be severely strained. Often this drives the project into a never-ending sequence of testing and error correction. These consequences often result because of management's inability to distinguish between effort and productivity.

By understanding and managing the interaction of the key variables of work, resources, and time, the project manager can productively plan and control systems development projects. Potential failures can be turned into successes. New projects can be launched with confidence in the likelihood of success—delivering systems that meet requirements on schedule and within budget and make the most productive use of the organization's systems development resources.

About the Editor

ROBERT E. UMBAUGH is principal consultant and head of Carlisle Consulting Group, an affiliated consulting firm specializing in productivity improvement in IS and the strategic application of technology. He is a consulting editor for Auerbach Publications and served for many years as chief information officer for Southern California Edison. As an adjunct professor of information systems at Claremont Graduate School (Claremont CA) and visiting lecturer at other schools, Umbaugh has helped educate many of today's IS managers. He can be reached at (717) 245-0825 or by mail at 700 West Old York Rd., Carlisle PA 17013.

Index